Unimportant Clerks

Unimportant Clerks

The New York School Poets
and the Culture of Bureaucracy

JASON LAGAPA

Cover art: "Writing Desk," G. Ellingwood Rich, *When mother lets us make paper box furniture* (New York: Moffat, Yard and Company, 1914), 55. The Library of Congress Collection. *Internet Archive.*

Published by State University of New York Press, Albany

© 2025 State University of New York

All rights reserved

Printed in the United States of America

No part of this book may be used or reproduced in any manner whatsoever without written permission. No part of this book may be stored in a retrieval system or transmitted in any form or by any means including electronic, electrostatic, magnetic tape, mechanical, photocopying, recording, or otherwise without the prior permission in writing of the publisher.

Links to third-party websites are provided as a convenience and for informational purposes only. They do not constitute an endorsement or an approval of any of the products, services, or opinions of the organization, companies, or individuals. SUNY Press bears no responsibility for the accuracy, legality, or content of a URL, the external website, or for that of subsequent websites.

EU GPSR Authorised Representative:
Logos Europe, 9 rue Nicolas Poussin, 17000, La Rochelle, France
contact@logoseurope.eu

For information, contact State University of New York Press, Albany, NY
www.sunypress.edu

Library of Congress Cataloging-in-Publication Data

Name: Lagapa, Jason, author.
Title: Unimportant clerks : the New York School poets and the culture of bureaucracy / Jason Lagapa.
Description: Albany : State University of New York Press, [2025]. | Includes bibliographical references and index.
Identifiers: LCCN 2024059982 | ISBN 9798855803341 (hardcover : alk. paper) | ISBN 9798855803358 (ebook) | ISBN 9798855803365 (pbk. : alk. paper)
Subjects: LCSH: New York School of poets and painters. | American poetry—New York (State)—New York—History and criticism. | American poetry—20th century—History and criticism. | Bureaucracy—United States—History—20th century. | New York (N.Y.)—Intellectual life—20th century. | LCGFT: Literary criticism.
Classification: LCC PS255.N5 L34 2025 | DDC 811/.5093581—dc23/eng/20250209
LC record available at https://lccn.loc.gov/2024059982

*For my parents, Godofredo and Dorothy Lagapa,
and for the jobs that they worked*

Caesar's double-bed is warm
As an unimportant clerk
Writes I DO NOT LIKE MY WORK
On a pink official form.

—W.H. Auden, "The Fall of Rome"

Contents

Acknowledgments		ix
Introduction	Unimportant Clerks: the New York School Poets and the Culture of Bureaucracy	1
Chapter 1	I'll Concentrate More on My Work: W.H. Auden and Poetry as Serious Play	25
Chapter 2	To Ignore the Rules Is Always a Provocation: Frank O'Hara and the End of Bureaucracy	47
Chapter 3	Accounts Must Be Reexamined: John Ashbery and the Bureaucratic Mind	67
Chapter 4	Barbara Guest's Office Inventory: Three Desks, a Water Cooler, and a Dictaphone	91
Chapter 5	It Won't Last: Monuments, Counter-Monuments, and James Schuyler's Trials of Affiliation	117
Chapter 6	On Being Companionable: Eileen Myles's *Afterglow* and the Administration of Care	143
Conclusion	Toward a (New) Bureaucratic Sublime	169
Notes		185
Works Cited		195
Index		203

Acknowledgments

This book has as its genesis an invited talk I presented at the Arizona Quarterly Symposium in 2018. Chapter 2, "To Ignore the Rules Is Always a Provocation: Frank O'Hara and the End of Bureaucracy," was the eventual outcome of the talk and was originally published as an article in the *Arizona Quarterly* (vol. 75, no. 1, Spring 2019). I am grateful to Lynda Zwinger and Daniel Crumb for convening the AZQ Symposium and for hosting me and my fellow presenters, Dana Nelson, Eric Savoy, and Joanna Hearne, to whom I am also thankful. I owe a particular debt to Tenney Nathanson for introducing me to the New York School poets when I was a graduate student at the University of Arizona and for his indispensable and brilliant instruction in the reading of poetry. I could easily dedicate this book to him as I did my last, such is the magnitude of the intellectual, professional, and personal debt I owe to him.

    I would also like to thank colleagues with whom I've worked throughout my academic career. At the University of Texas Permian Basin, I had the pleasure of working with Sophia Andres, whose mentorship, friendship, and guidance helped me move, happily, through the ranks, from assistant to full professor. Rebecca Babcock likewise enriched my time at UT Permian Basin, and I value our collaboration on the NEH-funded grant, "Boom or Bust: A Collection and Study of Energy Narratives," as a highlight of my years in West Texas. Annie and Chris Stanley are two stalwarts of the community in Odessa, both in the university environs and beyond, and their friendship enabled me to feel grounded for over sixteen years in the Permian Basin. Suzanne Rathbun, Don Allen, and Bob and Irene Perry also greatly contributed to the sense of home I felt in West Texas. Derek Catsam was always a proponent of research at UT Permian Basin, galvanizing myself and others in camaraderie, community and productivity.

Friendship and guidance were also in great supply in the time I spent at the University of Colorado Boulder, and I would like to thank Kirk Ambrose for our weekly conversations, many of which related to the subject of teaching and reinforced my belief in its great purposefulness as a vocation. Laurie Gries's support of and belief in me always provided me with a sense of uplift, and her example as an academic, at once exceptionally talented, personable, and generous, is truly extraordinary. Stephanie Foster made the Center for Teaching and Learning both rewarding and particularly enjoyable—our shared sense of intention, humor, and pedagogy was ground for both meaningful work and friendship. Karim Mattar read through an early version of a proposal for this book and kindly offered encouragement at a time when it was much needed.

There are also some people I have only briefly engaged with in literary and academic circles whose kindness and professional assistance has been quite meaningful to me, even as they are likely unaware of just how influential they have been. To remedy this in some small measure, I would like to thank Bob Perelman, Rob Wilson, and Jonathan Stalling, each of whom as outside reviewers graciously wrote letters of support when I went through the tenure and post-tenure process. John Yau also might not realize how much his correspondence meant to me in response to an article I wrote about his poetry, but it was an interaction I value beyond measure. I would also like to express my gratitude to Norman Finkelstein, whose endorsement of my first book and incredible thoughtfulness encouraged me in ways that are hard to put into words.

I have dedicated my book to my parents, Godofredo and Dorothy Lagapa, who are its driving force and essence: they endured managers and long hours at their jobs, withstood the vagaries of bureaucratic systems, and put in labor—all so that our family might thrive. Lastly, I thank my wife, Emily, who gives me hope and never fails to inspire me to better work.

Introduction

Unimportant Clerks: The New York School Poets and the Culture of Bureaucracy

> And indeed, the advent of this anthill society began with the masses, who were the first to be subjected to the framework of levelling rationalities. The tide rose. Next it reached the managers who were in charge of the apparatus, managers and technicians absorbed into the system they administered; and finally it invaded the liberal professions that thought themselves protected against it, including [people] of letters and artists.
>
> —Michel de Certeau, *The Practice of Everyday Life*

> The question I want to consider is whether the kind of affirmation at the heart of the work ethic can be used successfully in the struggle for better work: is it possible to demand both better work and less work without one demand neutralizing the critical force of the other?
>
> —Kathi Weeks, *The Problem with Work: Feminism, Antiwork Politics, and Postwork Imaginaries*

Almost as a matter of routine, the subject of work and the act of the writing appear as topoi that preoccupy the New York School poets. A determined commitment to work—represented as scenes of writing, reflective moments typing at a desk, or the setting down of ideas in a notebook—suffuses the poetry of the New York School. Accordingly, the management of time, the habits of writing, and acts of the imagination become common and integral markers of their poems. For Frank O'Hara,

John Ashbery, Barbara Guest, and James Schuyler, the references in their poetry to their own writing processes directly concerned—and became a means for—creative expression, but the references to work also stemmed from, and were an engagement with, the historical period of the American mid-twentieth century and the prevailing bureaucratic discourse of the time. Whether in imagery of office work or references to business discourse, the cultural milieu of bureaucracy inhabits the poetry and the imaginations of the New York School poets to such a degree that a pattern not only suggests itself but calls for critical attention. Questions that begin to emerge from this pattern include how the New York School poets might be situated within the social and economic conditions of bureaucracy: Are the references to offices and clerical work in the poems merely a reflection of the era, or is there an oppositional stance that the poets assume—one that is critical of the ethos of bureaucracy and its strictures, regimentation, and confining rationality? Additionally, if the New York School poets have a self-reflexive propensity to discuss work and the creative process, is this, too, somehow determined by the need to support one's art with clerical work, with day jobs at the office, or is the subject of creative work in the poems a parodic rebuke of what the bureaucratic age demands?

Writing within the predominant socioeconomic and cultural age of mid-century American bureaucracy and its aftermath suggests that answers to the questions above might just entail a mixture of both mimetic and oppositional stances. The depiction of bureaucracy in the work of the New York School poets involves both an imitative impulse that reflects the clerical and bureaucratic ethos of the period and a subversive critique of an overarching administrative cultural dominant within the United States. The New York School poets' aversion to bureaucracy notably coincided with emerging skepticism in the 1950s about the expanding influence of bureaucratic administration in both corporate and governmental sectors of the United States. William Whyte, for instance, identified in 1954 the American bureaucratic cultural milieu in his book *The Organization Man*, noting the increase of "economic and political consequences of big organization—[including] the concentration of power in large corporations . . . the political power of the civil-service bureaucracies, and the possible emergence of a managerial hierarchy that might dominate the rest of us" (4).[1] The increase in "big organization" in the postwar era resulted in the development of a specific type of individual, Whyte argues, an "organization man" who "left home, spiritually as well as physically, to take the vows of organization life" (3).

The problem, as Whyte saw it, was that "in our attention to making organization work we have come close to deifying it. We are describing its defects as virtues and denying that there is—or should be—a conflict between the individual and organization" (13). The New York School poets found themselves situated squarely within the conflict with "big" organization that Whyte characterizes; their poetics, consequently, both reflect and contest the political and cultural determinants of mid-century American bureaucracy. The influence of bureaucratic norms were indeed inescapable, yet the New York School poets purposefully resisted administrative systems as a dominant cultural dynamic. Against bureaucratic principles of rationality and organization, the New York School poets would mobilize irrationality as a poetic force, elevating in their poetry the unconscious workings of the imagination. The role—and primacy—of the imagination within the writing of the New York School poets signaled the means with which they opposed the regimentation of organized and administered existence that had become all-encompassing at midcentury: imaginative work and the labor of poetry writing would be their response to the rigidity of bureaucracy as a cultural mindset.

A paradox arises, though, from the repudiation of bureaucratic systems: administrative and business discourse periodically filtered its way into the New York School poets' writing despite their antipathy for bureaucracy. Within a society that idealizes work, productivity, and efficiency, bureaucratic and business terminology was an available, if seemingly incongruous and contradictory, discourse with which to frame and describe their literary output and creative labor. In this regard, the New York School poets were a product of the midcentury era of big organization and bureaucracy, caught, as Kathi Weeks might contend, within a state of consciousness defined by work: "The problem with work is not just that it monopolizes so much time and energy, but that it also dominates the social and political imaginaries" (36). Matters of employment and labor, indeed, constitute key elements of such a political and social imaginary in the writing of the New York School. For instance, O'Hara's *Lunch Poems* were so titled because many were written or conceived during his lunch break while at New York's Museum of Modern Art and often concluded with statements about the necessity of heading back to work. The office, for these lunch poems, stood as an impinging counterpart to the release of a noontime walk and the reveries—by turns joyous and gravely contemplative—that came with his excursions.

The wry titles of Ashbery's poems, including "Business Personals," "Flow Chart," "The Leasing of September," and "A White Paper," similarly invoke matters of employment, commerce, or governmental policy, even if the subject matter within the poems largely diverges from what the titles would intimate. In "Fragment," another such poem invoking the language of business, Ashbery reconsiders his relationship to his late father by using bureaucratic terms to convey his grief. As John Shoptaw writes, the focus of "Fragment" involves Ashbery making "what peace he can with the dead, the remembered, and himself," yet the work of recollection throughout the poem is written in the discourse of bureaucracy and office work, where Ashbery comments, "the accounts must be reexamined, / [amid] shifting ropes of figures" (Shoptaw 118, 299). In O'Hara's *Lunch Poems* and Ashbery's "Fragment," administrative terminology is arguably at hand because of the prioritized place that work occupies in social existence. "Work," as Weeks has contended, "is the primary means by which individuals are integrated not only into the economic system, but also into social, political, and familial modes of cooperation. That individuals should work is fundamental to the basic social contract" (8). Despite the New York School poets' efforts to contest the ideology of work, it was, nevertheless, the cultural atmosphere within which they worked.

Bureaucracy, and the office work entailed within it, might then be said to be, to use a phrase from Fredric Jameson, an integral element of the New York School poets' "political unconscious" (*Political Unconscious* 20). A pervasively administrative society forms the conditions and ideological horizon that loom over their work, frequently delineating the discursive terrain of their writing. A principal dilemma that Jameson identifies for textual analysis is thus relevant for analyzing the poetry of the New York School: "is the text a free-floating object in its own right, or does it 'reflect' some context or ground, and in that case does it simply replicate the latter ideologically, or does it possess some autonomous force in which it could be seen as negating that context?" (*Political Unconscious* 38). The premise of this book is that the writing of the New York School of poets does both, at times replicating a midcentury ideology of bureaucracy and, at other times, and more persistently, offering a repudiation of administrative and bureaucratic culture's more inhibiting and oppressive practices. The ambivalent statements of the New York School about bureaucracy are expressive of rival and vying impulses: to yield to the prevailing ideology of midcentury America or to contest it. The tendency of the poets, accordingly, is to employ bureaucratic and administrative terminology, with the aim either to appropriate it for their own purposes or to parody its values and language outright.

In a prescient manner, the critical strain of the New York School poets' resistance to bureaucratic work and their sense of being enmeshed within its confining strictures in the 1950s and '60s predict many twenty-first-century labor critiques, particularly as their poems and plays anticipate present-day analyses of precarity and protests over workplace conditions, job instability, and the extreme rationalization of labor.[2] The New York School poets' repudiation of office work thus also prefigures the post–COVID-19 movement of quiet quitting, the Great Resignation, bare minimum Mondays, or the cultural phenomenon in China of *tang ping* ("lying flat"), all of which are a means of objecting to the long hours and workweek demands placed on office laborers by late capitalism. While it is certainly clear that the writing of the New York School poets did not mobilize others into an organized movement of social protest, their distrust of bureaucracy and questioning of principles of work are identifiable conceptual strands that both tie their literary works together and reflect an incipient rejection of capitalist labor imperatives, a repudiation whose very skepticism resounds with questions surrounding work and employment today.

To fathom both how and why matters of bureaucracy and the discourse of office work might filter into the writing of the New York School poets and arise from their particular historical and cultural moment at midcentury, it is important to note that their earliest work and professional experiences were often clerical in nature. James Schuyler's role as secretary to W.H. Auden is an oft-mentioned detail within New York School poetry lore. What is less well known is that Frank O'Hara, as Geoff Ward has pointed out, worked as a "private secretary to photographer Cecil Beaton" (36). O'Hara would later become a curator at the Museum of Modern Art in New York, but his initial, clerical position at the museum involved sitting at the front desk and selling tickets and museum merchandise.[3] Ward goes on to propose that the New York poets likely considered themselves "a secretarial generation," owing to their work "as museum curators, reviewers, young middle-men" (80). Adding to the clerical jobs carried out by the New York School poets is Barbara Guest's time as Henry Miller's typist as well as an after-college stint doing entry-level office work at CBS. Like Guest, Schuyler worked during the

1940s for a broadcast company, NBC, at Voice of America, which he stated had "nothing to do with the creative part, like programming. It was a clerical job" ("Interview with James Schuyler" 158). John Ashbery notably held the position of copywriter, first at Oxford University Press in New York and then at McGraw Hill, the latter being the job that inspired "The Instruction Manual," his well-known poem about the far-reaching fantasies of a technical writer. Clerical work was not central to Kenneth Koch's job experiences, yet he still had ties to the business world and the material trappings of bureaucracy. Koch's father and uncle owned C. Loth Inc., an office furniture supply company in Cincinnati, Ohio, and Koch's poem "To My Father's Business" details the younger Koch's disinterest in joining the operation, wary that he "might go crazy in the job" (595).

That the New York School poets would gravitate toward office work when seeking out their first jobs makes some degree of sense considering the key role that writing plays within bureaucratic operations. As Max Weber—the foremost social theorist of bureaucratic organization—first acknowledged in *Economy and Society*, the nexus between writing, paperwork, and bureaucracy has long been integral to bureaucratic administration. Writing is so central to modern bureaucracy, Weber contends, that "the principle that all administrative work is done in writing is maintained, even when oral discussion is the actual rule" (*Economy and Society* [2019] 346). In the earliest bureaucracies, being a specialist in writing was an essential skill: "a degree of empirical education became necessary very early on, especially the ability to read and write, which was originally considered to be a very rare 'art'" (359). Inclined to pursue clerical work as a first foray into employment, the New York School poets resembled early "humanists" who, Weber notes, were "recruited from the social rank of the literati" into the role of bureaucrats (359).[4]

Despite the affinity between humanists or literati and bureaucratic work, or perhaps even because of such an affinity, there has long been a quarrel between literature and bureaucracy, the basis of which has been a deep skepticism of administrative systems, office regimentation, and clerical work. Franz Kafka is perhaps the principal name in literature associated with bureaucracy and its esoteric and intricate logics of banality, contradiction, and obstinance. In *Catch-22*, Joseph Heller so astutely captured the hindering mechanisms of bureaucracy that his novel's title became shorthand for contradictory administrative regulations and the absurdity of trying to comply with them. Among modernist poets, as is well known, T.S. Eliot worked as a bank clerk, a role correlative to Wallace

Stevens's own employment as an insurance executive. Contemporaries of the New York School poets, the Beat generation—Jack Kerouac, Allen Ginsberg, and Williams S. Burroughs—produced their own caustic critiques of American conformity and capitalist bureaucracy, yet their relation to office work, except for Ginsberg's short employment as a market researcher, seems less central to their writing than that of the New York School. The long list of male writers known for writing about bureaucracy, of course, should be adjusted to include women, as Lydia Kiesling rightly does in "The Office Politics of Workplace Fiction by Women," though her particular focus is on the twenty-first century. Perhaps coming closest in spirit and attitude to the New York School is Herman Melville, despite writing in the nineteenth century. Melville himself had been employed as a bank clerk among his first jobs, and his short story "Bartleby the Scrivener" articulates a central rejection of clerical work. The title character's recurrent objection, "I would prefer not to," expresses a persistent, headstrong desire, like that of the New York School poets, to undermine office protocols—and the demand of work itself.[5]

Literature's enduring and multiple-period-spanning objection to bureaucracy might suggest that the antagonism between literature and administrative organization is transhistorical. Though the New York School poets share sympathies with writers from other eras critical of bureaucracy, this book argues that their rejection of administrative organization came at a particular historical moment of midcentury America and the Cold War. The sheer, exponential growth of bureaucracy at midcentury was an inescapable facet of culture for the New York poets. The Cold War era saw an unprecedented rise in bureaucracy, as Louis Galambos relates: "In the years that followed Pearl Harbor, federal authority grew rapidly, as did the federal budget and the federal bureaucracy. By 1962 there were over 2.5 million persons working for the national government, and the federal budget constituted about 19.5 percent of the gross national product. By 1970 the comparable figures were over 3 million employees and 20.2 percent of the GNP" (14).[6]

The expansion of bureaucracy during the Cold War was not limited to the federal government alone but was matched by bureaucratic increases in corporate and military sectors, leading, as C. Wright Mills argued in *The Power Elite* (1959), to a consolidated, administrative privileged stratum, spanning across three sectors—politics, the military, and business: "Within each of the big three [sectors] the typical institutional unit has become enlarged, has become administrative, and, in the power of its decisions, has become centralized. . . . As each of these domains becomes enlarged and centralized, the consequences of its activities becomes greater, and its traffic with the others increases. The decisions of a handful of corporations bear upon military and political as well as upon economic developments around the world" (7).

The rise of the Cold War led to anxious moments in the United States, stirring uncertainty as how best to deal with perceived communist threats. The turn toward administrative culture and big organization seemed not only a viable and effective solution but one that could expand to meet the magnitude of the historical moment. The recourse to enlarging bureaucracy during the Cold War was indeed a predictable consequence of the era's organizational and administrative mindset. Bureaucratic systems are self-propagating, Weber repeatedly reminds us in *Economy and Society*: "the bureaucratic apparatus itself has compelling and purely material . . . interests in its own perpetuation" ([2019] 351). The New York School poets nevertheless proved themselves to be wary of such inevitable expansion, at both personal and institutional levels. For most clerks, continued work within an office would typically and inexorably lead to an entrenched position. A clerk's tendency would be to "treat [their] official appointment as their sole or principal occupation," as "the role of specialist qualification is constantly increasing" (Weber, *Economy and Society* [2019] 347, 349). Such an intensive, single-focused commitment to routinized office work, however, was something the New York School poets were unwilling to do.

Resisting the call to specialized, bureaucratic knowledge, the New York poets would become—to adapt Marianne Moore's phrase from "Poetry"—not "literalists" but, instead, specialists "of the imagination" (27). References to typewriters, work schedules and deadlines, proofreading, and office memoranda in their poetic works indicate that the New York School poets heeded Moore's additional advice in "Poetry" *not* to "discriminate against 'business documents,'" yet they nonetheless placed the imagination, and the workings of the unconscious, at center of their poetics (27). The poet, as Guest explains in her essay "Forces of Imagination," must maintain "a balancing act between reality or rules, and the imagination." (106).[7] The imagination, in all its openness to possibility, including its rejection of rules, provides an indispensable means for poetry to operate in a manner contrary to the rational, efficient procedures of bureaucracy that had informed their early professional careers.[8]

The primacy placed upon the imagination by the New York School, writing in the midst of the Cold War and in an age of increased bureaucratization, not only signals a move away from rational thought within administrative culture but also notably reveals ways in which the New York School was particularly indebted to the Surrealists and Dadaists, whose own postwar aesthetics after World War I relied heavily on the unconscious and the irrational. The emphasis placed on the imagination as a poetic force, of course, is most often associated with Romanticism, but the aesthetic and political imperatives of the Surrealists and Dadaists provide a more direct analog for the New York School, especially when a deliberate critique of bureaucratic culture is taken as an aesthetic objective. In the *Manifestoes of Surrealism*, André Breton points to increased rationalization as a particular detriment to society, one that inhibits personal experience and artistic creativity: "We are still living under the reign of logic: this, of course, is what I have been driving at. But in this day and age logical methods are applicable only to solving problems of secondary interest. The absolute rationalism that is still in vogue allows us to consider only facts relating to our experience" (9). Breton's denouncing of logic and rationalism gains full context, though, when these targets are associated with bureaucratic measures that drive capitalist economies. As Abigail Susik contends in *Surrealist Sabotage and the War on Work*, Breton's "surrealist viewpoint arguably resonates with [Marxist and Weberian] conceptualisations about the negative effects of capitalist-industrialist mode of production and the bureaucratization of daily life" (iii). Breton placed the imagination in direct opposition to an administered society, where efficiency, utility, and capitalist productivity dominate: "The imagination which knows no bounds is henceforth allowed to be exercised only in strict accordance with the laws of an arbitrary utility" (4).

Antecedents for the New York School poets' aversion to bureaucracy exist as well in Dadaism, whose parodic appropriation of institutional discourse to name its supposed subsidiary branches—such as the Dada Graphological Institute and Dada Health Department—sought similarly to ridicule the extent to which European society had become administratively managed. The sardonic slogan to "Join Dada!" as if it were a governmental institution or military branch indicated another ironic jab at bureaucracy (Foster 102). While the exact degree of Dadaist and Surrealist influence on the New York School poets has been a matter of some dispute or downplaying, a sharp critique of bureaucracy as a restrictive, inhibiting force on the imagination undergirds the anti-administrative politics of each of the movements.⁹

Ashbery's "The Instruction Manual"— Daydreaming Labor at Work

Perhaps no poem is as indicative of the New York School reproach of bureaucracy and corresponding espousal of the imagination as John Ashbery's "The Instruction Manual," whose very conceit turns upon a clerk's wearied loathing of office work and his compensatory daydream of a trip to Guadalajara. Ashbery writes in the poem from the perspective of a technical writer who contrives to counteract the dreariness of his job with a fantasized escape from his office duties: "As I sit looking out of a window of the building / I wish I did not have to write the instruction manual on the uses of a new metal" (*Some Trees* 14). The speaker's wish is, importantly, self-granted, spawned from his own imagination: "And, as my way is, I begin to dream, resting my elbows on the desk and leaning out of the window a little" (14). Material objects from the office give way to a dream, as the clerk appropriates his work desk and inventively repurposes it: the bureau upon which his elbows rest now serves as the foundation of a dream as he suddenly conjures an otherworldly, sublime image of Guadalajara, the "City of rose-colored flowers!" (14).

The dream of Mexico rests, additionally, upon his antipathy for work, spawned from his dismay that there are others, unlike himself, exempt from bureaucratic strictures and deadlines: "I look down into the street and see people, each walking with an inner peace, / And envy them—they are so far away from me! / Not one of them has to worry about getting out this manual on schedule" (14). For Ashbery's technical writer, Guadalajara is the

> City I most wanted to see, and most did not see, in Mexico!
> But I fancy I see, under the press of having to write the
>   instruction manual,
> Your public square, city with its elaborate little bandstand!
> The band is playing *Scheherazade* by Rimsky-Korsakov.
>   (*Some Trees* 14)

The structure of Ashbery's conceit in "The Instruction Manual" is antipodal, with the imagination opposed to reality, leisure contrasted with bureaucratic work, and unbound creativity held distinct from a capitalist, instrumental mindset concerned with the "press" of deadlines. The allusion to Scheherazade and *One Thousand and One Arabian Nights* serves to reinforce the opposition between bureaucratic obligations and the imagination, as Ashbery's technical writer will only be able to forestall his return to office work by continuing to unfold fictive scenes and serial installments of his narrative of Guadalajara.

John Shoptaw, tracing the literary influences in "The Instruction Manual" from Walt Whitman's elongated lines, Elizabeth Bishop's travelogues, surrealist Max Jacob's "novelistic discourse" (39), and Charles Baudelaire's "modern imaginary voyages" (40), suggests about the daydreaming technical writer that "we are left to declare whether or not the functionary is a poet" (39). The open question that follows from Shoptaw's comments is whether the clerk's daydreaming could thus itself be considered equivalent to the act of writing a poem, for the technical writer "knows Guadalajara only by name" and wholly creates its facsimile in his mind (40). Ashbery's elaborate conceit consequently reveals that "The Instruction Manual" is, of course, a poem not about Mexico at all but about poetic invention and the workings of the imagination. With its allusive nods to other poems and a framing device foregrounding the act of writing—even that of a stymied technical writer—"The Instruction Manual" proves itself to be a manual of sorts on how to create something anew or, more precisely, how to go about writing a poem.

In its portrayal of the unconscious at work, "The Instruction Manual" endeavors to illustrate daydreaming to be a form of labor, one that mirrors yet inverts clerical routine. Ashbery has related that the situation of "The Instruction Manual" corresponds to his own experience of boredom while at McGraw Hill "writing and editing college textbooks" (Gangel 18). Within "The Instruction Manual" and in commentary about the poem, Ashbery makes creative activity the obverse of office work, where clerical tasks are not only source material for the imagination but also the impetus for challenging or resisting bureaucratic directives and obligations, a strategic principle of defiance to which he and his fellow New York School poets repeatedly adhere.

Workplace Resistance Strategy #1: *La Perruque*

The rejection of managed work and bureaucratic timelines exhibited by Ashbery's escapist, daydreaming clerk typifies a set of behavior that Michel de Certeau in *The Practice of Everyday Life* has called *la perruque*, or "the wig," wherein a worker ignores job duties to focus on his or her own personal interests: "*La perruque* is the worker's own work disguised as work for his employer. It differs from pilfering in that nothing is stolen. It differs from absenteeism in that the worker is officially on the job. *La perruque* may be as simple a matter as a secretary's writing a love letter on 'company time' or as complex as a cabinetmaker's 'borrowing' of a lathe to make a piece of furniture for his living room" (25). As a form of resistance, *la perruque* diverges from bureaucratic principles of productivity and efficiency and instead pursues an outcome determined by the gratification of one's creative interests: "the worker who indulges in *la perruque* actually diverts time (not goods, since he only uses scraps) from the factory work that is free, creative, and precisely not directed toward profit" (25). The overwrought, sensual, and pleasure-filled daydream of Ashbery's technical writer, which amounts to a cessation of work, is not only a form of *la perruque* but also—in its advocacy of the imagination—a transmutation of bureaucratic principles and conventional administrative values.

The actions of *la perruque*, for de Certeau, constitute an entire politics, fueled by tactics of subterfuge and diversion: "we can create a network of connivances and sleights of hand . . . and in these ways we can subvert the law that puts work . . . at the service of the machine" (28). Diverting time from work not only affords one the opportunity to create art, but, as de Certeau suggests, becomes a form of art itself: "To deal with everyday tactics in this way would be to practice an 'ordinary' art, to find oneself in the common situation, and to make a kind of *perruque* of writing itself" (28). The New York School poets approach writing in such a manner, making a conscious departure from workplace or office routine, even as they embrace the quotidian as subject matter.[10] O'Hara's *Lunch Poems* in particular bears an affinity with the type of practice that de Certeau associates with *la perruque*, elucidating how writing itself—done on company time—might constitute a form of such subversive behavior.

The midday departure from the office presented in several of the *Lunch Poems* would initially suggest that O'Hara wrote outside of work hours and therefore was not in dereliction of his employment responsibilities. However, it is hard to fathom O'Hara obediently observing a strict demarcation between office work and his own creative activity. As Ashbery remarks of his close friend, such boundaries around work were permeable for O'Hara, for he would dash "the poems off at odd moments—in his office at the Museum of Modern Art, in the street at lunchtime or even in a room full of people . . ." (*Collected Poems of Frank O'Hara* vii). Schuyler confirms O'Hara's furtive work habits: "The first time I saw him working at the museum . . . he was in the ticket booth with a yellow legal pad writing a poem in the intervals between selling tickets. And later, when he worked upstairs at the museum, he would very often come back from lunch and, before he got back to work, sit down and write a poem, which is how he wrote the short poems that are in the collection *Lunch Poems*" ("Interview with James Schuyler," 160).

Workplace Resistance Strategy #2: The Refusal of Work

The *perruque*'s turning away from job responsibilities, endorsed in actuality by O'Hara at the Museum of Modern Art and fictively by Ashbery in "The Instruction Manual," unwittingly anticipates the nearly contemporaneous Italian Marxist strategy of political resistance of the 1960s entitled "the refusal of work." A tactic of subterfuge, the refusal of work challenges the conditions of labor—its duration, regulation, compensation, and monitoring—and thereby promotes the autonomy of the worker. Much recent critical attention has turned to the refusal-of-work movement as a means for understanding contemporary neoliberal policies and the corresponding precarity that such policies engender, but such criticism proves relevant for comprehending the New York School poets' perspectives on work as well.[11] The Italian autonomists, as Weeks has explained, shifted focus away from previous Marxian concerns about private property and control of the means of production to concentrate instead on "self-valorization, separation, and antagonism" in reaction to repressive capitalist labor practices (Weeks 96). The turn toward work as a focus for critique, the autonomists believed, was essential: "work—not private property, the market, the factory, or the alienation of our creative capacities—is understood to be the primary basis of capitalist relations, the glue that holds the system together. Hence, any meaningful transformation of capitalism requires substantial change in the organization and social value of work" (Weeks 97).

The Italian autonomists primarily sought the liberation of laborers rather than the improvement of conditions for the clerical class, yet their critique of capitalism nevertheless encompassed a related and explicit rebuke of rising bureaucratization in society. Mario Tronti, a leader within the Italian refusal-of-work movement, took pains to highlight the organizational and administrative practices of capitalism: "capitalists, themselves, constitute a social class not of entrepreneurs so much as organisers: the organisers of workers through the medium of industry. A history of industry cannot be conceived as anything other than a history of the capitalist organisation of productive labour . . ." (Tronti 336–37). Skeptical of such organizational impulses, Tronti cautioned that bureaucratic regulation was creeping into other social spaces. As Sarah Ferris has contended, Tronti's concerns about the encroachment of capitalist organization into society owe much to Weber's influence: " 'Rationalisation,' a pre-eminently Weberian concept, thus became [for Tronti] a key concept for understanding increasing 'factorisation,' that is, the progressive extension of capitalist relations to the entire society . . ." (34).

The increased rationalization or bureaucratization of workplaces and of everyday life diagnosed by Tronti and other Italian autonomists in the 1960s and '70s has bearing on how to understand the New York School poets and their writing. Michael Hardt, for example, gleans from the refusal of work and the Italian autonomist movement an inherently creative capacity that runs counter to bureaucratic and capitalist imperatives of productivity and efficiency, such that the refusal of work "did not mean a refusal of creative or productive activity but rather a refusal of work within the established capitalist relations of production" (Hardt and Virno 1). Cultivating a creative impetus separate from the work environment could consequently "generate and sustain social forms and structures of value independent of capitalist relations of production . . . [and] the domination of the State" (3). The impulse of the New York School poets to continue writing even as they worked office jobs reveals analogous and corresponding concerns to those of the Italian autonomists who were interested in maintaining a fuller lived experience premised upon creative output and independent from the obligation to work.

Toward a Politics of Desirable Work

To appreciate the New York poets' rejection of work and bureaucracy more fully, one might return to the question of surrealist influence on the New York poets. Susik has argued that the surrealist attitude toward work and labor elucidates their practices of artistic experimentation, for the surrealist embrace of the unconscious and the irrational closely coincided with a rejection of capitalist rationalization. Like the Italian autonomists, the surrealists sought a place for creativity within the strictures of the administered capitalist workspace: "though the surrealists rejected with hostility their rationalized, wage-based society as dehumanizing, they did not condemn the basic idea of desirable work, or engaged, creative activity as a form of self-motivated and self-rewarding making and producing. They valued unproductive over productive labour" (Susik 5). The value that the New York School poets themselves placed on "unproductive" labor is evident in Ashbery's "The Instruction Manual," in O'Hara's peripatetic departures from work in his *Lunch Poems,* and in his stolen moments at the office writing poems, just as their creative output as a whole indicates a valuing of poetic endeavors over the instrumentalist concerns of capitalism.

The surrealists are important to apprehending the New York School poets' antipathy for bureaucracy in another regard as well, for the surrealist critique of waged labor extended beyond the concerns of the working class to those of office workers. As Susik contends, "In terms of their work critique, the surrealists did not make a strict distinction between proletarian labour in the factory and white-collar jobs in the office, although their protest statements, aligned with the Communist Party, focused on blue-collar labour. All waged work was alienated for the surrealists" (5).[12]

The Boredom of Clerks

The alienating effects of office work are matters to which the New York School poets recurrently respond, with their poems often elucidating the conditions of work within a society predominated by bureaucracy. In the chapters that follow, one can observe how entire poems and plays by the New York School poets address the subject of bureaucracy, yet even offhand remarks suggest their antipathy for officialdom and a heavily administered society. In "A City Winter," for instance, O'Hara draws from personal experience with office work to make a familiar claim about the drudgery and repetition inherent to bureaucratic employment:

> I understand the boredom of the clerks
> fatigue shifting like dunes within their eyes
> a frightful nausea gumming up the works
> that once was thought aggression in disguise (*Collected Poems* 75)

O'Hara's remarks, sympathetic to the office worker's plight, not only reveal compassion for the clerk's tiredness but a clear understanding that bureaucratic work is detrimental—even existentially nauseating—to an individual's being. O'Hara, however, is also discerning about conditions of labor here: the administrative system that gets "gumm[ed] up" and promotes "aggression" articulates common beliefs about the intransigence of bureaucracy and the resultant apathy of clerks.[13]

The comments by O'Hara about bureaucracy indicate a typical perspective: that the mechanisms of bureaucracy are cold, stultifying, obscure, and anonymous. Such cultural beliefs about the mechanistic impersonality of administrative systems reinforce what is commonly found in scholarly studies of bureaucracy. As Weber remarks, bureaucratic operations obey "the formal rule of impersonality: *sine ira et studio*, or 'without hatred and passion,' and so without 'love' and 'enthusiasm'; impersonality impelled by concepts of simple obligation" (*Economy and Society* [2019] 353). Weber's pronouncements, here, are inadvertently equivocal: what serves as the virtue of bureaucratic systems—the promise of equal, impersonal treatment of all—also signals bureaucracy's faults, when jobs are undertaken "without 'love' [or] 'enthusiasm,'" or, put more negatively, with apathy and indifference.[14]

David Graeber's trenchant assessment of bureaucracy also cleaves closely to popular opinion as he contends that bureaucracy operates much like a machine, without regard for actual people. Graeber offers in *The Utopia of Rules: On Technology, Stupidity, and the Secret Joys of Bureaucracy* a sophisticated analysis of bureaucracy wherein everyday regulation is premised upon threats of penalty and violence,[15] yet he also explains how bureaucratic systems simply reduce human interaction to formulaic, impersonal routine: "Bureaucratic knowledge is all about schematization. In practice, bureaucratic procedure invariably means ignoring all the subtleties of real social existence and reducing everything to preconceived mechanical or statistical formulae. Whether it's a matter of forms, rules, statistics, or questionnaires, it is always a matter of simplification" (75). The disregard of subtlety in social interactions outlined by Graeber follows from Weber's perception of bureaucracy, where enthusiasm is replaced by neutral, obligatory duty. Both speak to a bureaucratic principle of rote detachment and impersonality that seems to infuse so many dealings with big organization and large-scale administrations.

Poets in an Age of Bureaucracy: A New York Paradox

About bureaucracy the New York School poets would thus have much to object, and their poems routinely raise opposition to the impersonal social interactions, the rigid regulation of everyday life, and the reduction of human existence to calculation and expedient administration. A uniform rebuke of bureaucracy in New York School poetry would seem warranted, yet there obtains a complex, paradoxical aspect to their treatment of bureaucracy: when discussing their own work habits as poets, they often appropriate terms from office administration to depict their diligence and the gravity of their work as poets. Rather unexpectedly, positive associations of bureaucratic efficiency come to mark their creative output and productivity. The New York School poets' attitudes toward bureaucracy prove, then, to be particularly ambivalent in the specific moments that they adopt bureaucratic discourse and business language to discuss the labor of writing poetry.

Weber's observations about the inherent practicality and reliability of bureaucratic practices help to clarify why the New York School might draw on positive bureaucratic metaphors: "Experience has demonstrated that [bureaucratic administration] provides precision, consistency, discipline, rigour, reliability, and hence predictability" (*Economy and Society* [2019] 350). Bureaucratic organization can promote a beneficial type of dependability and efficiency, thus offering a disciplined model of steadiness necessary for the commitment to artistic work. While New York School poets may not have taken their day jobs so seriously, their interest in the very work of writing poetry was nevertheless determined and sincere. Appropriating the language of clerical work was therefore somehow only fitting: the New York School poets approached their own writing with a persistence that could best be conveyed using the language of consistency and discipline oft ascribed to bureaucratic work.

The alignment of office work and poetry in the work of the New York School can also be anticipated if W.H. Auden's influence on the group is taken into account. Auden's role as an important figure and mentor for the New York School poets is well known, yet his own ambivalent take on governmental and corporate administration also serves as an important precursor to the ways in which both bureaucracy and the work of poetry writing is represented for the New York School. In such poems as "The Unknown Citizen," "The Fall of Rome," and "Forty

Years On," Auden wrote scathingly of bureaucratic institutions and their impingement on individual freedoms, yet he also repeatedly employed clerical work as a figure for the act of composing poetry, a tendency that reflects the esteem in which he held writing. Auden believed that a level of professional seriousness and rigor should necessarily mark the labor of poets: "every European poet, I believe, still instinctively thinks of himself as a 'clerk,' a member of a professional brotherhood, with a certain social status" (*Dyer's Hand* 365). Auden's sense of professionalism similarly finds its way into the writing of the New York School poets, as they likewise often embrace the image of clerical or office work as a figurative means of conveying the requisite work for writing poetry.

The New York School poets' ambivalent use of figures of office work to depict the activity of poetry writing underlines what Michael Hardt suggested about the refusal of work movement and what Susik remarked about the surrealists; each group not only rejected salaried work for its oppressive rigidity and repetitiveness but simultaneously sought outlets for creative productivity and imaginative undertakings. The twin impulse to critique bureaucratic strictures and to seek outlets for imaginative labor informs the New York School poets' attitude toward employment and their practice of poetry and reveals the degree to which they existed within—and labored under—the prevailing ideology of bureaucracy and an era of "big" organization. Work, as Weeks has argued, is a "site of interpellation," where one's job "produces not just economic goods and services but also social and political subjects . . . and generates not just income and capital, but disciplined individuals, governable subjects, worthy citizens, and responsible family members" (8).

The New York School poets understood well the type of interpellative, domineering effects of work that Weeks outlines. They also understood Weber's warning at the end of *The Protestant Ethic and the Spirit of Capitalism* about the "tremendous cosmos of the modern economic order" (123). Weber had cautioned that capitalism "determine[s] the lives of all the individuals who are born into this mechanism, not only those directly concerned with economic acquisition" (123). Workers of all types under this bureaucratic and economic order, Weber feared, would become "specialists without spirit, sensualists without heart" (124). The New York School poets, in seeking an outlet for their poetic imaginations, consequently aimed to escape the working conditions and economic order that Weber would ultimately—and famously—describe as an "iron cage" (123).

The search for avenues for creative expression led the New York School poets to find other jobs and better work than the clerical positions of their earliest employment. O'Hara, Ashbery, Guest, and Schuyler were all able to work as art critics or as museum curators and to continue in their vocations as poets and playwrights. The ability to move out of low-level clerical positions displays degrees of privilege, social connection, and fortune not attainable by all workers, yet their career mobility also illustrates a rejection of predominant bureaucratic imperatives of what work should look like. Prioritizing the work of writing poetry and carving out time to write it while having professional careers, for the New York School poets, became indicative of a cultural aim that rejected the single-mindedness of the Protestant work ethic, in which corporate productivity and the expansion of profits are chief goals. The archives of the New York School poets' writing thus exist as evidence of an alternate set of priorities and a different conception of work, wherein time is afforded to creative pursuits and an existence outside of the parameters of office work. Their poetic labor thereby stands as a repudiation of their cultural moment in mid-century America and its valuation of work. The stance adopted by the New York School poets amounts to their own version of a "refusal to work," which Weeks suggests can be "understood as a rejection of work as a necessary center of social existence, moral duty, ontological essence, and time and energy" (109). Properly embraced, the refusal of work has "the potential not only to contest the necessity of capitalist control, but to reduce the time spent at work, thereby offering the possibility to pursue opportunities of pleasure and creativity that are outside of the realm of economic production" (103).

∼

The New York School opposition to bureaucracy and their refusal of office work in favor of poetry traces, as stated earlier, back to W.H. Auden as a key progenitor of the school. I begin, accordingly, in chapter 1 with Auden's antipathy for the managerial class and his distrust of the invasive, administrative oversight of the lives of citizens by state governments (a sensibility that is articulated in the epigraph for this book and generative of its title). In the governmental, bureaucratic management of everyday lives, Auden identifies an incipient form of the tyrannical, at once absurd and foreboding, corresponding to what Michel Foucault has termed the "administrative grotesque" (Foucault, *Abnormal* 12, 13). Against the sobering and grave disciplinary power of governmental bureaucracy, Auden will advance his belief in the necessity of play, following the Dutch historian Johan Huizinga's argument in *Homo Ludens: A Study of the Play Element in Culture*. For Auden, poetry is the ultimate version of play, a subversive force powerful enough to undermine the administrative and proto-authoritarian inclinations of the bureaucratic State. The ambivalence of the New York School poets to bureaucracy, though, is evident in Auden's own paradoxical position: poetry, as a form of imaginative play, must be undertaken seriously and thereby becomes an antidote to the rigid sensibility of bureaucracy.

In contrast to Auden's advocacy of play, responsibility and duty in O'Hara's *Lunch Poems* initially seem to mark an alert consciousness of noontime schedules, reflecting an apparent concern on his part to get back to work and return to the office. As I discuss in chapter 2, however, O'Hara's seeming adherence to work hours and routine tasks betrays his awareness of his historical moment, including not only the age of midcentury bureaucracy but the threat of nuclear aggression in the Cold War era. O'Hara's hyper-consciousness of time and impulse to tabulate and organize the fast-paced happenings of a New York avenues give way to imagining a different conception of time, one that counters bureaucratic-capitalist imperatives of efficiency, productivity, and profit. Behind O'Hara's flippant remarks about New York's urban spaces are discerning observations about the United States' geopolitical position among rival communist nations like Russia and China, with nuclear annihilation appearing as the culmination of such competition. The bureaucratic drive behind economic and political competitiveness leads O'Hara to consider the anti-bureaucratic principles of poetry, wherein urgent deadlines and incessant demands for productivity might yield to the slow contemplation of a world not bent on war, mutual destruction, or competitive economic production but dedicated to humane principles of possibility and survival.

John Ashbery's relation to bureaucracy may be the most ambivalent of the New York poets discussed here, due, in no small part, to his conflicted relation to work and the process of composing poetry. Images of an artist or poet secreting himself away in a room are rife within Ashbery's poetry, and such scenes rely upon the figurative language of the office and of clerical work to convey the industry behind producing creative work. Beyond explicit references to bureaucratic tasks or foreboding administrative systems, the figures of office work can be difficult to discern unless one situates Ashbery alongside another writer, Franz

Kafka, whose aesthetic influence and own engagement with bureaucratic culture have provided Ashbery with a means to articulate both the torment and the pleasure of the writing process. In chapter 3, I discuss the ways in which Ashbery labors under what Kafka calls *Beamtengeist*, or the "bureaucratic mind," a state in which work at the office is felt to be both sanctuary and a confining trap (qtd. in Heinemann 257). The office becomes, for Ashbery, a preeminent figure not only for creative work and productivity but poetic consciousness itself. It is there, in Ashbery's offices and amid his bureaucratic figures for creative work, that one can most comprehend his vexed relation to the process of writing.

A concern with bureaucracy particularly manifests itself in Barbara Guest's writing in the material objects and office accessories that populate her plays and poetry. The most telling example is in the play *The Office*, whose minimal stage directions ("There are three desks. A water cooler. A Dictaphone. A loudspeaker. A blackboard. The desk of X1, who portrays the Executive, is placed in front of the other two desks") indicate the degree to which an ethos of organization and administrative rank is central to the drama. These administrative devices and clerical items from *The Office*, and poems like "Olivetti Ode," as I argue in chapter 4, are not mere matter to fill in the background but convey Guest's critique of an entire set of bureaucratic, hierarchical, and patriarchal social relations. Guest employs material objects from the office in her writing precisely to castigate the dehumanizing direction in which society is headed due to the culture and ideology of bureaucracy. In place of bureaucracy's more alienating principles, Guest seeks to establish an alternative, where a job's capacity for isolation is halted and administrative culture is replaced by interpersonal connection and cooperation amidst the refusal of work.

It is the monumental vastness of American bureaucratic culture to which James Schuyler's poetry attests. Court-martialed by the Navy in 1944, Schuyler was pitted against the US government and dishonorably discharged after the discovery of his sexual orientation. The judgment had lasting repercussions: in poems like "Hymn to Life," Schuyler expresses the shame of disaffiliation from his country as he walks the streets of Washington, DC, whose very monuments to freedom belie the infringement of his individual liberty. As I contend in chapter 5, Schuyler proceeds with his poetry to construct counter-monuments, poems that recount and memorialize personal friendships and romantic relationships that challenge the governmental and military bureaucracy that has denied his right to being. The counter-monumental stance of Schuyler's poetry, however, also extends toward literary reputation, about which he has always been dubious. In his later poems, Schuyler's retrospective accounting of his own poetic career and literary works downplays the career aspirations he once had, as he ultimately dispenses with his typical need to tabulate and record, leading to a diminished, vanishing, yet wholly appropriate, counter-monument to his literary output and past relationships.

Among second- and later-generation New York School poets, the subject of bureaucracy can be found in Alice Notley's *Disobedience* and *The Descent of Alette* or in a poem like Douglas Crase's "The Elegy for New York," though it is Eileen Myles's *Afterglow: A Dog Memoir* that provides a special, novel case for an analysis of bureaucracy as the New York School scrutiny of hierarchical, administrative culture unexpectedly turns back toward themselves with heightened self-awareness. Myles's critique of themselves as a bureaucratic "manager" or official in *Afterglow* is prompted when their dog, Rosie, alleges that it is she, and not Myles, who is responsible for Myles's literary production and career. As I discuss in chapter 6, the conceit of *Afterglow* is that Rosie has retained counsel and files a notice letter to seek redress for the theft of literary production that she considers her own. Rosie's lawsuit positions Myles as an illegitimate manager of Rosie's care, an example of Foucault's concept of the administrative grotesque, or the incompetent and failed execution of clerical, managerial, political, or other bureaucratic duties. As the memoir unfolds, Rosie admits that her lawsuit is not real, written not by a lawyer but by herself. The fictive letter threatening legal action, nevertheless, prompts Myles to reconsider the ways in which Rosie's being and perspective did make substantial contributions to their writing and career. The insight allows Myles to acknowledge their former participation in a hierarchical, organizational apparatus, highlighting the ways in which they had "grotesquely" mismanaged Rosie's life, acting as an authoritarian figure, precisely as Rosie's pretend lawsuit had alleged. Myles's subsequent aim in *Afterglow* is to approach Rosie with an ethics of care, a change that renders their companionship to be coequal rather than hierarchical in nature.

Resistance to bureaucracy and its apparatuses has been consistently operative in the writings of the New York School poets, gleaned in response to the midcentury era in which they lived and rooted in Auden's earlier articulated aversion to the State and the managerial class of his own day. At the same time, what Weber had called an age of "economic acquisition" lends its language to the New York School poets and becomes a part of their writing, suggesting that, again in Weber's terms, bureaucratic capitalism was less a cloak to be easily shrugged off than an "iron cage" circumscribing not just economic but social and cultural experience (*Protestant Ethic* 123). A parodic and sardonic strain nevertheless winds its way persistently into the poetic speech of the New York Poets, causing some dissonance in the message that bureaucracy would transmit, even when they adopt its terminology for their own purposes. It is, however, the very poems and plays of the New York School that offer the most opposition to the age of bureaucracy: as products of the imagination, eruptions within a rational, instrumentalizing order, the writing of the New York School poets refuses to work as expected.

Chapter 1

I'll Concentrate More on My Work
W.H. Auden and Poetry as Serious Play

> What could be more terrifying than a modern office building?
>
> —W.H. Auden, *The Dyer's Hand*

> If a poet meets an illiterate peasant, they may not be able to say much to each other, but if they both meet a public official, they share the same feeling of suspicion, neither will trust one further than he can throw a grand piano. . . . Whatever the cultural differences between them, they both sniff in any official world the smell of an unreality in which persons are treated as statistics.
>
> —W.H. Auden, *The Dyer's Hand*

Decades before John Ashbery developed his conceit in "The Instruction Manual" of a technical writer distracted by daydreams of Guadalajara City and worried that he might not finish a guidebook "on the uses of a new metal" on time, W.H. Auden had in his early childhood already ascertained how metallurgy and the imagination might be intertwined (*Some Trees* 14). In his commonplace book *A Certain World*, Auden states that "most of what I know about the writing of poetry . . . I discovered long before I took an interest in poetry itself," attributing the youthful rise of his creative faculties to a fascination for industrial mining (423). As Auden explains, "between the ages of six and twelve I spent a great many of my waking hours in the fabrication of a private secondary sacred world, the basic elements of which were (a) a limestone landscape mainly derived from the Pennine Moors in the North of England, and (b) an industry—lead mining" (423). Engrossed by the processes of heavy-metal extraction, Auden would ask his parents to "procure for [him] the necessary textbooks on geology and machinery, maps, catalogues, guidebooks, and photographs, and when occasion offered, to take [him] down real mines" (424).

While Auden's childhood self, captivated by mining practices, and Ashbery's bored technical writer might seem diametrically opposed in their interest in metal production, each has an identical aim: the construction of a fantastic or dream-filled alternate world. The primacy of place that Auden grants to imaginative thought at the start of his poetic career and the importance of daydreaming to "The Instruction Manual"—when read as an allegory for the act of writing poetry—reveal a continuity between Auden and the New York School poets, particularly in terms of the creative process, the habits of work, and the cultivation of a vivid and playful imagination. An ongoing tension between work and play underlies the composition of poetry for Auden and the New York School, with the activity of the unconscious—dreams and fantasies—seemingly winning out over the obligations of work. Within this dialectic of work and play, Auden pointedly and disparagingly associates work with a managerial class—anonymous, bureaucratic figures from the State and from business—who would impinge upon the freedoms of citizens and the imaginations of workers. However, even as Auden and the New York School poets align daydreaming or unconscious reverie with the act of writing poetry, the subject of work is not incidental but indispensable, paradoxically so, to their conception of poetic composition. Day-to-day office responsibilities function not merely as the ironic opposite of playful daydreaming within the poetry and poetics of both Auden and the New York School but also as a metaphor for the serious imaginative effort and commitment necessary to a career writing poetry.

This intersection or dialectic between work and play in Auden's poetry and the writing of the New York School, moreover, gains special significance in the context of American and European bureaucratic culture from the late 1930s to the mid-1970s. For Auden, nothing could be further from the liberating qualities of imaginative thought than the restrictions inherent to bureaucratic systems, which he views as pernicious and antithetical to the poetic process. The role of the poet, Auden believed, was to combat State and corporate bureaucratic interests. As Frederick Buell writes, Auden positioned himself as "a spokesman for . . . well-meaning, harried citizens of the modern bureaucratic, philistine age, a group irreverent toward and out of sympathy with the 'managers' who control such a society" (8). From the late 1930s onward, Auden grew concerned that large-scale, byzantine systems of political administration and corporate organization were beginning to beset the lives of individuals, shifting the human condition from one of self-determination and independence to one of domination and bureaucratic regulation. Accordingly, Auden sought to reject and refuse a State and corporate bureaucratic order reducing its citizens to anonymous, regulated statistics and its workers into managed and manageable units.

Auden's quarrel with bureaucracy additionally derives from his desire to safeguard the creative imagination from what would stifle or deter it and to align poetry with a pursuit of freedom from a heavily administered life. For Auden, the mind of the bureaucrat—rigid, focused on efficiency, humorless—proves incompatible with the imaginative realm—a site for games, play, and creativity—that he associates with writing poetry. In *The Dyer's Hand*, Auden makes his endorsement of games and other imaginative acts explicit, invoking the idea of *Homo Ludens*, or "man playing," as a means of declaiming the importance of creativity—of play—to society: "In our age, the mere making of a work of art is itself a political act. So long as artists exist, making what they please and think they ought to make, even if it is not terribly good, even if it appeals to only a handful of people, they remind Management of something managers need to be reminded of, namely, that the managed are people with faces, not anonymous numbers, that *Homo Laborans* is also *Homo Ludens*" (*Dyer's Hand* 88). Auden here follows Dutch historian Johan Huizinga's argument for the priority of play in human civilization in his book from 1938, *Homo Ludens: A Study of the Play Element in Culture*: "It is through . . . playing that society expresses its interpretation of life and the world. By this we do not mean that play turns into culture, rather that in its earliest phases culture has the play-character, that it proceeds in the shape and the mood of play" (46). The identification of office managers as a nullifying or dehumanizing force solidifies Auden's point about the necessity of play: managers here encapsulate all the administrative and bureaucratic imperatives hostile to playing and, in turn, to social existence. In curtailing the human impulse to create, managers become the callous adversaries of poets and the embodiment of bureaucracy's sober injunction against play.

That a similar critique of bureaucracy finds expression in the work of Ashbery and his fellow New York School poets might easily be predicted, as Auden's literary and personal impact on the group has been widely documented. David Lehman writes that, as a teenager, Ashbery sought out poetry that was challenging and difficult and "found himself drawn to W. H. Auden . . . precisely because [his] works baffled him" (128). Contending that the "earliest formulation of [Ashbery's] poetics arose from his reading of W.H. Auden," John Shoptaw notes that Auden later became the subject of Ashbery's "1949 undergraduate thesis at Harvard" (3). Auden, however, was not merely a remote literary figure whom the New York School poets read and studied from afar. In a well-known item of New York School literary history, Auden served as the judge of the Yale Series of Younger Poets competition in 1955. The final selection of the competition would come down to Ashbery and Frank O'Hara, with Ashbery winning. In yet another personal connection, James Schuyler worked as a personal secretary for Auden, performing such clerical tasks as the typing of his poems. In terms of subject matter and ideological critique, Auden's attitude toward managers and the State arguably constitutes an additional point of convergence between Auden and the group, for an aversion to bureaucracy frequently becomes a salient feature of the writing of the New York School poets as well.

Two brief instances from Auden's poems quickly illustrate the poet's contempt for the strictures of bureaucracy and indicate the critical perspective from which he will assail the administrative regulation of everyday life. In "The Fall of Rome," Auden tells of a disaffected ancient scribe—a precursor to Ashbery's technical writer—who cannot abide his plodding, desk-bound existence, amid the emperor's contrasting indolence: "Caesar's doubled-bed is warm / As an unimportant clerk / Writes I DO NOT LIKE MY WORK / On a pink official form" (*Collected Poems* [*CP*] 333). The clerk's defacement of office paperwork is an act of rebellion, one unlikely, however, to register beyond the scribe's individual sphere. Julius Caesar's wantonness, metonymically summoned by his "double-bed," only adds to the misery of the clerk who does not have time for such leisure, compelled as he is by imperial mandates to do his job. The anachronistic detail of a modern-day "pink official form" further derides the conditions of bureaucracy: its very ahistoricism implies that the rote conditions of clerical labor have remained constant for centuries.

Auden again speaks to the habits of bureaucrats in "Forty Years On," a quasi-occasional poem about his return to German Bohemia some four decades after his initial visit in 1928. Comparing alternate vocations to his chosen career as a poet, Auden muses in retrospect, "For a useful technician I lacked / the schooling / for a bureaucrat the *Sitz-Fleisch*" (*CP* 784). In its most positive idiomatic sense, *Sitz-Fleisch*—German for *sitting meat* or *sitting flesh*—connotes having the wherewithal to endure long hours at a sedentary job. *Sitz-Fleisch*, however, also conjures all the lethargy and physical debasement—the alienating and dehumanizing effects—of monotonous office work. With both "The Fall of Rome" and "Forty Years On" expressing the pernicious and stultifying effects of bureaucratic work, neither poem's treatment of office jobs is especially appealing. In each, Auden associates bureaucracy with insipidness, with work that is intellectually and existentially stultifying. Auden's view of a heavily administered society thus exhibits what Gerald M. Britan and Ronald Cohen, adapting the Marxist concept of alienation, have asserted about bureaucracy: "alienation is not only a function of class society, or of industrialization, but also of bureaucratization. Under capitalism, socialism, or any other political system, a citizen must still succumb to authoritarian control and to the dismemberment of [her] needs, wants, and options by dozens of organizations . . ." (25).

The dichotomy between bureaucratic work and play that Auden presents in his poetry often takes the form of an ironic critique of modern corporations and the corresponding managerial and employment practices in its office spaces. Auden's sardonic depictions of bureaucracy thus engage in what Michel Foucault calls the "administrative grotesque," a nightmarish, even dystopian, scenario in which inept yet tyrannical managers predominate, paperwork and documentation abound, and routine office tasks prove numbing (*Abnormal* 12). In opposition to such overbearing bureaucratic management, Auden promotes play—the imaginative and joyful realm of *Homo Ludens*—as the source of poetry. The valorization of play, however, cannot be diminished as an advocacy of mere leisure or inane recreation. For Auden, play—and its related activity, poetry—is an important correlative to social and political freedom. Much as Foucault does, Auden sees a continuum of repressive power wielded by bureaucracies and totalitarian regimes, both of which must be combated. About the "administrative grotesque," Foucault writes, "And what I say about the Roman Empire, what I say about modern bureaucracy, could also be said about many other mechanical forms of power, such as Nazism or Fascism. The grotesque character of someone like Mussolini was absolutely inherent in the mechanism of power" (*Abnormal* 13). Auden's own recognition of the dangers of bureaucratic power and totalitarian figures leads him to espouse poetry as a force to express personal freedoms and thereby contest both the smallest of administrative encroachments into daily existence and the most heinous acts of despotism.

The concern Auden had about restrictive social measures arose at a particular historical moment. In the months leading up to World War II, from February to September 1939, Auden would write a series of poems, including "The Unknown Citizen," "In Memory of W.B. Yeats," and "September 1, 1939," which all assail the impingement upon liberty that he associates with bureaucratic institutions, with the last poem also explicitly impugning authoritarian behavior. The three poems each culminate with an articulation of the necessity of individual and collective freedom, a condition whose very realization, Auden maintains, can only be safeguarded through poetry and corresponding acts of play.

Auden fully engages with the features of bureaucratic alienation and authoritarian control in "The Unknown Citizen," a poem that, with its singular focus on the ideology of administration, offers a more extensive treatment of large-scale bureaucracy and the State than the brief references in either "The Fall of Rome" or "Forty Years On." Written as a mock elegy, "The Unknown Citizen" encapsulates the life of a man through the many reports that have been generated in his life and includes, appropriately enough, a serial number and official statement as way of dedication, "(To JS/07/M/378 *This Marble Monument Is Erected by the State*)" (*CP* 252). For the poem, Auden adopts the voice of the State and presents a darkly comic scene corresponding to what Foucault has termed "disciplinary writing," or the "accumulation of documents, their seriation, the organization of comparative fields, [which make] it possible to classify, to form categories, to determine averages, to fix norms" (*Discipline and Punish* 190).

Assuming a tone of overwrought solemnity, the opening lines of the poem obliquely signal some of the irony and acerbic humor to come:

He was found by the Bureau of Statistics to be
One against whom there was no official complaint. (*CP* 252)

The absurd but all too plausibly named government office, the "Bureau of Statistics," develops the poem's sardonic humor further. Auden, though, quickly introduces a paranoid tenor to his absurdist treatment of administrative proceedings: while "no official complaint" has been made, the threat that a charge could very well be brought against the citizen adds a degree of frisson to Auden's parody of bureaucratic discourse. "The Unknown Citizen" rapidly establishes itself as a poem about disciplinary surveillance, wherein every aspect of the unknown citizen's behavior is both monitored and highly administered: "Yet he wasn't a scab or odd in his views, / For his Union reports that he paid his dues, / (Our report on his Union shows it was sound)" (*CP* 253). The self-enlarging, Byzantine nature of bureaucracy nightmarishly surfaces here, as the paperwork redoubles, layering one administrative report onto another. So much information accrues around the unknown citizen excluding, of course, one key element: a name. The dehumanizing effects of bureaucracy are such that they render humans anonymous—unknowable beyond a generic set of statistical information. To make matters worse, the individual's anonymity is uncannily and ominously matched by the bureaucratic State's own faceless status.

Whatever symmetry that obtains between citizen and State ends there, though, for the State builds its organizational structures not in an equal but in a hierarchical manner. With multiple official reports all implying a potential violation of rules, the Unknown Citizen finds himself positioned as an enemy of the State, an antagonistic motif that stems from the earliest of Auden's poetry: that of Mortmere. An ominous and imaginary place created by his friends Christopher Isherwood and Edward Upward while at Cambridge University, Mortmere found its way into Auden's writing as well. The setting for Mortmere was a fictional school, and as part of this collective fantasy, Auden and his friends would invent adventurous stories where young students were pitted against authority figures, including university dons and administrators. The antagonistic relationship was, as Frederick Buell argues, key to the mood of Mortmere: "The most striking of these would be Mortmere's idea of the enemy; on the one hand the enemy is the rigid society. . . . On the other hand, latent in the Mortmere notion of an enemy is the idea that the individual is up against a 'combine,' one that works against him in secret and devious ways" (71). Though "The Unknown Citizen" is not explicitly a Mortmere poem, the relation between the State and individual citizen enacts a similar mood of adversarial hostility. An accusatorial tone and a diffuse sense of enmity prevail in the poem, as the bureaucratic State takes the form of a shadowy enemy and the individual citizen must contend with a system or society—a devious "combine"—that appears to conspire against him or her.

The hermetically closed world that Auden develops in "The Unknown Citizen" is one in which the modern bureaucratic system has infiltrated every facet of human existence. Though the State is the primary form of bureaucracy, the Unknown Citizen is also a "Modern Man" who labors under a watchful eye of a corporation, where "[e]xcept for the war till the day he retired / He worked in a factory and never got fired, / But satisfied his employers, Fudge Motors, Inc." (*CP* 252). As with the phrase "no official complaint," Auden again employs a negative ("never got fired") to imply that this very penalty of being laid off was a persistent and real threat, particularly because the name of his factory employer—Fudge Motors, Inc.—invokes the idea of unscrupulous or dubious practices. "The Unknown Citizen," with its constant depiction of an underlying possibility of unemployment, thus anticipates the socioeconomic moment of precarity in the twenty-first century, foreseeing, as Lauren Berlant writes, "the instability of the ongoing present as the ground for living," a social order in which "the economic and political conditions of contingency refract in singular, simultaneous, and yet collective bodily performances . . ." (196). The Unknown Citizen's anonymity here comes into play once more, as his precarious situation, the poem suggests, relates to an exponential number of others beyond himself who are equally vulnerable.

The Unknown Citizen's precarious employment is not the only form of uncertainty he must endure. He also navigates a health care system and its bureaucratic regimen of insurance paperwork. Auden's attention thus turns toward what Foucault describes as biopolitics: the State's monitoring of not only matters of population, including "the birth rate, the mortality rate, longevity, and so on," but also "accidents, infirmities, and various anomalies," all of which introduce a corresponding regulatory set of "rational mechanisms: insurance, individual and collective savings, safety measures, and so on" (Foucault, *Society* 243, 244). The Unknown Citizen of Auden's poem finds himself enmeshed in a monitoring apparatus of biopolitics wherein "Policies taken out in his name prove that he was fully insured, / And his Health-card shows he was once in hospital but left it cured" (*CP* 253). Due to the solitary hospital visit, Auden seemingly presents the medical outcome as positive. The ratio of multiple policies to actual use, however, suggests an industry whose outsized profits come from leveraging fear and minimizing liability in its own favor. Each line of "The Unknown Citizen" contributes to a sweeping portrait of a bureaucratically administered life, evoking echoes of totalitarianism with the State's efforts toward eugenics and population control: "He was married and added five children to the population, / Which our Eugenist says was the right number for a person of his generation" (*CP* 253).

The ironies that Auden laces into "The Unknown Citizen" come into full, equivocal effect with the poem's final couplet:

Was he free? Was he happy? The question is absurd:
Had anything been wrong, we should certainly have heard.
  (*CP* 253)

Auden mocks the State for its haughty dismissiveness and bureaucratic rigidity: the two short questions about freedom and happiness are absurd precisely because these conditions lie outside the State's sphere of interests, surveys, and instruments of calculation. Even as Auden depicts the State as hopelessly incompetent or, worse, callously uncaring in its failure to register the affective and existential intricacies of human experience, a more menacing vision of the State as an enemy—hostile to the rights and being of the individual—returns. The absence of complaints filed by the citizen implies that the State does not brook discord; the system of bureaucratic surveillance is so complete and intimidating that it likely stifles any criticism in advance. Hearkening back to the world of Mortmere, Auden here registers his skepticism and antipathy toward authority, as the State dismisses the categories of *freedom* and *happiness* directly out of hand. Despite the oblique and ironic treatment of bureaucracy, Auden's message becomes readily clear: the State's pursuit of a statistically identifiable norm for personal behavior actively operates a pernicious denial of individual identity and social liberty.

For all of Auden's suspicion of bureaucracy, there is, however, a contradictory element to his representation of the State and its administrative organization: in both essays and poems, Auden frequently adopts a common office clerk as a figure for the poet. This choice, though, is not nearly as odd as it initially seems, nor is it ultimately inconsistent with his rebuke of bureaucracy. Auden sees in the clerk an apt metaphor for the industrious poet who works long hours in isolation to attain the status of an expert, a quality that Auden much admired. As Callan notes, "Auden represented himself not in the high Romantic manner as a lover of the Muse—an *amateur*—but as a professional who could produce verse for a play, a libretto, an epistle, or an elegy as the occasion demanded" (10).

Discussing the meticulous care necessary for a career in poetry in *The Dyer's Hand*, Auden specifically summons the image of an office clerk: "however fantastic . . . his notion may be, every European poet, I believe, still instinctively thinks of himself as a 'clerk,' a member of a professional brotherhood, with a certain social status irrespective of the number of his readers" (*Dyer's Hand* 365; quoted also in my introduction). The office worker's assiduous habits approximate what is to be expected of an adept poet, an expertise honed out of duty toward one's job.

Max Weber's description of the demeanor and responsibilities of a civil servant confirms why Auden would select an office clerk as a figure for the dedicated, serious poet: "when a civil servant appears in his office daily at a fixed time, he does not act only on the basis of custom or self-interest which he could disregard if he wanted to; as a rule, his action is also determined by the validity of an order (viz., the civil service rules), which he fulfills partly because disobedience would be disadvantageous but also because its violation would be abhorrent to his sense of duty" (*Economy and Society* [1978] 31). Auden similarly held himself to a code of responsibility and professionalism, firmly believing that "a poet's first duty was to master the technical elements of his craft" (Callan 10). This impulse toward expert proficiency informs the lines from "At the Grave of Henry James," where Auden notes that, for the masterful James, "the beautiful" is "the common locus / Of the master and the rose" (*CP* 311). James is, as Lucy McDiarmid writes, "the patron saint of [socially or politically] disengaged writers, a holy celibate whose dedication to art was a religious vocation" (117). Later in the poem, Auden is consequently inclined to ask James to forgive "the treason of all clerks," that is, the disloyal acts of writers like Auden himself who betrayed his art with the distraction of politics.

Auden's endorsement of the clerk as a figure for the poet had its limits, however. While the office worker's dedication to his or her profession and its craft might have appeal as a means of conveying the expertise or technical proficiency necessary for the writing of poetry, Auden was wary of the ill effects of management strategies and protocols on actual office workers. Consequently, Auden would continue to rail in several of his poems against the hierarchical organization of bureaucracy and its alienating social effects. Toward this end, Auden develops the figure of the clerk or office worker as a stand-in for not just the writer but also the average individual or common person hindered or undone by the confines of bureaucratic organization. Accordingly, the everyday office clerk in Auden's poems becomes a counterforce to excessive administration—an anti-managerial presence who embodies the desire for freedom despite the constrained circumstances of her work life.

Auden's skepticism toward business affairs and his portrayal of the beleaguered office clerk promptly surface in his elegy "In Memory of W.B. Yeats," as he condemns administrative practices that impinge upon personal liberty. The occasion and primary focus for the poem is, of course, the death of Yeats, yet Auden's concerns also shift toward society, including not only its class stratifications and corporate institutions but also the collective impact of the poet's passing on society. The communal response to Yeats's death, Auden observes, is relatively minimal: "A few thousand will think of this day / As one thinks of a day when one did something slightly unusual" (CP 247). Though Auden here registers the paucity of public reaction, the depiction of civic mourning sets up the framework that he will utilize for the rest of the poem, in which the individual is positioned in relation to the larger social body. As "In Memory of W.B. Yeats" proceeds, Yeats becomes somewhat displaced as the subject of the poem as it turns to a consideration of the purpose of poetry and its function within society.

The turn toward collective experience allows Auden to address the day-to-day business, financial markets, and corporate entities all of which occupy Europe's attention in lieu of an awareness of Yeats's death:

> But in the importance and noise of to-morrow
> When the brokers are roaring like beasts on the floor of the Bourse
> And the poor have their sufferings to which they are fairly accustomed
> And each in the cell of himself is almost convinced of his freedom (CP 247)

Auden diagnoses the social condition as one alternately predominated by animal instinct or routinization, with high-level financiers fiercely hounding after money and the impoverished feeling inured as they succumb to economic mechanisms hostile to their interests. The average citizen does not fare much better than either the poor or the wealthy stockbrokers, becoming habituated to a rote, dreadful daily existence herself. Though Auden does not identify bureaucratic norms as the sole, stifling force besieging individuals, the prevailing context of commerce implies that the angst-ridden, repetitive obligations of an office career forcefully intrude upon a fully realized selfhood.

With each person occupying a "cell of himself," the Yeats elegy anticipates the tropes of ideological imprisonment and bureaucratic surveillance in "The Unknown Citizen"—a poem written only a month later. The common man of "In Memory of W.B. Yeats" is ideologically predisposed to believe in his individuality, nearly "convinced of his freedom," just as the Unknown Citizen enjoys, in Auden's caustic phrase, "everything necessary to the Modern Man," who buys on a corporate-controlled installment plan such standard merchandise as "A phonograph, a radio, a car and a Frigidaire" (*CP* 247, 253). The ideological situation that confronts both the Unknown Citizen and the "Modern Man" is something Fredric Jameson describes as the illusory circumstance of the "contemporary capitalist city," where "the most standardized and uniform social reality in history . . . reemerge[s] as the rich oil-smear sheen of absolute diversity and . . . human freedom" (*Seeds of Time* 31, 32). Auden deplores such captive lives, whether made so by the appeal of consumerism or the seductive draw of complacency, for in either case choice is freely discarded by the individual.

To dramatize further the ideological imprisonment of consumers and workers, Auden invokes a familiar enemy, the managerial class, as he contrasts the cold productivity of business interests with the viability of poetry. "Poetry makes nothing happen," Auden avows in perhaps the elegy's most famous line, as he concedes poetry's inability to enact social or political change (*CP* 248). Nevertheless, as he subsequently states, poetry "survives / In the valley of its making where executives / would never want to tamper" (*CP* 248). The invocation of executives remains tellingly consistent with Auden's antipathy for bureaucracy and its regulation of individual lives. Executives here function as shorthand, a metaphor for corporate efficiency and calculation with their orientation toward profit and financial gain being antithetical to that of poetry. As Buell has observed, Auden treats the businessman, like the Oxford dons of Mortmere, as a "new social enemy" to revile: "the managers are the figures whom all members of a bureaucratic society suspect and dislike" (192). Auden's use of the verb "to tamper" only augments this point: poetry is a purer entity, a value unto itself, resistant to and able to ward off management's corrupt and meddling influence.

The proclamation that "poetry makes nothing happen" has customarily been taken as Auden's repudiation, between 1938 and 1940, of poetry that is overtly political. It was, as Buell writes, a time that marked "Auden's re-evaluation of politics (or, in other terms, recantation of his old commitment)" (186). However, Auden's statement about poetry's lack of utility might also easily be understood as the reckoning of politics of another sort—a politics of daily existence rather than momentous historical events. The Foucauldian notion of biopolitics—including, specifically, the strategic instruments used to measure and calculate human existence for the purpose of productivity or human longevity—again is helpful here, as it elucidates Auden's perspective on poetry and its purpose. The inutility of poetry, as Auden conceives it, means that poetry is incalculable from the standpoint of a manager's valuation or capitalist interests, its worth resistant to quantification or measurement. Following Foucault, Michel de Certeau identifies such resistance as "the practice of everyday life," wherein disciplinary surveillance and biopolitical calculation and measurement are thwarted by the daily activities or practices of individuals. For de Certeau, this daily practice is imperative to discern: "it is all the more urgent to discover how an entire society resists being reduced to [the grid of 'discipline'], what popular procedures (also 'miniscule' and quotidian) manipulate the mechanisms of discipline and conform to them only in order to evade them . . ." (xiv). Taken as a statement about daily activity and political resistance, poetry's futility, its inability to "make [things] happen," operates as a countermeasure to the economic and administrative order of society. The inutility of poetry veritably makes it a willful counterstatement to—and sabotage of—bureaucratic productivity.

To appreciate fully the statement that "poetry makes nothing happen," and comprehend its implications as a political stance of resistance, it is important to recall how closely Auden aligns poetry with play and also to return to Huizinga's remarks about play from *Homo Ludens*. Rather than devaluing poetry by implying its inutility, Auden affords poetry its proper due, asserting its integrity as something that does not reach beyond itself. As Huizinga argues, play "stands outside the immediate satisfaction of wants and appetites, indeed it interrupts the appetitive process. It interpolates itself as a temporary activity satisfying itself and ending there" (9). If poetry "survives," residing "[i]n the valley of its making," it thrives by virtue of being consistent with—and carried out for—itself (*CP* 248). Poetry is thus like a game or instance of play undertaken for its own ends: "Play is superfluous. The need for it is only urgent to the extent that the enjoyment of it makes it a need. Play can be deferred or suspended at any time. It is never imposed by physical activity or moral duty. It is never a task. It is done at leisure . . ." (Huizinga 8). The taskless, leisurely quality of play is, moreover, but another way of saying that it is not productive of the economic, industrial, or bureaucratic order: play, like poetry, makes nothing happen. As Huizinga remarks, play is "an activity connected with no material interest, and no profit can be gained from it" (13).

The non-utility of poetry does not mean, however, that its value is nil. What joins poetry and play together is that each, undertaken with no other end than itself, exhibits or embodies freedom. For Auden, poetry *is* freedom, particularly when it epitomizes the spirit of play, much like when he would invent an imaginary world of industrial mines as a child. Auden makes the connection between poetry and freedom explicit in the third and final section of "In Memory of W.B. Yeats," where he condenses the departed Yeats and all subsequent poets to a single figure who offers insight into the freeing properties of poetry:

> Follow, poet, follow right
> To the bottom of the night,
> With your unconstraining voice
> Still persuade us to rejoice (*CP* 248)

Exemplary of freedom, the poet's voice is not merely unconstrained but *unconstraining*, with the present participle actively pointing to the possibility of human liberation going forward. Such liberation is open to humankind, Auden affirms, if all can partake of the poet's activity and imperative: to "rejoice." The release of emotion inherent to rejoicing, and the implied physicality tied to it, makes clear poetry's proximity to play once more, for this unrestrained expression of joy coheres with some of the earliest definitions of play: "We recall Plato's conjecture that the origin of play lies in the need of all young creatures, animal and human, to leap" (Huizinga 37). Such spontaneous, self-generating action of play is, as Huizinga argues, a guarantee of freedom: "First and foremost, all play is a voluntary activity. Play to order is no longer play: it could at best be but a forcible imitation of it. By this quality of freedom alone, play marks itself off . . ." (7).

The final two lines of "In Memory of W.B. Yeats" further elaborate Auden's equation of poetry with freedom and revisit his antipathy for a bureaucracy-laden society. Auden bids the poet to demonstrate the means of liberation for the average citizen burdened by bureaucracy:

> In the prison of his days
> Teach the free man how to praise. (*CP* 249)

The individual, whom Auden earlier referred to as being "almost convinced of his freedom," here returns, the "cell of himself" now a "prison of his days," where bureaucratic work schedules and office regulations impinge on his daily existence. Auden does make, however, a slight shift, an ameliorating change, where the "imprisoned" citizen is—paradoxically—already a "free man." With this phrase, Auden implies that each person already has the capacity to realize the freedom presently within herself: by rejoicing, by praising, and thereby committing to the act of playing. The ideologically and bureaucratically trapped citizen might learn from poetry and the poet how to alter what is finally and fully the one thing under a person's control: one's immediate reaction to lived circumstances. In this regard, Auden remains consistent; neither the poet nor poetry *makes* anything happen; the individual only accesses freedom by undertaking action herself.

Other means of protest and resistance to the administrative curtailment of daily freedoms are left unstated by Auden, yet the implication is that each person can take subtle and perhaps even furtive steps in establishing her independence. Auden's advice for the average citizen to exercise her freedom within the bureaucratic confines of her job amounts to stealing, and recalls de Certeau's notion of "*la perruque*," as first discussed in my introduction (25). *La perruque* is a form of thievery, where a worker ignores her job duties on "company time" to create, develop, or fabricate something of her own. As de Certeau states, "Accused of stealing or turning material to his own ends and using machines for his own profit, the worker who indulges in *la perruque* actually diverts time (not goods, since he only uses scraps) from the factory for work that is free, creative and precisely not directed toward profit" (25). For Auden's "In Memory of W.B. Yeats," the characteristics of *la perruque* hold true: to praise, though a seemingly inconsequential act, can deliver the worker from constraints of the most menial or laborious task and is widely available to the "free man." Finding a clandestine moment to give joy and to praise—or, in Auden's view, to act and play like a poet—is a rewarding and surreptitious game, a daily practice conducted at work or office as a means of altering the "prison of [one's] days." As De Certeau explains about *la perruque*, "In the very place where the machine [the worker] must serve reigns supreme, he cunningly takes pleasure in finding a way to create gratuitous products whose sole purpose is to signify his own capabilities through his *work* . . ." (25). The gratuitousness and pleasure of *la perruque* accord with Auden's equation of poetry with games and with freedom. Despite the departures in "In Memory of W.B. Yeats" from a singular focus on Yeats, the elegy remains a fine acknowledgment of Yeats's work and life, arriving ultimately at a tribute to poetry itself. Yeats's death, however, also importantly provides Auden with the occasion to reassess the obligations of work and one's station in life: one must rejoice, he avers, or live as if imprisoned.

Auden's critique of the biopolitics of bureaucracy continues in "September 1, 1939," where he once again invokes the perspective of the common citizen. Perhaps unexpectedly, it is Auden himself who occupies the individual's—the average person's—point of view at the poem's start, having just heard the chilling news of Germany's invasion of Poland: "I sit in one of the dives / On Fifty-Second Street / Uncertain and afraid" (*Selected Poems* [*SP*] 95). Horrified by the historical moment, Auden condemns Hitler and his barbarism, and the poem rightly stands as one of the great literary rebukes of totalitarianism of the twentieth century. The poem offers a lucid meditation on the psychology of wickedness and ponders the correct communal response to malevolent acts of war. Later, Auden would regret having written the poem, discounting various lines as aesthetically dishonest and ultimately disavowing the poem as a whole. Edward Mendelson writes that Auden conceived the poem in the end to be one that was "grand, emphatic, and false" (78). Auden agonized over the similarities between the tyrant and the poet, where each might exert influence over the populace due to the willfulness of egos. As Callan notes, Auden over time "became acutely conscious of a kinship between the cult of the poet as a national Bard and the cult of the 'inspired' national leader—Hitler, Mussolini, Stalin—that threatened the survival of European democracy in the thirties" (146).

Auden's reservations about the political nature of poetry notwithstanding, "September 1, 1939" does cohere with the critique of biopolitics—of State and corporate bureaucratic powers—of his other poems and offers a cogent refutation of the repressive tendencies that Foucault associates with totalitarian regimes and bureaucratic systems. "September 1, 1939" functions as a societal warning, initially concerning itself with the rise of fascism yet going on also to assail individual apathy, collective inaction, and the constraints on freedom instituted by administrative strictures. Gone is Auden's imperative to rejoice in "In Memory of W.B. Yeats," replaced with a foreboding wariness: "Waves of anger and fear / Circulate over the bright / And darkened lands of the earth, / Obsessing our private lives" (*SP* 95). Confronted with Hitler's dictatorial, bellicose acts, the citizenry feel compelled to retreat into a frightened, sullen, and anxious contemplation of the historical moment. Hitler's invasion of Poland marks the day as unequivocally exceptional, but the bar at which Auden sits—at once in isolation and among others—only seems to register the dull despair of modern existence: "Faces along the bar / Cling to their average day: / The lights must never go out" (*SP* 96). Auden's forlorn apprehension is that the historic day will revert to the statistical and quotidian mean, an anomalous blip in the bureaucratic imagination, and thereby become forgotten or ignored as "average" and unremarkable.

In his long eclogue, "The Age of Anxiety" (1944–46), Auden will later revisit the scene of a bar for a setting, establishing in that poem an insular space where patrons feel encumbered by the stasis of their existence as they seek refuge from the war. "September 1, 1939" and "The Age of Anxiety" have not just the communal—if also gloomy—space of the tavern in common but also the narrative context of bureaucratic office work that drives patrons to the bar. Quant from "The Age of Anxiety," for example, is an office clerk, whose self-engrossed mirror-stare summons Auden's familiar correlation of bureaucratic work with imprisonment:

> Looking up from his drink, QUANT caught the familiar eye
>   of his reflection in the mirror
> behind the bar and wondered why he was still so interested
>   in that tired old widower who would never be more now
>   than a clerk in a shipping office near the Battery. (*CP* 449)

The mirrored reflection congeals the scene, bringing time to a halt: all is familiar and unchanging; Quant's dull fate as a clerk is permanently sealed. A model of bureaucratic complacency, Quant perversely relishes a mediocre existence, as his subsequent comments make clear: "The safest place / Is the more or less middling: the mean average is not noticed" (500).

In "September 1, 1939," Auden designates the average office worker with a similar sense of constriction and entrapment:

> From the conservative dark
> Into the ethical life
> The dense commuters come,
> Repeating their morning vow (*SP* 96)

Auden accomplishes a great deal in classifying the office workers as "commuters," whose very beings even before they get to work are densely compacted and circumscribed. *Dense*, moreover, conveys not only the subway, bus, or train car's confinement but also the unthinking existence of an office automaton whose shuttling back and forth will not end upon arrival at the workplace. The repetitiveness of the morning commute spills over as well into "their morning vow," the recurring quotidian pledge the company workers employ to coax themselves to the office.

Auden's portrayal of daily bureaucratic existence as stifling and loathsome indeed deepens with the specifics of the vow that propel the office workers forward. As far as oaths go, this one is particularly tepid, breeding skepticism that it will actually be carried out:

> "I *will* be true to the wife,
> I'll concentrate more on my work" (*SP* 97)

Inherent to the vow—and its use of italics and the future tense—is an admission of a present lapse in character, a concession that one has not been working quite hard enough, that the original declaration of fidelity must necessarily be reaffirmed and cemented into place. By introducing levels of dubiety into the pledge, Auden implicitly questions the average individual's tolerance for ethical commitment and action, particularly if habit and rote compliance typically determine the commuters' behavior. Undercut from the start, the commuters' vow thus reads ironically, revealing fissures in the institution of marriage or the worker's loyalty to the corporation, for each seems compulsory and not freely chosen.

Homosexuality, and Auden's vexed relationship with his own sexual orientation, might explain the guilt that prompts the archetypal businessman to renew his vow, but, coupled with the promise to work harder, the commuter's pledge signals Auden's critique of unreflective thought and the complacency that incapacitates society.[1] For the majority of "September 1, 1939," until the final two stanzas, the tone alternates between a morose contemplation of impending war and a numbed admission of personal and collective ineffectualness. In search of a means to understand the state of current affairs, Auden looks toward an oracular figure in Thucydides, whose chronicles of history could offer guidance. Having read Thucydides, Auden asserts, Western European civilization should already know "what dictators do, / The elderly rubbish they talk," for it was "[a]nalysed all in his book" (*SP* 95). Despite historical knowledge and forewarning, the collective European fate was to endure in Hitler another dictator due to a lack of public vigilance:

> The enlightenment driven away,
> The habit-forming pain,
> Mismanagement and grief:
> We must suffer them all again. (*SP* 95)

Reconciling with the fact that enlightened, social progress has been halted, Auden confronts the collective cost of acceding to a dictator's aggressions. Here he echoes Emily Dickinson's diagnosis of great pain, where "The Feet, mechanical, go round—/ A wooden way," as he describes the present moment as historical stasis, marked by a repetitive "habit-forming pain" (Dickinson 162; Auden, *SP* 95). The listless habituation to pain and grief, moreover, prefigures Auden's invocation of the "dense commuters" and their bureaucratic automatism later in the poem. Telling, also, is Auden's use of the term *mismanagement*: the failed diplomatic acts leading up to the German invasion further correlates with Auden's dislike of bureaucracy. Britain's diplomatic mishandling of events lamentably had ensured a continuance of suffering.[2]

England's diplomatic blunders render its officialdom yet another ineffectual bureaucracy, proving consistent with the "managerial" class that Auden has long despised and critiqued. In contrast to England's diplomatic and political leadership, Auden positions himself as an anti-bureaucrat: he is, rather, an individual and poet who must transcend the trappings of bureaucracy in protest of Germany's invasion of Poland. All around him, Auden observes an administrative torpor settling in. As the "dense commuters" travel numbly to work, they arrive only to find a class of supervisors and bosses void of leadership:

> And helpless governors wake
> To resume their compulsory game:
> Who can release them now,
> Who can reach the deaf,
> Who can speak for the dumb? (*SP* 97)

Using the British term for a boss or a person in a position of authority, Auden notes that the "governors" have many questions but no answers. The serial questions, suspended as they are and left immediately unanswered, announce society's prevailing sense of panic and anxiety. With no recourse or "release" seemingly available, the rhetorical questions suggest futility, and Auden's figurative references to "the deaf" and "the dumb" reveal a widespread political unwillingness to thwart Hitler's aims.

The managers' "compulsory game" of asking empty, rhetorical questions about what to do, though, is reconfigured by Auden in the next stanza into a playful game of his own: a riddling exercise that necessitates a set of answers. As Huizinga has contended, riddles are but another form of play, a challenging competition of mental gamesmanship: "Questions may be put demanding an answer. The competition may take the form of an oracle, a wager, a lawsuit, a vow or a riddle" (105). Though at one point seeming rhetorical, the question of who can speak is taken now to be literal, as Auden answers,

> All I have is a voice
> To undo the folded lie,
> The romantic lie in the brain
> Of the sensual man-in-the-street
> And the lie of Authority
> Whose buildings grope the sky (*SP* 97)

The riddling features of these lines situate them alongside other of Auden's question and answer poems, like "O What Is That Sound" or "The Witnesses." As John Hollander has written, there is a discernible poetics of riddles focused upon "the nature of questions," which are then "solved by means of the . . . answering process" (51). Auden's answer to the governors' question about who may speak is forthrightly humble ("All I have is a voice"), yet its true power lies within its desire to act, a feat accomplished by speaking out. The aspiration for Auden is to expose society's generalized apathy and to call to account the inaction he associates with bureaucracy and its atomizing tendencies.

Auden makes his antipathy for the isolating effects of bureaucracy explicit in the subsequent lines, as he lambastes the government as an imagined, abstract monolith known as the State: "There is no such thing as the State / And no one exists alone" (*SP* 97). Auden's strategy is a radical one in which he dismantles the very concept of the State, its administrative hierarchies and networks of governmental organization to reveal what is substantively and actually—not abstractly—there: people. In the same moment, though, Auden also reinforces the idea that society is best understood as a collective of individuals whose power is real only when properly coordinated:

> Yet, dotted everywhere,
> Ironic points of light
> Flash out wherever the Just
> Exchange their messages (*SP* 97)

Above, the pivotal conjunction *yet* distinguishes Auden's ideal of social cooperation from the ineffectualness of the State. In contrast to the centralized machine of the bureaucratic State, a loose yet coordinated collective of just individuals can announce their solidarity and act. In their assessment of twenty-first-century political movements and social activism, Michael Hardt and Antonio Negri have advocated for a similar spirit of cooperation and coordination that echoes Auden's call for collective action: "cooperation and composition arise as mechanisms by which a plurality of diverse political forces act in common" (*Assembly* 37). Compelled by the collective spirit of cooperation and the Just who "[e]xchange their messages," Auden utters a new vow for his own time, one to replace the hollow one of the isolated, "dense" commuter: "May I, composed like them / Of Eros and dust, / Beleaguered by the same / Negation and despair, / Show an affirming flame" (*SP* 97).

In his affirmation of democratic action, Auden hopes to be "composed like them," that is, both just *and* part of coordinated multiplicity of individuals. The aspiration marks his desire not to be the poet-leader whose overblown and undue influence he feared but a coordinated part of the masses. Though Auden worried that "September 1, 1939" smacked of the ego-driven force of the dictator, the poem itself renounces such an undemocratic, tyrannical stance. Nor does Auden see a solution in the consolidated power of the bureaucratic State. Instead, he understands the importance of a common purpose and the ethical call to collective action that generates between people who act in accord. Such agreement, Auden believes, is not an impossibility and exists as the only remedy in the face of challenging events.

As Hardt and Negri argue, the proposed call for collective social action is less naïve than it is reflective of what really and practically occurs, when individuals, together, are faced with large-scale catastrophes and crises: "Today security can derive only from the freedom and cooperation of singularities in the common. We find a powerful foretaste of this real security, which neither private property nor the State can accomplish, in the forms of community and cooperation that emerge in the midst of social and ecological disaster" (*Assembly* 102). What Auden confronted in "September 1, 1939" was the onset of a catastrophic, disastrous war, and while the coordinated efforts of Allied governments were certainly necessary to combat Hitler, it was the communal response and sacrifice of the mass populace of the Allied countries to which Auden spoke most directly. At the center of the poem is a conception of freedom that is besieged, Auden believed, by the infiltration of bureaucratic measures on everyday lives and its accompanying effects of alienation that separate one person from another.

Auden's stance against bureaucracy is an anti-atomizing one, where he decries the pernicious effects of administrative regulation on community. The antidote to atomizing bureaucracy is to play and therefore to realize what makes us human. Chiefly, for Auden, this means that poetry, as a form of play, must be championed, and though poetry may serve no end other than itself, it achieves something important in its own doing. As Huizinga says of play, "It adorns life, amplifies it and is to that extent a necessity both for the individual—as a life function—and for society by reason of the meaning it contains, its significance, its expressive value, its spiritual and social associations, in short, as a culture function. The expression of it satisfies all kinds of communal ideals" (9). Auden is a defender against any entity that would delimit all that poetry and play offers society, and he views bureaucracy as a particularly stifling impediment to such human drives for such personal expression. To combat bureaucracy, Auden would have the average person or the common clerk rejoice, for this is what guarantees our humanity. He would also replace the officiousness of prevailing social organization with an ethics of human coordination that is less hierarchical, more egalitarian, and largely spontaneous. Auden's proposal for changing society might even look, from the outside, like a game, but games, he believes, should be taken seriously, of course: "among the half dozen or so things for which a man of honor should be prepared, if necessary, to die, the right to play, the right to frivolity, is not the least" (*Dyer's Hand* 89).

Chapter 2

To Ignore the Rules Is Always a Provocation

Frank O'Hara and the End of Bureaucracy

> Rather [Frank] talks about himself because it is he who happens to be writing the poem, and in the end it is the poem that materializes as a sort of monumental backdrop against the random ruminations of a poet seemingly caught up in the business of a New York working day. . . .
>
> —John Ashbery, introduction,
> *The Collected Poems of Frank O'Hara*

> I understand the boredom of the clerks.
>
> —Frank O'Hara, "A City Winter"

At once "enthusiastic and bored" is how John Ashbery described Frank O'Hara when a publisher had asked the latter to cull poems together for a book manuscript (introduction, *Collected Poems of Frank O'Hara* vii). The task before O'Hara was all the more demanding and tedious because he kept his writing haphazardly located in various "drawers and cartons" throughout his apartment and work office (vii). Donald Allen, editor of *The New American Poetry: 1945–1960* and O'Hara's *Collected Poems*, confirms Ashbery's remarks about the disorganized state of O'Hara's papers. While many of O'Hara's poems could be found in multiple copies, still others could only be recovered through letters that he had previously sent to his friends (vi). That O'Hara's poems might not be in order likely does not surprise those who associate his writing with the crowded avenues, late-night jazz clubs, and frenetic pace of New York City. One is even tempted to forgive O'Hara, the poet, for not filing away his poems in the methodical manner of an office clerk. For if O'Hara was not a painter, as he famously avowed, it is hard to imagine him as a meticulous bureaucrat either.

Nevertheless, O'Hara wrote his poems in an American work environment that was, at mid-century, becoming increasingly defined by bureaucratic imperatives. It seems appropriate, then, to examine O'Hara's poetry in light of bureaucracy and its corresponding ethos of organization, efficiency, administration, and paperwork. To do so, to read O'Hara in this manner, raises vital questions about his adherence to—and departure from—the mechanisms of bureaucracy, yet it also lays bare the degree to which he considered America to be driving toward an overly rational, rigidly structured, and even self-destructive end in the Cold War era. O'Hara's reaction to bureaucracy was undoubtedly mixed: though his work periodically contains signs that he found administrative routine and structure appealing, including prominent references to work schedules, deadlines, and office tasks, he was ultimately not able to ignore what he perceived as dehumanizing and even perilous about bureaucratic norms. Accordingly, to object to and counter the deleterious nature of a highly administered society, O'Hara sought to explore the utopian purpose of his writing, wherein the poetic imagination and poetry itself might offer an alternative to bureaucratic schedules and temporality, the stultifying tedium of office work, and the bellicose mentality of the Cold War period. Repudiating administrative culture for its belligerent principles and orientation toward war, O'Hara ultimately inaugurates a poetic conception of open-ended, utopian time that runs counter to—and refuses—bureaucracy and its regimented management of time. In doing so, he shifts workplace priorities from the office to his own acts of poetic imagination and composition.

The campy stance of being simultaneously "enthusiastic and bored" when collating his poems speaks directly to O'Hara's ambivalence toward bureaucracy. O'Hara, whose book *Lunch Poems* was composed in part during midday escapes from the office, showed a surprising predilection—and enthusiasm—for clerical work. Brad Gooch has described O'Hara's job as special assistant in the International Program at the Museum of Modern Art in New York as one filled with dull, repetitive tasks at which he nevertheless excelled: "O'Hara's job (at eighty-five dollars a week) consisted mostly of paperwork—writing business letters to lenders and paying attention to minute organizational details. Deceivingly organized, [he was able to] . . . sail through the first assignment and prove his administrative abilities" (257). O'Hara's keen appreciation of dates and affinity for recordkeeping led to his ascendancy within the organizational hierarchy of the Museum of Modern Art, where he eventually would be promoted to curator. Beyond merely being an interesting, if unexpected, biographical anecdote, O'Hara's capacity for accomplishing mundane office tasks is something that corresponds closely with formal features of his poetry. Gooch goes on to explain that O'Hara's detailed and attentive nature influenced the manner in which he wrote some of his most famous poems: "His listing and dating skills were reflected in notes for dates kept in increasingly busy agenda books, as well as in the dating of most of his poems, a habit that extended to the slightly jokey specifying of times and dates" in his poetry (257). The busy, bureaucratic work of attending to schedules and administrative duties—seemingly foreign to the act of writing poetry—nevertheless held a significant place in O'Hara's lived experience and noticeably influenced the composition of his poetry.

The impulse to date, list, and organize does indeed speak to integral elements of O'Hara's poetics, with specific regard to the representation of time and also history. The temporal, routine nature of bureaucratic agendas and schedules particularly coheres with the aesthetics of the quotidian, the mode in which O'Hara's poems have frequently been interpreted. As David Lehman writes, for instance, O'Hara "discovered a way to elevate the prose of everyday life—the diary entries, bread-and-butter letters, memos, and obituaries—into the stuff of lyric poetry" (169). However, these daily motifs also resonate with a larger historical significance extending beyond the everyday. Michael Davidson has argued several of O'Hara's poems illustrate "ongoing concerns with Soviet-American foreign relations" during the Cold War (68–69). In a similar manner, Barrett Watten contends that the quotidian aspects of O'Hara's poems ought not to be "mistaken as natural" or empty of political significance (33). This nexus between daily events and the geopolitical moment of the Cold War becomes especially evident when O'Hara addresses bureaucratic principles. Perhaps better than any other subject matter, O'Hara's references to bureaucracy oscillate between the quotidian and historical, wherein daily schedules and organizational tasks not only indicate the administrative obligations under which he labored and lived and but also ultimately point to his anxious preoccupation with the Cold War. A release of these Cold War anxieties only arrives—ultimately and conclusively—after he rejects office work and affords time to composing poetry.

O'Hara's quotidian organizational impulses—his desire to chronicle time, plan tasks, and portion out his day—find direct expression in the poem "Getting Up Ahead of Someone (Sun)." Within the poem, O'Hara sets down his early morning agenda in detail: "hours and hours go by I read / van Vechten's Spider Boy then a short story by Patsy Southgate and a poem / by myself it is cold and I shiver a little / in white shorts the day begun" (*Lunch Poems* [*LP*] 341). Such record keeping is an administrative, bureaucratic undertaking, especially as O'Hara attempts to initiate a change in behavior, one that is determined by timeliness and efficiency: "I / am for once truly awake letting it all / start slowly as I watch instead of / grabbing on late as usual" (*LP* 341). O'Hara's self-reflexive habit of listing his artistic endeavors and recording the time here squarely situates his poetics within a quotidian work experience, wherein he would like to be equal to the day—on time and aware—and perceptive of time's movement.

O'Hara's quotidian description of his poetry, however, also performs an additional bureaucratic task: that of placing or classifying his poetry into a new literary category. With a "sketch pad" in hand, O'Hara announces in "Getting Up Ahead of Someone (Sun)" that he will "commence to write one of [his] 'I do this, I do that' poems," a sub-genre of his own invention, one that second generation New York School poet Ted Berrigan would later adapt for his own purposes (*Collected Poems* [*CP*] 341). The tendency toward classification indicates O'Hara's impulse toward the organization of experience within poetic terms. Harold Bloom charts a similar inclination in Wallace Stevens's "The Idea of Order in Key West," arguing that the "rage to order" on Stevens's part is "an assertion of the power of the poetic mind over the sea, or such a universe" (*Poems of Our Climate* 103). Though O'Hara would himself sometimes confront the ocean at Fire Island, his veritable universe was the city of New York, and he immersed himself within its multiform spaces—its institutional settings, corporate office buildings, street scenes, apartments, local taverns, and artist studios. Intent to organize and put in order the experiences of New York, O'Hara will rely on his administrative tendencies to make sense of the world he inhabits.

The inclination to organize, though, is only one half of what I am describing as O'Hara's ambivalent and contradictory relation to bureaucracy. Despite displaying a zeal for orderliness and efficiency, O'Hara also remains deeply skeptical of bureaucratic systems and frequently conceives of bureaucracy as it is has long been widely and negatively understood: as dehumanizing, overly methodical, and oppressive in its restrictiveness. Max Weber, perhaps the preeminent scholar of bureaucratic systems, raises this notion of the impersonal and machinelike nature of bureaucracy when he argues that it "develops the more perfectly, the more it is 'dehumanized,' the more completely it succeeds in eliminating from official business love, hatred, and all the purely personal, irrational, and emotional elements which escape calculation" (*Economy and Society* [1978] 975). For Weber, the impersonal aspect of bureaucracy is its chief virtue, for it provides the functioning of governmental agencies and corporate offices with an objective, predictable basis and promotes maximum efficiency. The consequence of bureaucratic principles, as Wolfgang Mommsen further elaborates, is a highly codified society, whose goal is to neutralize personal or individual traits that would interfere with productivity: "In Weber's view, routinization and rationalization pave the way for the eventual rise of a new human species—namely the fully-adjusted men of a bureaucratic age . . ." (20).

The things that Weber would eliminate from the bureaucratic process—"all the purely personal, irrational, and emotional elements"—could not, however, be more antithetical to the tenets in O'Hara's mock manifesto "Personism," which, despite its many ironies, still speaks seriously to O'Hara's purpose in writing. The movement of Personism, according to O'Hara, is founded on "being totally opposed to [the] kind of abstract removal" of the personal found in works of other poets like "Keats or Mallarmé" (*CP* 498). Instead, "one of [Personism's] minimal aspects is to address itself to one person (other than the poet himself), thus evoking overtones of love without destroying love's life-giving vulgarity" (*CP* 499). With Personism, the poem "is at last between two persons instead of two pages" (*CP* 499). O'Hara's jocular espousal of personal, affective dimensions of poetry thus distances him from the administrative mindset seeking to expunge all human elements from bureaucratic operations.

O'Hara's skeptical view of bureaucratic systems as dehumanizing, rigidly logical, and disposed toward war also owes something to his interest in Dadaist aesthetics.[1] An assault on the rational was an explicit aim for the Dadaists, and their art and literature sought to negate the primacy of place that reason and logic held in society, particularly if such "rational" thought had led to large-scale war. As Kenneth Coutts-Smith writes, "for the Dadaists, the 1914 war confirmed the total bankruptcy of nineteenth-century bourgeois society, a society presently engaged in tearing itself to pieces. . . . [T]he logic of society and the reason of the bourgeois was [accordingly] seen as being manifestly illogical and unreasonable" (21). The Dadaists had contempt for the inflexible logic and rationality of bureaucracy as well, which they saw as an extension of society's warmongering. The Berlin Dadaists, Hanne Bergius explains, would invent official sounding "positions, titles, and institutions" for themselves in order to parody "Prussian hierarchical thinking, the bureaucracy of the November Revolution, the fixation on authority, and the confusing simultaneity of offices [in the] civil service" (40). Though O'Hara confronts in the Cold War an altogether different historical moment than the Dadaists after World War I, he does share the view that war—and the bureaucratic systems supporting it—is nonsensical and absurd and, moreover, antithetical to the purposes of art. O'Hara thus shares in the pacifist principles of Dada, even if the historical periods were different, and Dada thus offered O'Hara a precedent for an artist's anti-war sensibilities. As Éva Forgács details, the anti-war sentiment of Dada was substantial: "Zurich Dada was not just another oppositional trend. It was a bitter, fundamental revolt against the entirety of Western culture that had not been able to prevent an all-out war . . . no matter how erudite and highly educated its citizenry was" (354).

If the principles of "Personism" establish O'Hara's belief in an interpersonal dynamic of poetry, wherein social interaction between people is foremost, and if O'Hara upholds a Dadaist antipathy for warmongering and the regimentation of society, what is to be made of those moments in O'Hara's poetry when he actually indulges in and even seems to value the impersonal calculability, rationality, and efficiency of bureaucracy? One manner of appreciating O'Hara's complex, ambivalent attitude toward bureaucracy is to comprehend what is contradictory about bureaucracy itself. As anthropologist David Graeber has argued in his book *The Utopia of Rules*, there is something fundamentally paradoxical about bureaucracy, for despite being nearly universally detested, bureaucracy also unexpectedly possesses traits that people find not just beneficial but desirable. Graeber explains that the "experience of operating within a system of formalized rules and regulations, under hierarchies of impersonal officials, actually does hold—for many of us much of the time, for all of us at least some of the time—a kind of covert appeal" (149). Citing the early stages of the German postal system, the development of the Internet by the US military, and even ATMs as examples, Graeber proposes that *some* bureaucratic operations undoubtedly enhance human existence. In fact, the advantage of "[c]old, impersonal bureaucratic relations" stems from their neutrality, particularly as they are "simple, predictable, and—within certain parameters, at least—treat everyone more or less the same" (152).

Expressive of the contradictory emotions surrounding bureaucracy, O'Hara's poetry frequently discloses both the positive and negative of regimented, bureaucratic existence in mid-century Manhattan. For examples of O'Hara's embrace of an organizational, bureaucratic ethos, one need not look further than some of his most well-known "I do this, I do that" poems. In "A Step Away from Them," for instance, O'Hara is at lunch, off the clock at "12:40 of a Thursday," yet he still dutifully and meticulously manages to inventory the cityscape before him (*LP* 15–16). Surveying the scene, he records taxicabs, construction workers, Times Square chorus dancers, and bright neon signs, producing a catalog of the various elements that enliven the street. The very plenitude of vibrant, urban activity, however, leads O'Hara to think of what is absent, as he tabulates those friends of his who recently had passed: "First Bunny died, then John Latouche, then Jackson Pollock." There is an anguished turn to O'Hara's record keeping, and, in his attempt to manage grief, he cannot quite balance the mortal ledger, asking: "But is the / earth as full as life was full, of them?" (*LP* 16). By the poem's end, O'Hara consequently looks toward self-comfort in a "glass of papaya juice" and the consoling, bureaucratic routine of both office and schedule as he heads "back to work" (*LP* 16). Though the deaths that interrupt O'Hara's quotidian activities here have nothing to do with geopolitics, "A Step Away from Them" does present the poet's unease about the precariousness of life, something that is later amplified in the poems that overtly invoke the Cold War and the prospect of nuclear annihilation.

Another of O'Hara's elegies, "The Day Lady Died," offers similar bureaucratic accounting to that of "A Step Away from Them." The beginning of "The Day Lady Died" displays O'Hara's enthusiasm for the comforting orderliness of the train schedule on his way to a dinner party:

> It is 12:20 in New York a Friday
> three days after Bastille day, yes
> it is 1959 and I go get a shoeshine
> because I will get off the 4:19 in Easthampton
> at 7:15. (*LP* 25)

The bureaucratic exactitude in the timetable reflects a wish for efficiency, speed, and well-administered transportation, especially as O'Hara conveys his desire in a rapid—perhaps even breathless—manner. Maggie Nelson, citing later-generation New York School poets Eileen Myles and Alice Notley, designates such characteristically hurried speech as "fast talk," borne of the quick-paced tempo of life in the five boroughs (149). O'Hara, furthermore, keenly structures "The Day Lady Died" so that the bureaucratic principles of swiftness, order, and efficiency at the start of the poem give way to disorder and uncertainty, as Billie Holiday's death eventually becomes revealed. As the poem progresses, time begins to slow for O'Hara with the realization of Holiday's passing; his rushed pre-dinner activity is replaced by a memory of a Holiday performance so sublime and arresting that "everyone and I stopped breathing" (*LP* 26). The slippage between order and chaos is even obliquely presaged by a minute lapse in clerical protocol, near the middle of the poem, when O'Hara observes—in a bit of campy surprise—that the bank teller "Miss Stillwagon (first name Linda I once heard) / doesn't even look up my balance for once in her life" (*LP* 25). Exempted from bureaucratic scrutiny, O'Hara gets the first glimpse that the day has veered from the routine and has moved, inexorably, toward the extraordinary and tragic.

While "A Step Away from Them" and "The Day Lady Died" provide evidence of O'Hara's engagement with bureaucratic systems and spaces, two poems, "Rhapsody" and "Adieu to Norman, Bon Jour to Joan and Jean-Paul," not only exemplify O'Hara's interest in bureaucracy but also highlight the dismay that O'Hara feels toward an increasingly regimented, rule-based America, one that he believes is speeding toward self-destruction. In "Rhapsody" O'Hara addresses his anxious concern for the American nation whose annihilation he believes is the teleological end of bureaucratic systems at the height of the Cold War. To counter this, O'Hara will modulate his work habits in an attempt to slow down and deter society's militaristic machinations. "Adieu to Norman," as a kind of corollary to "Rhapsody," proposes O'Hara's belief in poetry an alternative to—and refusal of—office work, where poetry functions as a utopian corrective to the bureaucratic regulation of time and thereby suggests that, despite threats to the contrary, the continuance of life is manifestly possible.

"Rhapsody" begins with geographic precision as O'Hara locates himself at 515 Madison Avenue in New York, the address of the DuMont Building. The ornate Art Deco entrance of the DuMont Building provides

O'Hara with an object for absurdist contemplation, as he ponders—quite disjunctively—whether the entry is not also a "doorway to heaven" (*LP* 37). Designed by the architect J.E.R. Carpenter, the DuMont Building housed multiple corporate office spaces, a quarter of which were owned by the Coca-Cola Company, yet O'Hara reimagines the building space to be a divine "portal," where the building's "bronze" and "elevator cables" substitute for heavenly "marble" and Edenic "lianas" or vines (*LP* 37). This unreal scene—fusing paradise with commercial enterprise—sprouts fantastically and irrationally from O'Hara's unconscious, seemingly like a Dadaist exercise of automatic writing. Fellow New York School poets John Ashbery and James Schuyler are perhaps more rightly known for using Dadaist techniques of cut-up and collage in their work, yet O'Hara's fusion of contrasting imagery here owes much to the Dadaists as well. As Coutts-Smith writes, the Dadaists sought the "discovery of a new figurative 'reality' brought about by the chance meeting of previously unrelated images" (107). O'Hara likewise renders a corporate office anew by infusing the space and its "stopped real[ity]" with discordant imagery of "eternal licentiousness" and transforming it into a "jungle of impossible eagerness" (*LP* 37).

Amid O'Hara's dreamwork envisioning an exotic alternative lurking within an office building, there exists the poet's corresponding impulse to implement some kind of bureaucratic order and organize his environment. In the subsequent lines, O'Hara sounds like a poet-cum-urban planner whose administrative concerns lie as much with Eros as they do with traffic conditions:

> while everywhere love is breathing draftily
> like a doorway linking 53rd with 54th
> the east-bound with the west-bound traffic by 8,000,000s
> o midtown tunnels and the tunnels, too, of Holland (*LP* 37)

The management of erotic possibility is at the forefront of O'Hara's fantastic urban renewal project. His plan is to open up the very space of the city, redesigning the DuMont Building to join 53rd and 54th streets in a facilitation of ardor. Apostrophes to the Midtown and Holland tunnels complete his design, as O'Hara rhapsodizes about New York commuters as enthusiastically as Walt Whitman does about the Brooklyn Ferry and its passengers. O'Hara's bureaucratic sensibility, here, makes him accountable to eight million bodies, as he tries to keep the East Side of Manhattan in balance with the West Side. Such ratios and numeric calculations are not new for O'Hara. In "Personal Poem," O'Hara has played before with such figures, quotients, and percentages, asking—albeit a bit wistfully—"if one person out of the 8,000,000 is thinking of me," a statistic that would, if true, tilt heavily in O'Hara's romantic favor (*LP* 33).

Numbers accumulate in the rest of "Rhapsody" as well, particularly as O'Hara speaks to New York's primacy as an architectural center and financial capital. Shifting attention from the doorway on Madison to the rest of the city, O'Hara beholds the "sight of Manhatta in the towering needle," wherein the needle—the antenna atop the structure—functions as a synecdoche for the Empire State Building (*LP* 38). There are multiple levels to this synecdochic relation of part to whole, for just as the relatively small "needle" represents the larger structure beneath it, the Empire State Building also has often come to signify all of New York itself. Perhaps by necessity for his quasi-bureaucratic poetics, O'Hara has turned to a figure of speech in synecdoche that operates—economically, efficiently—in terms of proportion, scale, and ratio. As Kenneth Burke writes, synecdoche, as a rhetorical figure, "stresses a *relationship* or *connectedness* between two sides of an equation, a connectedness that, like a road, extends in either direction, from quantity to quality or from quality to quantity" (509).

Tellingly, it is the very stature and colossal size of the Empire State Building that prompts a decisive turn in O'Hara's predilection for bureaucracy. In a seemingly offhand remark, O'Hara lightly mocks the monumentalism of a building whose prominence is meant to be a sign of economic—and therefore also bureaucratic—excellence: "Canada plans a higher place than the Empire State Building" (*LP* 38). The reference to New York's signature work of architecture thus keeps enlarging in scope and scale, its significance expanding beyond the merely municipal level, and O'Hara has difficulty abiding by the aim to be first among rival nations. Such competitiveness epitomizes an expansionist ethos of capitalism, one that is underwritten by—and coincides with—bureaucratic principles of endlessly increasing efficiency, productivity, and profitability. As O'Hara extends his reference to the Empire State Building and its towering antenna, or "needle," his dismay with bureaucracy continues (*LP* 38). Alluding to the Greek myth of Theseus, O'Hara calls the surrounding streets of Manhattan a "stringless labyrinth," yet with no thread from Ariadne to guide him, he conceives of himself as lost in a maze, caught up in the Byzantine, bureaucratic, and capitalist relations of New York

(*LP* 38). Bewildered within the vast network of the city, O'Hara unhappily confronts an economic and administrative environment indifferent to the concerns of individuals, where, in Max Weber's words, the "discharge of business primarily means a discharge of business according to *calculable rules* and 'without regard for persons'" (*Economy and Society* [1978] 975).

The disconcerting feeling of alienation is one to which O'Hara's fellow New Yorkers can readily attest. O'Hara continues to describe a depersonalized, highly administered Manhattan where metropolitan existence gets crunched into a slew of numbers, as he gets "into a cab at 9th Street and 1st Avenue" (*LP* 38). Numerical figures remain prominent in the poem's verse, as the African American taxi driver tells O'Hara of a "$120 apartment" and the city's tight housing market for a worker such as himself:

"where you can't walk across the floor after 10 at night
not even to pee, cause it keeps them awake downstairs"
no, I don't like that "well, I didn't take it" (*LP* 38)

If New York is bewildering, a hard-to-navigate labyrinth, it is also a complex puzzle that spreads both vertically and horizontally, making existence trying to navigate. For the taxi driver, one's domicile necessarily entails calculation: a dollar amount signals the upper limit of living expenses beyond which his subsistence will be precarious, his life made uncomfortable, particularly if basic human functions ("you can't walk across the floor after 10 at night") must be restricted out of neighborly courtesy. O'Hara's rejection of such an administered life is as swift as the conversational exchange, a quick give and take where O'Hara's negative reaction to such precarity and restricted living ("no, I don't like that") is nearly matched syllable for syllable by the cab driver, who likewise objects to an overly administered life ("well, I didn't take it"). The virtual symmetry and parity of their verbal responses counter a city dweller's common feeling of being reduced to a mere number and thereby returns some dignity and humanity to the driver's housing plight.

O'Hara concludes "Rhapsody" with an even sharper condemnation of the type of rule-bound, highly administered existence that he sees overtaking many parts of New York. The poem culminates with an image of collective death that O'Hara considers to be the teleology of bureaucracy in the Cold War era, though the superpower of concern here is China and not Russia. Seeing widespread destruction and death as a logical endpoint for American culture should the Cold War persist, O'Hara invokes once more the logic of ratios and equations in the poem's final lines to castigate the dangerous and violent national mindset by asking, "is Tibet historically part of China? as I historically / belong to the enormous bliss of American death" (*LP* 39). Though these questions do not expressly partake in the figure of synecdoche, the relation of part to whole still obtains, as O'Hara ponders just how he might fit within or belong to a national ideology of death and obliteration.

The precise meaning of O'Hara's paradoxical statement, "the enormous bliss of American death," has generated a good deal of critical interpretation. Terrence Diggory, drawing on the work of Jean-Luc Nancy, contends that the phrase indicates O'Hara's interest in subsuming the individual ego to the group ego of an artistic collective or community, something the individual experiences as a kind of death. Mutlu Konuk Blasing, by contrast, links O'Hara's statement about death to the American Empire, an interpretation owing to the poem's previous reference to the Empire State Building and Blasing's view of O'Hara's complicity with the politics of racial and economic exploitation, no matter how much he, as a writer, art critic, and museum curator, would like to remain positioned outside oppressive structures of power. As Blasing writes, "poetic creation partakes of the whole economy of empire building" (52).

My own understanding of O'Hara's poetry and his reference to "the enormous bliss of American death" allows for a more oppositional stance on O'Hara's part than what Blasing's analysis might concede. I consider O'Hara's paradoxical combination of bliss and death in his poem to be a sublime invocation of the terrifying potential of atomic weaponry, whose massive, lethal force O'Hara contests. The concern over war and nuclear annihilation has been a consistent feature of O'Hara's writing. The very first work of *Lunch Poems*, "Music," for example, attests quite clearly to the anxiety O'Hara experiences in 1953: "my nerves humming / Close to the fear of war" (*LP* 1). In "Poem (Khrushchev Is Coming on the Right Day!)," what seems like casual wind imagery ("my tie is blowing up the street / I wish it would blow off") assumes a gloomier, catastrophic hue, as Michael Davidson has discussed, within the "age of atomic testing" and mushroom clouds (*LP* 29; Davidson 68). Similar images of nuclear catastrophe and widespread death, as I have argued elsewhere, also figure in O'Hara's plays, including his eclogue, *Amorous Nightmares of Delay*, wherein a character cautions the audience to assume a "duck and cover" position, presumably in anticipation of a bomb dropping (Lagapa, "Homely Persons" 185).[2]

These recurrent concerns about the disastrous end of the world register O'Hara's opposition to a large-scale militarized and bureaucratic government apparatus and the state of aggression building between the United States and the Communist regimes of China and the Soviet Union.

O'Hara's query into national belonging, framed in the logic of ratios, weighs the degree to which he himself might be associated with the American military industrial complex and the Cold War ideology that drives it. The predicament that O'Hara finds himself in certainly raises matters of citizenship, individual rights, and coercive actions of the State. The other part of O'Hara's compound question about national affiliation, where he asks "is Tibet historically part of China?," only reinforces such concerns about political aggression and militant actions at the state level. O'Hara wrote "Rhapsody" in July of 1959, just four months after the Tibetan Uprising on March 10th, a rebellion spurred by escalating skirmishes between the Communist Chinese army and Tibetan rebel forces and by rumors of a planned abduction of the Dalai Lama.[3] With the battle lines so drawn, O'Hara aligns himself with Tibet's exiled spiritual leader, saying that "they are coming and we holy ones must go" (*LP* 39). To be certain, O'Hara's claim to holiness is ironic; nevertheless, he does register a pacifistic desire, in "Rhapsody" and his other Cold War poems, not to be part of an American agenda headed toward war and annihilation.

The irony O'Hara infuses into his self-portrait as a "holy" monk-like figure extends into the pose that he will strike, leaving no doubt at his intention for caricature. O'Hara will depict himself at rest, caught up in a calm state of poetic, if not spiritual, contemplation:

> I have always wanted to be near it
> . . . .
> lying in a hammock on St. Mark's Place sorting my poems
> in the rancid nourishment of this mountainous island (*LP* 39)

"Sorting [through] poems" in such a campy, lackadaisical posture, O'Hara fancifully imagines himself doing paperwork, an activity long attended to by monk-scribes throughout the centuries. From his hammock, O'Hara assumes, however, a stance belonging less to a reclining Buddha and more to a slow-moving bureaucrat, whose singular aim is to overturn the Weberian ideal of a well-functioning, industrious office space. Accordingly, O'Hara's embodiment of lethargy performs an—intentionally passive—act of protest against an American bureaucratic ethos of speed and efficiency and refuses conventional office dictates that require workers to be endlessly industrious.

Blasing argues that O'Hara, as a relatively affluent member of an art world driven by capitalism, "cannot be holier than what is around him," but he need not be (52). O'Hara's objective is a refusal of the bellicose, rational mindset of his era, and his means of doing so is to lie down on the job, think otherwise, and announce his lack of belonging. Graeber contends that there is an inherent link between bureaucracy and violence, in which the smooth running of bureaucratic systems "ultimately depends on the threat of physical harm" (58). O'Hara here in "Rhapsody" advocates a campy, disobedient protest in the form of a work stoppage or slowdown—a refusal of work—whose power derives from its audacious weariness, or from what Susan Sontag has described as camp's comically lackadaisical stance of "underinvolvement, of detachment" (288). Somehow both ironic and sincere, the refusal of labor constitutes O'Hara's means of removing himself from an American work environment that he believes only serves to escalate geopolitical hostilities.

O'Hara offers an altogether different view of working conditions and labor in "Adieu to Norman, Bon Jour to Joan and Jean-Paul," where he promotes a perception of work and time based not on regimentation but on individual and aesthetic liberation. The newfound conception of time involves a rejection of office work in favor of prioritizing his own imagination and poetic composition. In "Adieu to Norman," moreover, O'Hara pivots away from the warmongering he sees at the core of American culture during the Cold War and moves toward a contemplation of the end of bureaucracy and its strictly structured temporality. As the title of the poem signals with its French farewell and salutation, O'Hara finds himself at a moment of transition, between seeking a departure from the past and a welcoming of the new. As opposed to the death-driven, dystopian image of America at the end of "Rhapsody," there is a utopian release at the conclusion of "Adieu to Norman," premised upon a deep, open-ended conception of time, whose very continuity and fullness is registered in cascading lines of parataxis and anaphora. In a purposeful re-conception of work, the bureaucratic, rigorously scheduled time that O'Hara presents in other poems is replaced by an unregulated sense of time that stretches into an open-ended, utopian future, or what Ernst Bloch has called "the unclosed capability of becoming" (*Principle of Hope* 196).

Before O'Hara can unfurl his thoughts on deep, capacious time, he first encumbers himself to establish a specific starting time and point.

O'Hara thus begins "Adieu to Norman" in line with one of his "I do this, I do that" poems:

> It is 12:10 in New York and I am wondering
> if I will finish this in time to meet Norman for lunch
> ah lunch! I think I am going crazy
> what with my terrible hangover and the weekend coming up
>   (*LP* 34)

The hurried pacing of O'Hara's words and the very specificity of time—ten minutes past noon—reveal that he is on deadline, concerned about making his appointment, even if it is only lunch with a friend. From the immediate context, it is unclear precisely what O'Hara is working busily upon; that is, it is uncertain whether he is worried about finishing a work project for the Museum of Modern Art or the very poem "Adieu to Norman" itself. Though it remains unstated what preoccupies O'Hara's attention, the initial lines of the poem importantly dramatize a dichotomy between work and leisure. The weekend—and the potential of not being at the office or on the clock—looms in the future, and O'Hara must choose how to dispense with his energy and time.

"Adieu to Norman" subsequently reveals that O'Hara is not so determinedly opposed to work itself, especially if doing work means being far from the bureaucratic obligations of his office and laboring away, instead, at his poetry. The aforementioned plans involve a leisurely weekend "at excitement-prone Kenneth Koch's," though O'Hara prefers occupying his time in another manner: "I wish I were staying in town and working on my poems / at Joan's studio for a new book by Grove Press / which they will probably not print" (*LP* 34). Despite the prospect of the book project's futility, O'Hara still considers writing to be a better course of action than a weekend getaway. While O'Hara's gregariousness and allegiance to his friends has often been noted by critics like Terrence Diggory, Lytle Shaw, and Andrew Epstein, the desire for solitude is an equally important modality that structures O'Hara's poetry, particularly when it intersects with work and poetic composition.[4]

The doubt that O'Hara here expresses about spending his energy and time efficiently proves pivotal to the rest of the poem, for O'Hara introduces an alternate value system to bureaucratic principles of speed, tight schedules, and work deadlines, one that is premised instead upon potential and perseverance:

> but it is good to be several floors up in the dead of night
> wondering if you are any good or not
> and the only decision you can make is that you did it. (*LP* 34)

In just a few lines, O'Hara presents a repudiation of several bureaucratic ideals: he abandons the specific time stamp that started the poem for the long duration of "the dead of night." By "wondering if [he is] any good or not," O'Hara also jettisons the pose of the expert. In bureaucratic systems, Weber proposes that, "the more complicated and specialized modern culture becomes, the more its external supporting apparatus demands the . . . strictly objective expert" (*Economy and Society* [1978] 975). By contrast, O'Hara finds wavering, almost amateurish deliberation and uncertainty to be a good in its own right. The creative task is such that it lends itself to a continual, open-ended evaluation in which process is paramount. The last anti-bureaucratic perspective thus is an affirmation of poetic composition and creative productivity: for O'Hara, there remains only the fact of possibility, the final prospect "that you did it."

With artistic, and not bureaucratic, productivity definitively affirmed, O'Hara turns to a meditation on time and the utopian future that projects from it. O'Hara's contemplation of time future begins paradoxically in a moment from the recent past: "yesterday I looked up the rue Frémicourt on a map" (*LP* 34). The map-reading activity here is important, for it sets up a conceit for the rest of the poem, as O'Hara conjures an image of himself flying over Paris, away from his work and social obligations in New York. This imagined flight, moreover, stems from the slightest of surreal gestures; looking for rue Frémicourt on the map abruptly and dreamily transforms O'Hara:

> and [I] was happy to find it like a bird
> flying over Paris et ses environs
> which unfortunately did not include Seine-et-Oise which I
>   don't know (*LP* 34)

In the daydream, O'Hara will go on to explore various parts of Paris, its neighborhoods, its museums, and other places of interest. This conceit of reverie and travel is one that O'Hara borrows from fellow New York School poet John Ashbery, whose poem "The Instruction Manual" (1956) features the poet taking a break from his boring office job and from his bureaucratic "worry about getting out [a] manual on schedule" to daydream about a trip to Guadalajara City (*Some Trees* 14). For Ashbery and O'Hara, life is somewhere else—in Mexico or Paris—rather than in an office building in New York.

The reference to Seine-et-Oise, moreover, represents another disavowal, whether conscious or not on O'Hara's part, of an existence defined by bureaucracy, for Seine-et-Oise was an official administrative division, or *département*, surrounding Paris. These *départements* came into being in the aftermath of the French Revolution as a means for organizing France into political and administrative districts. As Leo Gershoy relates, bureaucratic orderliness was the goal: "France was divided into eighty-three departments, each department into districts, each district into cantons and each canton into communes. . . . [T]he deputies were concerned with establishing a new territorial unit that would make local administration simple and efficient" (149). O'Hara's offhand remark that the map does "not include Seine-et-Oise which I don't know" effectively marks—with its double negation—an erasure of the political *département* and the bureaucratic impulses behind it. O'Hara's allusion to Seine-et-Oise, moreover, likely gave rise to his conceit of flying: though Oise names a river that intersects with the Seine, O'Hara presumably employs the word due to its close proximity to the French word for a bird, *oiseau*. O'Hara thus enacts a reversal of bureaucratic imperatives: the image of a bird gets its genesis and takes flight from the name of an administrative district, thereby eclipsing the bureaucratic regimentation from which it springs.

From this point onward in "Adieu to Norman," O'Hara will devote nearly the rest of the poem converting his doubts about writing and his poetic abilities into a contemplation of possibility. What ensues after O'Hara's consultation of his map of Paris is a protracted declaration of creative potential in response to any limitation or impediment—whether bureaucratic or artistic. Toward this end, O'Hara conducts an interview with himself so as to hold himself accountable to what is possible within the creative process:

> the only thing to do is simply to continue
> is that simple
> yes, it is simple because it is the only thing to do (*LP* 35)

With the repetitions of the infinitive "to do," the terms here being negotiated involve poetic will and necessity. O'Hara even goes so far to remove a question mark from his dialogue ("is that simple") in a seeming effort to ward off reservations about his being determined to work. In contrast to a bureaucratic mindset skewed toward achieved results and completed projects, the imperative for O'Hara is "simply to continue," a phrase that ushers into the poem a utopian dimension. This utopian potential centers on the artistic imagination and takes the desire to solve a creative block or crisis as its impetus.

Ernst Bloch has argued for a correlation between self-consciously literary works—such as the *Künstlerroman* or the novel of the artist—and the utopian impulse, in which the very difficulty of the creative process mimics the challenge of engaging in utopian thought, as both specifically entail a problem being solved and overcome. At the heart of such self-referential literary works like the artist's novel, Bloch states, is "the desire to break new ground . . . to head for the envisioned utopian castle or to that which corresponds to its formation in shape, sound, or word" (*Utopian Function* 277). The pivotal moment of the *Künstlerroman* arises as the artist overcomes a creative block, when "the adventure of the *breakthrough* occurs, the difficult midsummer day of the new work . . . as though it were being conceived right now" (270–71).

For O'Hara, his breakthrough arrives not during summer at midday but at dawn, as he flies in his imagination over the environs of Paris and answers his own questions of artistic doubt in the affirmative:

> can you do it
> yes, you can because it is the only thing to do
> blue light over the Bois de Boulogne it continues (*LP* 35)

O'Hara shores up his confidence by distilling his poetic drive into a singular, determined necessity, as "the only thing to do," and by witnessing how the blue light traveling beyond the Bois de Boulogne "continues" unabated.

In subsequent lines of "Adieu to Norman," the refrain of "it continues" persists, as if O'Hara is attempting to enact possibility with the utterance of a mantra. The daydream flight over Paris takes O'Hara past the city's landmarks, as he notes what remains ongoing:

> the Seine continues
> the Louvre stays open it continues it hardly closes at all
> the Bar Américain continues to be French
> de Gaulle continues to be Algerian as does Camus (*LP* 35)

The litany of examples of continuity concludes in a crescendo of anaphora and parataxis, one that is primarily triumphant in tone and expressive of utopian yearning. O'Hara observes:

> and the Flore continues to have tables and newspapers and
>   people under them
> and surely we shall not continue to be unhappy
> we shall be happy
> but we shall continue to be ourselves everything continues
>   to be possible
> René Char, Pierre Reverdy, Samuel Beckett it is possible isn't
>   it (*LP* 36)

O'Hara here momentarily hedges, admitting to a prevailing sense of unhappiness or collective gloom. The acknowledgment of unhappiness, however, is short-lived, its double negative swiftly converted to a proclamation in the affirmative: "we shall be happy." The happiness here espoused, articulated in the future tense, is replete with utopian promise, an uplifting moment in the poem that might qualify for what Norman Finkelstein describes as one of "the few genuinely utopian passages in O'Hara's work" (58). Though Finkelstein does not read O'Hara's work overall to be utopian, the concluding lines of "Adieu to Norman" do speak to the type of utopian potential that Finkelstein sees as essential to literary projects. In a manner that echoes O'Hara's persistent refrain on continuity, Finkelstein maintains that utopian works must entail qualities of development and progress: "If poetry is to be of *continued* worth, then it must in some ways be a means to greater cognitive powers, schooling human thought and feeling to allow for the *continuance* of creativity. 'This is what we are' must be translatable into 'this is what we might be'" (51, emphasis added).

To believe O'Hara's utopian message at the end of "Adieu to Norman," one must ultimately contend with the poet's vacillating reflections about what is or is not possible. In the poem's penultimate line, O'Hara invokes a triumvirate of writers who serve as inspiration for what is creatively possible: "René Char, Pierre Reverdy, Samuel Beckett it is possible isn't it" (*LP* 36). O'Hara's list of writers is apposite. Reverdy writes in his poem "That Memory" of such potential and possibility, suggesting that "[e]verything continues / No one knows where time will stop" (69). Samuel Beckett's *The Unnamable* also would seemingly provide an object lesson in continuity, with the well-known, concluding words of the novel ringing forward: "I can't go on, I'll go on" (414). However, the next and very last line of "Adieu to Norman" seemingly backtracks from all that O'Hara has said about possibility—about things continuing forward—for he writes, "I love Reverdy for saying yes, though I don't believe it" (*LP* 36).

A question arises if the final words "Adieu to Norman" ought to undercut the thirteen times O'Hara has said that things must "continue" or the two times that he avers that all is "possible." The preponderance of O'Hara's affirmative language would appear to outnumber—and therefore outweigh—the last, anxious statement of O'Hara's that he cannot quite believe in saying "yes." One might do well by understanding O'Hara's final equivocation to be a superstitious gesture on his part, intended to ward off an overly glib, unwarranted belief in the future. In "Personal Poem," O'Hara admits to such superstition, declaring that he walks around with "two charms in my pocket / an old Roman coin Mike Kanemitsu gave me / and a bolt-head that broke off a packing case" (*LP* 32). These are talismans that O'Hara uses to encourage fortune and good grace and to keep himself steady "in New York against coercion" (*LP* 32). In "Adieu to Norman," O'Hara longs for the appropriate future, for all that is possible to be ensured, and he is seemingly superstitious enough in the end to claim that he cannot quite believe that all will continue or be possible as he has proposed. This final statement is a receding moment of ambivalence, a fleeting expression of doubt, and the reader must conclude whether or not O'Hara's cynical, final line should be believed at last.

As O'Hara knew well, what is foreclosed to the bureaucratic mindset is time unregulated. Under bureaucratic systems and their rules, proficiencies cannot be unmet without consequence, and explorations of open-ended possibility are highly discouraged. John Ashbery has said that O'Hara's poetry evinced a simple truth, wherein "to ignore the rules is always a provocation" (introduction, *Collected Poems of Frank O'Hara* vii). Though O'Hara had his moments when he adhered to, and even enjoyed, the structure that bureaucratic systems and rules might offer, he also urged us in his poems to go beyond bureaucratic imperatives and limitations to see what is possible. This would prove a difficult task, even for O'Hara. The historical moment of the Cold War weighed heavily upon him, as did the corresponding era of bureaucratization, which confined and closed in upon him. Nevertheless, O'Hara's poetry frequently stood as a rebuke to the delimiting nature of society, and he took its restrictions as a challenge to his being. In fact, he sought to provoke something in us as well, so that we, too, "might continue to be ourselves" and find that "everything continues to be possible."

Chapter 3

Accounts Must Be Reexamined

John Ashbery and the Bureaucratic Mind

> But once more, office desks, radiators—No! That is behind me. No more dullness . . .
>
> —John Ashbery, "The Skaters"

> "Mr. Samsa," the chief clerk called now in a louder voice, "what's the matter with you? Here you are, barricading yourself in your room, giving only 'yes' and 'no' for answers, causing your parents a lot of unnecessary trouble and neglecting—I mention this only in passing—neglecting your business duties in an incredible fashion."
>
> —Franz Kafka, "The Metamorphosis"

Of the many fictions embedded within "The Instruction Manual," beyond, that is, the daydream conceit of a festive and color-filled tour of Guadalajara, Mexico, there exists an additional one concerning the poem's composition and its source of inspiration. The office that gave rise to the writing of "The Instruction Manual" was actually an enclosed, windowless room in the thirty-five-story McGraw-Hill Building, where John Ashbery had worked as a copy editor. About the office, Ashbery remarks: "There wasn't any window in the room so that was an invention . . . The poem really ends with me returning to the boring task I have to do, where the poem began. It leads back into me, and is probably about the dissatisfactions with the work I was doing at the time" (quoted in Gangel 18). The invented detail about the office window is important not only to a poem explicitly about fabrication but also to Ashbery's writing as a whole, whose subject matter frequently invokes an office space as the site of the imagination and aligns the flowering of creativity with work accomplished in a circumscribed room and at a remove from the external world. In such limited, functional office spaces, Ashbery cultivates room for the poetic mind to flourish, leading to a triumph of another kind of work, one opposed to the bureaucratic labor that seemed everywhere to surround him.

The conceit of "The Instruction Manual," in which a bored clerk invents a vibrant imagined world, establishes a leitmotif for a surprising number of Ashbery's poems, where the tedium of work is contravened by bright acts of the imagination. Uninspired toil and flourishes of the imagination pair in Ashbery's writing consistently enough that the two—dull office work and poetic composition—become fused and made the obverse of each other. The fusion reflects the sense that administrative culture has pervaded almost every corner of society, yet it also importantly signals a potential means to contest the prevailing bureaucratic ethos. For Ashbery, work done in an office, as a site of bureaucratic labor, soon doubles as a paradoxical figure for creative labor, and the trials of poetic composition are transposed onto the monotony of clerical tasks. Within the wide realm of Ashbery's recurring images, the office—nondescript, clerical, routinized—makes for an ironic, inverse emblem of poetic invention and even play.

Insular spaces, though, are not the only means for Ashbery to address creative productivity, its inspirations, and its challenges. Corresponding and persistent bureaucratic terms and metaphors appear in Ashbery's poetry and point to his critique of administrative culture and its ideology. Adopting business terminology for his own poetic ends, Ashbery operates in the manner of *la perruque*, as discussed by de Certeau, by using corporate language against itself: "he succeeds in 'putting one over' on the established order on its home ground" (26; see also my introduction and chapter 1). The appropriation of bureaucratic language for poetry indicates a habitual desire on Ashbery's part not only to repudiate administrative culture but to bend it toward his own purposes. The use of office terminology, however, also notably reveals the complex—and, at times, particularly vexed—relationship he has to work, aesthetic production, and audience. Bureaucracy is an ever-shifting, equivocal trope for Ashbery, alternately indicating the trials of the creative process and the artist's precarious position facing both public scrutiny and self-doubt. With each instance of office language, Ashbery's stance becomes clearer, though; here is a poet who wants to cultivate within his poems an efficient workspace of the imagination, where he might manage risk to his productivity and hedge against any sort of impediment to his writing or his creativity.[1]

Ashbery's invocations of bureaucracy and administrative terminology, by turns subtle and explicit, are notable and frequent elements of his poetry, even if these aspects recede at times into the background. As Bonnie Costello has observed, Ashbery's many landscapes include not only the "pastoral, sublime, [and] suburban" but also, importantly, the "bureaucratic" ("Landscapes" 61). In such bureaucratic settings, high, multi-floored buildings assume an integral role, and administrative offices recur as conflicted spaces of work, privacy, and creativity. Feelings of being exposed—his writing laid bare to an audience or his own self-conscious appraisal—typically set in when Ashbery takes up the subject matter of bureaucracy, lending such moments a troubled sense of conflict and unease. In poems like "The Painter," "Self-Portrait in a Convex Mirror," "Litany," and "Fragment" to name just a few, the speakers—many of whom seem a facsimile of Ashbery himself—are regularly hampered by bureaucracy and its mechanisms. Depicting himself as anchored to a dull office desk is an ironic, figurative, and multifaceted means for Ashbery to convey not only the angst-ridden trials of artistic creativity but also his beleaguered attempts to overcome them.

The motifs of bureaucratic alienation, stasis, and demanding work that prevail in Ashbery's poetry owe much to the stories of Franz Kafka, a writer whom several critics have associated with Ashbery's writing and whom Ashbery himself cites and parodies in poems like "Wet Casements," "A Boy," and "The Skaters." David Shapiro, for instance, has argued in his reading of "The Skaters" that certain sections of the long poem are modeled on Kafka's "condensed tales of defeat and humiliation" (94). Similarly, John Shoptaw sees in Ashbery's poetry echoes of Kafka's writing, particularly the "minimal narratives in *Parables and Paradoxes*," which display a "transcendental urge" to find meaning in abstruse messages as well as in alienating situations (253).[2]

Kafka and Ashbery are arguably joined as well through their ambivalent attitudes toward writing, as Kafka's compositional struggles help to elucidate Ashbery's conflicted feelings about artistic productivity, in which the compulsion to write is experienced as simultaneously pleasure-filled and anguished. As is well known, writing was central to Kafka's existence, though it was often a vexed endeavor, something to which his diary entries repeatedly, and histrionically, attest: "Yesterday incapable of writing even one word. Today no better. Who will save me? And the turmoil in me, deep down, scarcely visible" (Kafka, *Diaries* 31).[3] Despite the tumult that the creative process produced, Kafka would also routinely declare his intention to write as if it were a personal necessity: "I will write in spite of everything, absolutely; it is my struggle for self-preservation" (*Diaries* 75). Ashbery's reflections on writing are more measured than Kafka's, yet they display a similar determination and aim to overcome the challenges of writing. In an interview with David Remnick, for instance, Ashbery describes his writing process as entailing both pleasure and pain due to the degree of concentration required: "It is sort of like a high when I write. It's kind of painful and pleasurable at the same time to be so attentive. It's nice when it's over, too" (Remnick).[4]

In Ashbery's more intense moments of ambivalence and vacillation regarding work, he seems trapped in what Richard Heinemann has labeled *Beamtengeist*, or the "bureaucratic mind," a mainstay of Kafka's stories where the office is paradoxically both a refuge and a space of confinement (Heinemann 257). As Heinemann further explains, *Beamtengeist* is a condition of debilitating stasis and restriction that Kafka's characters simultaneously loathe and depend upon: "the only way for Kafka to break the spell of *Beamtengeist* is to leave his office and his residence, which signify the self-protectiveness and security he seeks, and to abandon himself to a future fraught with risk" (259). For both Ashbery and Kafka, the appeal of escaping the office—of jettisoning work—is strong, though the idea of quitting also conjures equally intense feelings of guilt and dread. Possessed of a bureaucratic mindset, of *Beamtengeist*, one is consequently predisposed "to protect oneself by making calculations rather than by acting" (Heinemann 259).

Ashbery's "Untilted" [sic] is a poem that typifies the bureaucratic mindset for its very premise revolves around the drive to work and a desire to renounce it. The speaker of "Untilted" details rival impulses of an isolated life of writing and one that is less arduous in a recognizable and familiar manner: at the center of the poem is a tall building like that of "The Instruction Manual" from which the speaker looks down—at once longingly and apprehensively—onto the streets below. Ashbery begins the poem with an exhilarating feeling approaching the sublime:

> How tall the buildings were as I began
> To live, and how high the rain that battered them!
> Why coming down them, as I often did at night,
> Was a dream even before you reach the first gullies (*Shadow Train* 26)

As in the dream-space of "The Instruction Manual," Ashbery configures what occurs below to be a temptation, a space of play and leisure to be contrasted with dutiful work completed overhead. That the building above is a site of work and responsibility is implied in Ashbery's subsequent declamation as he longs to join others taking a break from job duties: "Forget / The tourists—other people must travel too" (*Shadow Train* 26). This cavalier comment announces his longing: Ashbery's speaker would like for work—or poetic composition—to be neither an obstacle to being sociable among others nor an impediment to pleasure found outside of the space of work. As the title suggests, the desire to which "Untilted" speaks is balance, where work and play are properly offset, made equal. Corresponding questions of self-preservation also arise, so that the risk of exposure—whether to artistic failure or an unsympathetic audience—might be contained: "And [you] gave yourself over to thoughts of your own welfare" (*Shadow Train* 26).

As he weighs his options between work and leisure and isolation or engagement with an audience, Ashbery comes to a realization about himself in the final lines of "Untilted" about his conflicted predilections: "Why not just / Breathe in with the courage of each day, recognizing yourself as one / Who must with difficulty get down from high places?" (*Shadow Train* 26). Indicative of *Beamtengeist*, the default inclination for Ashbery is to remain industrious at work, yet a visit to the social spaces below also tempts, even if such a trip would require a daily ritual of inspiration and self-encouragement. Ashbery's rhetorical question at the end of "Untilted" suggests that its speaker is forever stymied by his situation, caught in a state of suspension and calculation, as he must choose between remaining secure in his building or exiting it. It is an equivocal proposition: the speaker instructs himself to recognize—yet not necessarily overcome—his fears of descending from his room, leaving the decision to depart or not ultimately uncertain. These vying impulses have led Andrew Epstein to recognize in Ashbery's poetry a "balancing act [between] solitude and fraternity," a tension that Epstein argues can be traced to the American pragmatist tradition (130).[5] Though Epstein rightly draws attention to the once-overlooked social dimension of Ashbery's poetry, it seems equally fitting to understand the other side of Ashbery's conflicted choice between sociability and isolation. Friendship and societal acceptance beckon, but so does solitude and the security it brings.

Ashbery's insular shelter within a high-rise building in "Untilted" recalls another ambivalent, multifaceted space of seclusion, protection, work, and creativity: the habitat of the mole-like animal in Kafka's story "Der Bau," or "The Burrow." Throughout "The Burrow," the animal protagonist obsessively details his constant efforts to fortify his underground dwelling and ensure his safety. As with many of Kafka's stories, though, "The Burrow" intimates more than its ostensible narrative of an animal securing his underground home and reveals a secondary, corresponding subject: writing. Stanley Corngold has pointed out that the German "Der Bau" means "literally, 'The Building,' 'The Construction,'" words that allude "to Kafka's literary enterprise," for *Bauen* "is a recurrent figure of writing for Kafka, as is its cognate *Konstruktion*" (282).[6]

Elaborating on Corngold's reading of "The Burrow," Richard Heinemann contends that the animal's allegorical "'house of art' is [equally] a bureaucracy," particularly if "the creature's officialistic tone, pettiness, and love of routine and especially [the] prolific . . . calculations" of his burrow are taken into account (262). The mole's ceaseless renovations indeed render his project forever unfinished, similar to the stasis and postponement of action that besets many a bureaucracy. A perpetual mode of appraisal constitutes the bureaucrat's job, as David Graeber argues: "Much of what bureaucrats do, after all, is evaluate things. They are continually assessing, auditing, measuring the relative merits of different plans, proposals, applications, courses of action . . ." (41). What Kafka describes in the mole's continual tinkering and what Graeber characterizes as the bureaucrat's definitive task of evaluation resemble, moreover, an artist's deliberation over—and dissatisfaction with—the direction of a work in progress. Kafka's mole is at an impasse, unsure of the direction of his burrow. Correspondingly, the angst that predominates "The Burrow" matches the tone that commonly infuses Ashbery's writing, where anxiety about the creative process and concern over audience reception find available expression in bureaucratic circumstances and terminology.

In Ashbery's early sestina "The Painter," for instance, motifs of bureaucratic supervision, work-related stasis and indecision, along with comparable Kafkan subjects of artistic setback and failure, are fundamental elements of the poem. The ostensible narrative of "The Painter" revolves around thwarted attempts by an artist to paint his chosen subject matter: the sea. Of the sestina's repeated six end-words, *building*—that recurrent and quintessential architectural image in Ashbery's poetry—here signifies an urban and densely populated setting, yet it also obliquely alludes to bureaucratic oversight: "So there was never any paint on his canvas / until the people who lived in the buildings / put him to work . . ." (*Some Trees* 54). A subordinate, clerical passivity marks the volition of the painter, as he yields to administrative management by others. From this group come clamoring directives that more closely resemble the instrumental discourse of efficiency protocols than a discussion of aesthetic technique: "'Try using the brush / As a means to an end'" (54). Echoing the commentary of an office committee or focus group, the ensuing guidance from "the people . . . in the buildings" only reinforces the sense of a pragmatic oversight, as their facile suggestions and directions are thrown out in a haphazard manner: "Select, for a portrait, / Something less angry and large, and more subject / To a painter's moods, or perhaps, to a prayer" (54).

Toward the poem's end, the image that the painter has composed vanishes, "leaving the canvas / Perfectly white," a consequence that David Shapiro calls an "apt artistic defeat" and a "victory for the funny philistinism of the poet's audience" (*Some Trees* 55; Shapiro 47). The moment of inspiration indeed falters, with the artist's efforts thwarted: "Imagine a painter crucified by his subject!" (*Some Trees* 55). This derailed outcome and Kafkaesque defeat could perhaps have been predicted from the outset, for the painter is not, as in many of Ashbery's other poems, situated securely above the street—like the privileged spaces of "The Instruction Manual" or "Untilted." Had the painter remained isolated in his studio or office, sheltered by the principle of *Beamtengeist*, or the ingrained wariness of exposure to others, he might have avoided ridicule. The painter of Ashbery's poem is instead unprotected and vulnerable; he sits openly in a spot "between the sea and the buildings" (54).

The location makes the painter all the more subject to the whims of his audience, whose collective critical judgment and disembodied commentary ("news spread like wildfire through the buildings") contribute to the poem's overarching mood of paranoia and resignation (54). In this regard, "The Painter" exhibits what Costello calls a customary "pattern of mutuality and conflict" between the writer and audience in Ashbery's poems ("Idea of the Reader" 499). The final verdict about the painter is not positive, as the nondescript, menacing audience make their hostile sentiments known: "They tossed him, the portrait, from the tallest of the buildings" (*Some Trees* 55). With the antagonism of its conclusion, "The Painter" chronicles an artist's despair over his lack of creative output and inefficient deployment of artistic skill amid an audience skeptical of his abilities. At every turn, risk to creative production is continuously present for the painter, exposing him to ridicule and disapproval.

The impulse toward security and self-preservation that Ashbery had so keenly expressed in "Untilted" would thus seem fairly remote from the mood of "The Painter." Unless, that is, one might take the painter's very last artistic gesture of voiding his own painting to be an act of concealment and self-protection. At that moment, the painter ceases work, and "all indications of a subject / Began to fade" (*Some Trees* 55). The steps toward erasure, moreover, pertain not just to the painting but also to the painter himself, as "others" in the audience "declared it a self-portrait" (55). By absenting himself from his artistic work, the painter endeavors, albeit unsuccessfully, to fend off scrutiny. Ashbery here evinces, via the painter's attempts at aesthetic erasure and concealment, a tendency also employed by Kafka, who "takes up his themes and buries himself in them as an animal buries itself in its hole" (Albérès and de Boisdeffre 55). The effect is one of Kafka enclosing "himself and his narrative in a bunker . . . and creating a wall between himself and the outside world" (Albérès and de Boisdeffre 55). Ashbery's "The Painter" likewise illustrates a temptation of the artist to hide, with the successful execution of the sestina itself constituting yet another level of concealment: the painter's absurdly comical troubles and failures take precedence in the poem, while Ashbery's bravura management of the sestina's form itself withdraws into the background. To the extent that the painter—the poem's protagonist—fails, Ashbery's poem itself succeeds, wherein the poem's motifs of bureaucratic oversight and hostile, collective opinion ultimately yield to adroit, poetic achievement of the sestina form.

Lessons gleaned about the bureaucratic mindset that governs much of "The Painter" prove relevant to Ashbery's subsequent poetic output. Shoptaw has argued that "The Painter" forms something of "a preliminary sketch" for Ashbery's prize-winning "Self-Portrait in a Convex Mirror," and the subjects of artistic creation, public response, and shielding oneself from scrutiny correspondingly surface in the later poem as well (29). Parmigianino, the sixteenth-century Mannerist painter whom Ashbery details in "Self-Portrait in a Convex Mirror," likewise engages and shies away from his viewer, ultimately appearing trapped within the spaces of his own portrait, his outwardly gesturing hand, paradoxically and simultaneously, "swerving easily away, as though to protect / What it advertises" (*Self-Portrait* 68). In summing up Parmigianino's self-portrait, Ashbery offers a flat, truncated summation of the artist's rendering of selfhood: "It is what is / Sequestered" (68). Here, again, Ashbery fashions an image of the artist suspended in the moment of imaginative production, wary of what exposure to the audience might cost or risk. As with his other poems, and in a manner befitting the concept of *Beamtengeist*, Ashbery locates the handiwork and process of creativity within a closed-off, burrow-like workspace that guarantees its productivity only through self-protection and seclusion.

Ashbery further distills this feeling of burrowing and self-enclosure in the beginning sections of "Self-Portrait in a Convex Mirror," as he concentrates his attention on what the painting evokes, which is the sense of a soul having been trapped within the portrait itself:

> The soul has to stay where it is,
> Even though restless, hearing raindrops at the pane
> The sighing of autumn leaves thrashed by the wind,
> Longing to be free, outside, but it must stay
> Posing in this place. (69)

These lines give an indication of what Helen Vendler has broadly remarked about Ashbery's poetry, that "[l]ife for Ashbery, as everyone has noticed, is motion" (184). The passage's depiction of turbulent leaves and pelting rain undoubtedly intimates flux and movement, yet stillness and fixity are also crucially important to the passage. The soul, Ashbery maintains, "has to stay where it is," remaining installed within its repository for the painting to achieve its aesthetic effect. Indeed, the remarkable impact of Parmigianino's painting, the dynamic rendering of a soul, relies paradoxically upon a mundane, stationary object—the wooden hemisphere on which the self-portrait is painted. As Ashbery wryly observes, Parmigianino's being—the animated fullness of his soul—is stuck, immobile.

Ashbery's objective in "Self-Portrait in a Convex Mirror" is to create a poem that approximates Parmigianino's own portrait and even attempts to be its equal. Accordingly, the status of Parmigianino's soul—fixed in place—prompts Ashbery to contemplate both the artistic process and conditions of work, for not only Parmigianino but himself. The difficulty of rendering a self-portrait like Parmigianino's initiates in Ashbery a bout of writing anxiety and a corresponding contemplation of artistic defeat, particularly as Parmigianino's grand achievement leaves little room for mistakes, let alone failure. Appropriate to the mirror conceit of the painting and the poem, though, Ashbery transposes his anxiety onto Parmigianino and his studio, whose working conditions inspire claustrophobic sensations of entrapment: "There are no recesses in the room, only alcoves, / And the window doesn't matter much, or that / Sliver of window or mirror on the right" (*Self-Portrait* 69). Ashbery's anxious reaction to Parmigianino's studio is telling, for the negative feelings about the studio are but one half of Ashbery's ambivalent response to work; he remains both frightened by and committed to the prospect of carrying out his own poetic labor. Later in "Self-Portrait in a Convex Mirror," Ashbery will come to embrace his own office as a site of creativity and imagination, a place of abundant artistic fulfillment and dedication, yet he initially conceives his own attempt to produce a self-portrait to be a stifling endeavor, particularly as his work closely parallels that of Parmigianino's.

The difficulty of mirroring Parmigianino's artistic efforts results in Ashbery projecting onto Parmigianino feelings of exhaustion and despair. Rather incongruously, Ashbery adopts bureaucratic discourse and the language of the office to convey the sublime nature of Parmigianino's artistic process, yet the terminology is a fitting expression of Ashbery's daunting task. Beset by *Beamtengeist*, Ashbery is compelled to speak of artistic dedication in bureaucratic terms:

> I see in this only the chaos
> Of your round mirror which organizes everything
> Around the polestar of your eyes which are empty,
> Know nothing, dream but reveal nothing. (71)

Ashbery prioritizes organization as a chief aesthetic technique for Parmigianino, who achieves effects of depth and perspective through the use of a "round mirror." This organizing principle, though, simultaneously suggests the mechanisms of bureaucratic order and its dehumanizing effects: Parmigianino's eyes—a would-be inspired, guiding force—are subsequently rendered vacant, revealed to be "empty" and to "[k]now nothing." The circumstances are yet again akin to that of "The Instruction Manual," where Ashbery initiates a dialectic between work and play, between dull responsibility and dreams, and the vibrancy of artistic imagination is contrasted with dedication to work. Ashbery's sense that Parmigianino's eyes "dream but reveal nothing" (*Self-Portrait* 71) parallel the denouement of the earlier poem, where the unconscious act of dreaming dissolves into nothingness. By the end of "The Instruction Manual," work and its dissatisfactions still remain: "I turn my gaze / Back to the instruction manual which has made me dream of Guadalajara" (*Some Trees* 18). In "Self-Portrait," Ashbery similarly views Parmigianino as being attenuated and nullified, wherein the dexterous work of producing art seemingly necessitates an emptying or voiding of the artist's existence.

In Ashbery's bizarre mirror-world, bureaucratic work consequently becomes a fitting, if purposely distorted, figure for artistic labor and its challenges in "Self-Portrait." Immediately after acknowledging Parmigianino's vacant stare, Ashbery pivots away from the room in which Parmigianino paints in order to contemplate his own work desk, as he proceeds to compose his version of a self-portrait in verse. Caught within his bureaucratic mindset, Ashbery begins by depicting the environment of his office as stifling, with the scene of labor possessing the dread commonly associated with an administrative desk job:

> I feel the carousel starting slowly
> And going faster and faster: desk, papers, books,
> Photographs of friends, the window and the trees
> Merging in one neutral band that surrounds
> Me on all sides, everywhere I look. (71)

The bureaucrat's typical impulse for organization—what Richard Heinemann, following the work of Henri de Man, calls the "fetishizing . . . arrangement of desk, pen, and ruler"—here gets turned on its head (261). Instead of gratifying order, the office "carousel" goes "faster and faster," spinning out of control. Markers of bureaucratic plainness in the form of a generic and constricting "neutral band" induce the sense of workplace vertigo, an effect compounded by the claustrophobic compactness of an office space "that surrounds / [Him] on all sides."

Shoptaw has noted that Ashbery began "Self-Portrait in a Convex Mirror" under precarious employment conditions, when "in 1972, after new owners took over Art News, Ashbery found himself without a job as an art critic" (174). The constrained spaces of "Self-Portrait" thus likely refer to Ashbery's home office, yet the aftermath of downsizing and employment insecurity nevertheless filters into his rendering of artistic work. With his workplace seemingly spinning and uncertain, Ashbery experiences the prospect of aesthetic labor and the writing of his self-portrait with a terror summoned by the bureaucratic sublime: "And I cannot explain the action of levelling, / Why it should all boil down to one / Uniform substance" (*Self-Portrait* 71). Ashbery processes the daunting moment of artistic creativity with the only language that is immediately available to him: a neutral vocabulary of bureaucratic and administrative tedium, in which all action is "level[ed]" and the conditions of work are blandly made "uniform." Weber has argued that bureaucracy's "tendency toward levelling" democratizes the office by eliminating social rank, a process of homogenization that no doubt contributes to the anonymity and flatness oft associated with bureaucratic spaces (*Economy and Society* [2019] 353). For Ashbery, the task of accounting for both Parmigianino's work and his own poetic labor is formidable, yet the lackluster language of bureaucracy constitutes a paradoxical means of attesting to the beauty of artistic creation and the hazards in producing it. A bland, tedious workspace here functions as means to contain—and inversely convey—the risks involved in making art.

As Ashbery continues to chronicle his response to Parmigianino's extraordinary aesthetic achievement, administrative discourse persists, with bureaucratic terms superseding the language of art and art history. Ashbery finds himself struggling to articulate what he witnesses in the painting, succumbing as he does to effects of the sublime. For Edmund Burke, a defining characteristic of the sublime is its ability to impair or inhibit the rational mind, an experience that consequently stymies articulation of the sublime object: "the mind is so entirely filled with its object, that it cannot entertain any other, nor by consequence reason on that object which employs it" (57). This is the reason-defying state in which Ashbery finds himself: "Impossible now / To restore those properties in the silver blur that is / The record of what you accomplished" (*Self-Portrait* 72). In Ashbery's telling, Parmigianino's artistic achievement amounts to the bureaucratic sublime, a "sliver blur," difficult to grasp and perceive and summarily encapsulated in an understated, truncated administrative officialese: "the record." Within this framework of institutional rhetoric, even Ashbery's citation of art historian Giorgio Vasari ("sitting down / 'With great art to copy all that you saw in the glass'") takes on a shift in meaning, for it aligns Parmigianino's role with that of a humble scrivener, tasked with the job of routine copying. The working imperative, as with office clerks, is for dutiful and efficient record keeping and duplication, "So as to perfect and rule out the extraneous" (72).

Ashbery's "Self-Portrait" is a simultaneous accounting of Parmigianino's work and his own, a comparison of work ledgers that chronicles tasks accomplished and work still needed to be done. Consequently, the corresponding bureaucratic record of the poem is an office log of scheduled duties and outcomes, items he evaluates in diurnal segments: "Tomorrow is easy, but today is uncharted, / Desolate, reluctant as any landscape / To yield what are laws of perspective" (72). The subject of these remarks is ostensibly still Parmigianino's painting and its adherence to rules of visual perspective, yet Ashbery here also uneasily recounts his own immediate workday tasks, which, "uncharted," press upon him.

In contrast to the present day, the future seems promising, its dreamy, distant deadline being far from unnerving or demanding: "Some day we will try / To do as many things as are possible / And perhaps we shall succeed at a handful of them" (72). Though he is able to postulate some future, open-ended deadline, he must regretfully concede that "this will not have anything / To do with what is promised today" (72). Instead, Ashbery experiences the workload of the present day as mounting with pressure, with Parmigianino's convex "Self-Portrait" providing the apt metaphor of a capacious "bubble-chamber" that gauges and measures levels of work output (72). Continuously expansive, the workday bubble will grow exponentially: "everything gets 'programmed' there / In due course: more keeps getting included / Without adding to the sum" (72). This is Ashbery at his most despairing when confronting the bureaucratic sublime: "programmed" data about work inexorably accumulates, yet any accounting of it is faulty; the numbers disconcertingly do not add "to the sum," failing to compute as they should.

The task before Ashbery is forbidding enough that, true to a clerk's *Beamtengeist*, he will want to retreat, escaping to his customary motif of the sequestered room in order to accomplish his work. The day's labor, along with its expanding catalog of duties, proceeds with the pressure-filled "bubble-chamber" of an office, its daily obligations now converted figuratively into a timepiece: "So the room contains this flow like an hourglass / Without varying in climate or quality" (73). This sterile, climate-controlled room in which Ashbery finds himself initially seems to offer no refuge: his rhetorical figures of administered work "flow" and measured time ("hourglass") here appear only intended to enforce constant productivity and an unrelenting schedule of work.

Nevertheless, a shift will occur in Ashbery's bureaucratic mindset that redeems the work of writing into something positive. It is a feat that he achieves through the sheer determination of his labors. The arid office is, over time, transfigured into a perfect environment for poetic inspiration, a hothouse of the unconscious, wherein "What should be the vacuum of a dream / Becomes continually replete as the source of dreams / Is being tapped so that this one dream / May wax, flourish like a cabbage-rose, / Defying sumptuary laws" (73). Ashbery, at this moment, imaginatively remakes his office into an ideal workplace and studio, wherein the bureaucratic sublime that had once terrified him now yields a different sensibility, one of inspired aesthetic composition and flourishing creativity. Such oscillation between despair and exhilaration traces a continuum, a spectrum between listlessness and inspiration, that Rob Wilson has described as the "euphoric/dreadful source of the postmodern sublime" (219).

The room that Ashbery inhabits has become a privileged space for the making of art, yet there remains in New York the seductive lure of a city outside his office window. As with the protective spaces in Kafka's "The Burrow," the bunker motif in Ashbery's poetry will now fully reassert itself, particularly as Ashbery contemplates how his situation mirrors that of Parmigianino, who had to contend with a different set of demands and dangers just beyond the walls of his artist studio in Rome: "The shadow of the city injects its own / Urgency: Rome where Francesco / Was at work during the Sack: his inventions / Amazed the soldiers who burst in on him; / They decided to spare his life" (75). For Ashbery, it is the distraction from work, in the form of city life and social engagement that potentially loom: "New York / Where I am now . . . is a logarithm / Of other cities. Our landscape / Is alive with filiations, shuttlings" (75). As a preeminent center of art, entertainment, and social life, logarithmic New York *is* diversion itself, an exponentially distracting allure that persists in staking its claim:

> It wants
> To siphon off the life of the studio, deflate
> Its mapped space to enactments, island it. (75).

The hope that Ashbery maintains is that the studio—the office—would remain his refuge, his Kafkan burrow, from which all dangers could be foreseen and thwarted and the self remain protected. The precarious equilibrium between work and life, however, threatens to be upset, with the office becoming less the privileged space of creation and more a desert "island," if New York, from the outside, could indeed usurp—deflate—the breath and vitality contained within his studio.

The bureaucratic mindset—the self-protective mentality of *Beamtengeist*—proves all too easily to have limitations, as the impulse to remain indoors oscillates between the good and bad. The site of seclusion, whether Parmigianino's artist's studio or Ashbery's office space, can suddenly seem less protective and more stifling—a quaint, domesticated enclosure like "A cloth over a birdcage," intended to keep external fears at bay (77). Such a sheltered space can equally produce works of art and literature that are paradoxically boundless and all encompassing. As Ashbery avows, an exceptional painting, like Parmigianino's, or poem like his own "Self-Portrait in a Convex Mirror"—though singular and finite—can imply so much more than itself, so that "The sample / One sees is not to be taken as / Merely that, but as everything as it / May be imagined outside time—not as a gesture / But as *all* . . ." (77; emphasis added). Ashbery endeavors to make his office, despite its limitations, an all-encompassing burrow, a self-contained cosmos rivaling the known universe. The reduplication of Parmigianino's painting thus reinforces Ashbery's sublime purposes: a writer at work copying another artist at *his* work produces a hermetically sealed enterprise, closed off to—but also a substitute for—the outside world. The only remaining question is how fulfilling or satisfactory this arrangement might be: is his office a birdcage or total cosmos, an entire world or a suffocating, circumscribed existence? Ashbery's conundrum is that he must choose between the lived experience outside his office or the imaginative world he summons within it.

"Self-Portrait in a Convex Mirror" concludes much as it began, with an artist sequestered, though the focus is not on Parmigianino, finally, but on Ashbery himself, who occupies the solitary space of his home, secure within "the disguising radiance of [his] room" (82). Ashbery absconds once more to a space high in his building, his balcony offering the same overhead experience that he wrote of in "The Instruction Manual," as the populace glides on by below:

> We have seen the city; it is the gibbous
> Mirrored eye of an insect. All things happen
> On its balcony and are resumed within,
> But the action is the cold, syrupy flow
> Of a pageant. (82–83)

Hovering above and hesitant to engage with the streets below, Ashbery has situated himself upon a precipice. Outside his apartment, the city—a treacly parade of activity, its "cold, syrupy flow"—is far short of being appetizing. Ashbery turns back to his work, "resumed within," ambivalently acquiescing to the job at hand. Returning to his writing, Ashbery affirms once more that he is someone "[w]ho must with difficulty get down from high places" (*Shadow Train* 26). There is still a task to be done within his apartment office, though the prospect of such labor is uncertain as well: "One feels too confined, / Sifting the April sunlight for clues, / In the mere stillness of the case of its / Parameter" (*Self-Portrait* 83). Like Kafka's mole-like creature, Ashbery inhabits an encased, secure space of his own making yet remains uncertain if he truly wants to be there. The alternative is to descend into the streets to join in the pageant of everyday social existence, and that, he has decided, he cannot do.

A poem begun in 1964, eleven years prior the publication of "Self-Portrait in a Convex Mirror," Ashbery's "Fragment" offers insight into why the poet might look toward one's solitary room as a workspace for the poetic imagination. In its depiction of and advocacy for enclosed spaces, "Fragment" foregrounds the speaker's *Beamtengeist* or clerical mindset as a trope for the self-protection necessary to guard against traumatic circumstances. The narrative of "Fragment" primarily revolves around the death of Ashbery's father, though the occasion also prompts self-reflection, as the poet reconsiders his role within the family's history. Ashbery approaches the act of reappraisal and self-reflection in an oblique and guarded manner, adopting bureaucratic metaphors to contain the emotional tumult of the moment.

In coming to terms with his father's death, the speaker engages in acts of accounting—what Kafka calls *Berechnungskunst*, or the art of calculation (qtd. in Heinemann 259). Integral to "Fragment" is Ashbery's use of a figurative balance sheet, on which a settling of accounts between self and other, parent and child, might be reconciled and the power of the imagination upheld. The analogy to office work offers Ashbery some protective distance from the grief that the occasion summons, even amid the poem's elegiac gestures. What also provides a safeguard is the fact that "Fragment" never stipulates a specific, singular addressee: the strained relationship that Ashbery had had with his father disallows that possibility. Within "Fragment" and its investigations of the past, Ashbery's default is a self-protective mode associated with *Beamtengeist*: as with Ashbery's other poems, the secure space of the office in "Fragment" becomes the privileged site for both self-preservation and contemplation, offering the discursive means to cultivate both the poetic imagination and a reconciliation of self with family.

Organized into fifty dizains, "Fragment" has the formal and visual appearance of order, even if the poem's purpose to revisit familial affairs after a father's death threatens to become chaotic and overwrought. The invocation of office terminology midway through "Fragment"—like the poem's orderly structure—is, by design, a guarded way of registering or cataloging difficult emotions:

> Then the accounts must be reexamined,
> Shifting ropes of figures. Expressions of hope
> Too late, a few seconds before. Only normal
> Transparent width separated them from the smaller,
> Flame-colored phenomena of each settled day. (*Mooring* 299)

The standard business discourse of "accounts" and "figures" allows for a controlled affective release, even as a plaintive tone of mourning is subtly perceptible. The invocation of a balance sheet, moreover, provides a means for Ashbery to keep record of what had previously inhibited relationships. By comparison, direct communication of emotion seems all too attenuated alongside the prevailing bureaucratic terms: "Expressions of hope / Too late, a few seconds before" (299). Nevertheless, there is urgency to attend to the familial matters at hand: Ashbery's review of the ledger takes place solemnly, at the figurative close of business (the "Flame-colored phenomena of each settled day").

Couched within lines predominated by office jargon, this epiphanic moment of reckoning signals Ashbery's longing for composure when coming to terms with the familial past. The early, manuscript version of the first page of "Fragment" is telling in this regard: as Shoptaw has pointed out, an "oddly appropriate column of figures" are scribbled in the top left-hand corner (112–13). It is an instance of calculation and reassessment, something transmuted into the text of the poem itself as "Shifting ropes of figures" (*Mooring* 299). Within the narrative of "Fragment," the "figures" being counted and assessed are the individuals of the immediate family, including not just a paternal figure but surviving members, like his mother and Ashbery himself, entangled and bound together in kinship. Ashbery later in the poem will call this accounting work the "rough / Business of the long day" (302). The review of emotions is particularly trying or "rough" business for Ashbery because he and his father had a difficult, strained relationship. As Karin Roffman has written, Chet Ashbery had long been an irritable individual whose "already short temper became explosive" due to financial difficulties during the Depression (13). The two would further become estranged from each other after the passing of Ashbery's brother Richard, who was perceived to be the favored son.[7] To reopen the accounts to examination after his father's death amounts to revisiting painful memories and reviewing acrimonious quarrels of the past.

Such anguished feelings revolve around, for example, an incident from Ashbery's adolescence when his love letters are found, and his homosexuality inadvertently revealed. Lost, errant letters are recurrent motifs in Ashbery's poems,[8] all of which may trace back to the formative moment of an unexpected and calamitous sexual disclosure:

> Gradually old letters used as bookmarks
> Inform the neighbors; an approximate version
> Circulates and the incident is officially closed. (*Mooring* 296)

The ill-fated paper trail exemplifies what Ben Kafka has called the "demon of paperwork," or the infelicitous mishaps typical of bureaucracies, where "hundreds or thousands or . . . more opportunities to misspell a word, miscalculate a number, misread a blank . . . misaddress an envelope" can easily occur (10). In "Fragment," the bureaucratic elements of the episode extend beyond an adolescent's "misfiling" or mishandling of love letters, though. Ashbery here likens parental oversight and judgment to a disciplinary authoritarian "State," resolutely intent on alerting or "inform[ing] the neighbors." In this way, the paper documents of a personal and intimate relationship easily convert to a disciplinary juvenile record: an "approximate version" or a duplicate "circulate[d]" between families that have put an official end to the affair in the regulating of a queer sexual act.

The sense of violation and intrusion upon privacy repeats elsewhere in the non-linear narrative of "Fragment," indicating the incident's long-lasting damage. Prior to dizain 7 in which the letters are found, Ashbery invokes the familiar Kafkan motif of a burrow-like space in order to describe both loss and a breach of privacy:

> The hollow thus produced
> A kind of cave of the winds; distribution center

Of subordinate notions to which the stag
Returns to die: the suppressed lovers. (*Mooring* 292)

The "hollow" most immediately refers to the void left after the death of Ashbery's father, yet the overdetermined image of a cave equally speaks to the desire for one's own secure space. As the previous scene attests, Ashbery did not enjoy the privilege of privacy; his bunker/cave proved all too susceptible to encroachment and incursion. Nevertheless, calling his room a "distribution center" transforms the room not only into a productive, bureaucratic space but into a creative one. Ashbery thereby sublimates the intrusion, reconceiving the room as the very site of the imagination, from which poems, daydreams, fantasies, and other unconscious, "subordinate notions" might be manufactured and distributed. Though the relationship between the "suppressed lovers" may have been curtailed, Ashbery has sought retrospectively to construct a secure space—a burrow or cave of his own making—in which the dynamism of the imagination might prevail, buttressed from threats from the outside.

The recurring enclosed spaces of "Fragment" suggest that self-protection has been deemed a necessity, yet Ashbery will still wonder in dizain 13 what kind of self he can have if he encloses himself so securely. In a compensatory move, Ashbery will compare himself—his very being—to an englobed object, a sphere as enticing as a piece of fruit:

Like the blood orange we have a single
Vocabulary all heart and all skin and can see
Through the dust of incisions the central perimeter
Our imaginations' orbit . . . (*Mooring* 293)

To be "all heart and all skin" suggests an individual's emotional exposure or intense sexual responsiveness—or, perhaps, both. All of the citrus-like sensuousness, however, arguably here leads, as in Wallace Stevens, to Ashbery's real concern: to the mind and consciousness. Stevens, in "Description without Place," envisions the mind as a seed, whose encased and protected interiors will later bear fruit and a subsequent consciousness: "The intentions of a mind as yet unknown / The spirit of one dwelling in a seed, / Itself that seed's ripe, unpredictable fruit" (272–73). For Ashbery, thought and selfhood are likewise enclosed: interior to all, "central [to the] perimeter," is the active imagination setting up its own boundary to safeguard. The poetic, imaginative, daydreaming mind is the last bulwark against a hostile, outer world, where "Other words / Old ways are but trappings and appurtenances / Meant to install around us like a grotto" (*Mooring* 293–94). Self-preservation is indeed key to Ashbery, for he says, gravely, "There is nothing laughable / In this" (294). It is the mind—a grotto-like space—that offers such security, and Ashbery learns early that imaginative work seemingly tips the scales in favor of isolation, which forms its own protective imperative: "To isolate the kernel of / Our imbalance and at the same time back up carefully; / Its tulip head whole, an imagined good" (294). The precarity of lived experience might thus be cordoned off, the potential for harm kept at a distance by the activity of the mind, its longed for and "imagined good."

Marshaling the imagination as a dynamic, protective force enables Ashbery to carry out ever more brave acts of scrutiny, whether that entails the troublesome relationship with his father or a clear-sighted contemplation of self. These investigations in "Fragment" lead Ashbery to realize his selfhood is inextricable from his history with his father.[9] There is a shock of recognition, as Ashbery writes, "your face [is] the only real beginning, / Beyond the gray of overcoat, that this first / Salutation plummet[s] also to the end of friendship / With self alone" (*Mooring* 290). The scene reads as if Ashbery were looking into a mirror, yet the *you* invoked here most likely refers to Ashbery's dad, evoked in a businessman's attire. The pronoun, however, equally initiates an examination of self, as his father's original face, in its similarity, is superimposed, as in "Wet Casements," upon his own, and Ashbery is locked into a view of himself as the progeny of his father ("to see, as though reflected / In streaming windowpanes, the look of others through / Their own eyes . . . their correct impressions . . . overlaid by your / Ghostly transparent face" (*Houseboat Days* 28).

Ashbery could easily become trapped within such a staring contest, yet his inclination is to find a way out of what would be a confining predicament. Kafka's creature in his burrow speaks of reliable means of egress through "far-flung passages," where he had "the advantage of being in [his] own house and knowing all the passages and how they run" (326). Ashbery likewise knows intimately the territory and passageways of his domicile and his familial past:

> And in doing so open out
> New passages of being among the correctness
> of familiar patterns. The stance to you
> Is a fiction, to me a whole. . . . (*Mooring* 290)

As Ashbery returns to his hometown and navigates a world in which his father no longer exists, he must redefine his sense of self, a process that entails some dangers or hazards due to the contentious relationship with his father. Ashbery's "stance" is defensive, his "whole" being and sexual identity on guard from having hitherto been dismissed as somehow false—an unacceptable "fiction" in Ashbery's adolescence.

Reopening of familial "accounts" for examination is painful, and Ashbery's intent is to do so with courage. The task requires Ashbery to assume the heroic, battlefield stance of a cavalryman, one that would endow him with the strength "to persist in the revision of very old / Studies, as though mounted on a charger" (*Mooring* 298). In such a strained, war-like environment, every turn of the psychological undertaking is hazardous, where "an odor of explosives hangs" distressingly over the scene (299). Taking charge in this manner necessitates a change in Ashbery's demeanor and being, something that he depicts via a surrealistic shift. Attending to death certificates, legal forms, and actual testaments, Ashbery abruptly transforms himself from a battlefield cavalryman ("mounted on a charger") to a responsible clerk.[10] Ashbery must steel himself with newfound purpose:

> This presupposes a will
> To carry out all instructions, dotting the last i
> Though cancelling with one stroke of a pen all
> The provisions, revisions and so on made until now. (299)

The figurative scene of paperwork is important, as it affords Ashbery a means to achieve some kind of resolution with his father. Despite a sense of wariness and skepticism toward reaching a satisfactory, posthumous accord and settling of accounts with his father, Ashbery, as son and acting clerk, occupies a unique position to reassess the relationship: "dotting the last i" enacts a redefined identity with which he might "cancel out" past ill will and opprobrium. Paternal "provisions," accordingly, will no longer have the same standing or the same meaning; old arguments can be revised and otherwise put to rest.

In the latter half of "Fragment," Ashbery grows increasingly intent on measuring things, engaging in *Berechnungskunst*, or the art of calculation. He proceeds to size up old emotions as an office manager might, taking stock of the present as it relates to the past. Amid the somberness of death, Ashbery arrives at a position of lucidity and hopeful, clear perspective: "Soon all is shining, mined, / Tears dissolving laughter, the isolated clouds spent" (*Mooring* 300). The very structure and form of "Fragment," its method of orderly composition, seems to allow for clear, sharp scrutiny of the past. In describing Ashbery's compositional process of "Fragment," Shoptaw has invoked economic metaphors and workplace analogies to suggest that Ashbery adhered to a fairly regulated "mode of production" notable for its consistency: "Each of the twenty-five typescript pages of 'Fragment,' and each illustrated page of the Black Sparrow edition, thus represents one day's labor. Ashbery's work schedule shows in his work . . ." (111). The adoption of figurative language of work and labor by Shoptaw is not coincidental but instead reflective of the terms Ashbery himself employs. Business and office terminology ramps up in the concluding stanzas of "Fragment," formulating an efficient means for Ashbery to draw an end to the grieving period.

In the fourth to last dizain, for instance, Ashbery euphemistically announces an endpoint not only of his father's passing but of the onetime scandal surrounding his adolescent relationship with the use of the businesslike term the *affair*: "And the affair was concluded in snow and also in / The satisfaction of the outline formulated against the sky" (304). Post-*affair* and after his father's passing, the mood has shifted, as the conclusion and clearing of old business makes way for lighter household interactions, closer to the funeral:

> People were delighted getting up in the morning
> With the density that for once seemed the promise
> Of everything forgotten, and the well-being
> Grew, at the expense of whoever lay dying
> In a small room watched only by the progression
> Of hours in the tight new agreement. (304)

Ashbery orchestrates the domestic scene somewhat fantastically, as if it were experienced like a dreamy, collective workday full of "promise," with "people" being "delighted [to get] up in the morning" and head off to their jobs. Nevertheless, Ashbery is cognizant of the emotional toll. Whatever household levity achieved comes at a cost, "at the expense of whoever lay dying" in an adjacent room. The intensity of Ashbery's grieving finds reprieve when fashioned in bureaucratic discourse, as the mourning period gets attached to its own productive work ethic and schedule, whose "progression / Of hours" forge a "tight new" business "agreement" that older, familial injuries might be put to rest.

In the murky business of grieving, Ashbery attends to what the loss of a parent might mean, as death and his ability to cope with it occupies his mind with "absorbing interest" (*Mooring* 305). Ashbery aims to be disencumbered from past wrongs, including the unsympathetic, even hostile, response to his sexual orientation. With death yielding a newfound perspective, Ashbery experiences, if not forgiveness, then a dismantling or "whole raveling [of] discontent, / The sum of all that will ever be deciphered / On this side of that vast drop of water" (305). Ashbery here constructs a balance sheet that separates what is important now and what was undertaken so gravely in the past; vast sums of emotional investment to "be deciphered" and put to "this [or that] side" (305).

As Ashbery aligns expenditures of his feeling about the past to one side or the other, he reserves for his father a substantial level of compassion:

> They let you sleep without pain, having all that
> Not in the lesson, not in the special way of telling
> But back to one side of life, not especially
> Immune to it, in the secret of what goes on (305)

The appeal to equilibrium, of a balanced accord between father and son, is paramount here, with regret or acrimony pushed "back to one side of life" (*Mooring* 305). Ashbery knows, however, that forgiving all past wrongs is fairly idealistic. It is a realization he registers in the passage with three consecutive negative phrases ("Not in the lesson"; "not in the special way of telling"; "not especially / Immune to it"), all of which suggest the reconciling of the past may in fact be one-sided—an act of unburdening accomplished on his own. He understands that the act of forgiveness does not adhere strictly to the parameters of a financial deal, no matter how fitting commerce might be as a figure for reaching agreements and finding accord. Instead, it is poetry—not business—that allows for such an accord, as Ashbery sings for himself as much as for his father that both might be appreciated and understood: "The words sung in the next room are unavoidable / But their passionate intelligence will be studied in you" (*Mooring* 305).

That "Fragment" ends with several affirmations of accord and agreement does not mean that Ashbery is completely at ease after the death of his father, nor is he fully comforted by the state of forgiveness at which he arrives. Understandably, Ashbery finds himself at a loss at all that has transpired between himself and his father:

> But what could I make of this? Glaze
> Of many identical foreclosures wrested from
> The operative hand, like a judgment but still
> The atmosphere of seeing? That two people could
> Collide in this dusk means that the time of
> Shapelessly foraging had come undone (305)

The figurative framework of the passage remains businesslike and bureaucratic. Ashbery's question ("what could I make of this?") reads as a statement of incomprehension but also of purpose, particularly if Ashbery is determined to write—to make—a poem about the experience: the very thing he ends up doing with "Fragment." The resolve to seek out "foreclosures" corresponds to Ashbery's newfound ability to get beyond and shut down the memories of a painful past incident. If "Fragment" indeed ends with acts of forgiveness, then judgment is "wrested from / The operative hand" that had originally made the matter scandalous. Ashbery and his father were at odds in the past, but Ashbery's return home resulted in a sort of accord, the aimless searching for a rapprochement between father and son finally over, as if "two people could collide"—somehow beneficially—"in the dusk."

In so many of Ashbery's poems, from "Untilted" to "Self-Portrait in a Convex Mirror" to "The Instruction Manual," we see him at work in scenes of contemplation and of writing. The task is often an arduous one, completed in solitude with the full weight of work initiating a sense of burden. To give the seriousness of the writing process its due, Ashbery invokes business metaphors and bureaucratic discourse and invents solitary spaces intended to preserve acts of the imagination. In "Fragment," the labor of writing and of revisiting the past is intermixed with solemn indications why such secluded spaces were necessary: Ashbery builds his encasements as a means to ward off scrutiny of his self and being. Kafka's writing, with its own tropes of seclusion and labor, offers an indication of Ashbery's need to shield oneself from observations from without. Walter Benjamin glosses the uncanny phenomenon in this manner: "Why does the glance into an unknown window always find a family at a meal, or else a solitary man, seated at a table under a hanging lamp, occupied with some obscure, niggling thing? Such a glance is the germ cell of Kafka's work" (218). What Benjamin says about Kafka could be applicable to Ashbery. For Ashbery and Kafka, both ensnared in the bureaucratic mindset, it is hard to convey writing and its trials—and more difficult still to figure the imagination otherwise.

Chapter 4

Barbara Guest's Office Inventory

Three Desks, a Water Cooler, and a Dictaphone

Who are you?
. . .
GIRL 1 (*tough*): I'm an office person.

—Barbara Guest, *The Office*

Perhaps nothing seems further from the abstractions or metaphysical ponderings in Barbara Guest's writing than the prosaic features of mid-century American bureaucracy. Mundane office items, including desks, typewriters, lamps, and Dictaphones, would surely seem antithetical to Guest's abstract lyrical investigations into natural elements like air and water or the lovelorn relations between women and men, yet these common office objects fill her literary works nonetheless. Guest's drama from 1963, *The Office: A One-Act Play in Three Scenes*, for instance, indicates an abiding interest in bureaucracy and its apparatuses, as do "Olivetti Ode" and other poems that feature clerical and administrative devices imbued with auras of corporate power, hierarchy, subservience, and obligation. These bureaucratic objects are not rendered by Guest in a neutral fashion but are instead notably situated within a stratified, regulated world and its network of gendered norms and patriarchal order. As the title of her first book of poetry, *The Location of Things*, indicates, Guest's poems reveal an interest not only in material objects but also in their situation—their placement within a set of social relations. Objects in Guest's poetry, accordingly, hold significance for their ability to correspond to patterns of human convention that structure and govern the world. As a consequence, the topic and substance of bureaucracy—including not just material objects but also rigid, hierarchical relations—become an important means for Guest to critique patriarchal society and to call into question the corporate and bureaucratic values that detrimentally organize, divide, and administer so much of human existence at midcentury and beyond. The material trappings of bureaucracy and office work within Guest's poems function importantly as object lessons, not only underscoring and repudiating the alienating and dehumanizing aspects of administrative ideology but also revealing the degree to which a refusal of bureaucratic work and its principles can lead instead to human connection.

Clerical work, interestingly, has informed Guest's literary pursuits from early on in her career. As Guest's close friend, Nancy Robbin, recounts, "She spent her senior year at UC Berkeley. When she returned she found a job at Columbia Broadcasting. . . . She had found a second job which, unlike the one at CBS, was close to her real writing life. She was working for Henry Miller, typing his manuscripts or letters to editors and other writers—volunteer work" (139). Miller was at the time too destitute to pay for clerical assistance, yet Guest's interaction with him nevertheless held some benefit. Guest credits Miller with her move from Los Angeles to New York, a transition that she describes as transformative for her writing: "It seemed like civilization coming from the West Coast; I thought that I was coming to Paris. I knew Henry Miller and he suggested I go . . . I needed something to free me. I became freer" (Guest and Hillringhouse 23).

If Nancy Robbin had viewed Guest's clerical work and her poetry as existing along some sort of literary continuum, Guest herself makes a similar association between writing and the figure of the clerk in her re-creation—or staging—of a "dramatic meeting between two protagonists," the poets H.D. and Ezra Pound, in her critical work *Herself Defined: H.D. and Her World* (*Forces* 61). Guest depicts the historic meeting as follows:

> He is dressed in his Whistlerian garb, the velvet jacket, the loose tie. Together they are a pictorial couple. She is so tall and lean, beautiful with the squared jaw and the hair falling over her brow. He is certainly no ordinary clerk. His reddish hair is long and tumbled. . . . Neither at this moment is interested in appearances. There is a more direct reason for the meeting.

Hilda has consented to show Ezra Pound her new poems.
(*Herself Defined* 40)

Though Guest pointedly distinguishes Pound from an "ordinary" office worker, a clerk is nonetheless Guest's reference point, placing H.D.'s and Pound's attraction to each other within the context of employment and making their connection a quasi-office romance.[1] Tellingly, Guest's rendition of the interaction between H.D. and Pound retains a sense of an apprenticeship—a set of relations indicating a power differential between men and women in the literary world that H.D. and Guest would both attempt to dismantle throughout the rest of their careers. The anecdote about the meeting between H.D. and Pound is consequently instructive for Guest's own career. The intersections between poetic origins, allusions to bureaucracy, and gender-inflected obstacles to professional success form an identifiable pattern that courses through Guest's writing and reveals her steadfast intention to pursue her literary career. Work and Guest's vocation as a writer ascend as crucial motifs within her writing, as she purposefully and determinedly grounds her identity within her chosen profession.

H.D.'s nascent desire to ascertain her value as a poet has a parallel in Guest's own poem, "The Location of Things," which engages in an extended act of writerly self-appraisal. Sitting at her desk, Guest performs a task not unlike the office role she assigned to Pound. Being herself a not-so-ordinary clerk to the world, Guest notes and takes stock of what surrounds her:

> Why from this window am I watching leaves?
> Why do halls and steps seem narrower?
> Why at this desk am I listening for the sound of the fall
> of color, the pitch of the wooden floor
> and feet going faster?
> . . . . . .
> Recognitions (*Collected Poems* [*CP*] 3)

Outside Guest's window, things take shape and appear. Proximity and distance: these are basic coordinates of location for Guest, and she adeptly manages to register and classify the objects around her. To the questions quoted above, Guest will provide a single-word answer, a solitary line of verse, hovering between stanzas: "Recognitions" (*CP* 3). With the utterance, Guest's vocation is compellingly announced. Her life's work is singularly summed up like a job requirement for a poet: to recognize and discern—with acuity—the composition of her environment.

Guest's identification of her occupation makes her serial, yearning questions from "The Location of Things" easier to fathom as she orients the outside world to the material objects contained within her office: "am I to find a lake under the table / or a mountain beside my chair . . . ?" (*CP* 3). Here, on the one hand, Guest laments her physical detachment from the outside world, yet, on the other hand, she points to her office as a notable space of creation, where her imagination is grounded in the items surrounding her. The process of writing is thereby made substantive with the objects (her desk and chair) that she references. Maggie Nelson gets at something like this when she notes that Guest "explicitly sets out to conflate word and object" in her compositional process (37).[2] From Guest's sedentary position at her desk, she finds herself able to accomplish the work of poetry and her task of regarding "dramatic afternoons / through this floodlit window" by principally attending to and situating the objects around her (*CP* 4).

The primacy that Guest places on the material objects of her office signals her engagement with what Georg Lukács has identified as the "totality of objects," the primary means through which the epic novel aims to represent society. As Lukács argues, the "totality of objects"—a term he draws from Hegel—offers writers a comprehensive way to convey socioeconomic reality: "human society cannot possibly be represented in its entirety, unless the foundations encompassing it, the surrounding world of things forming the object of its activity, is also represented" (*Historical Novel* 93). Beyond merely existing as the things that compose a scene or comprise the environment of a literary work, objects reveal the social relations between people and the economic and political conditions under which they live. As Judith Butler puts it, Lukács's concern is with "social totality," in which "every detail will be compelled to bespeak the social whole" (2, 14). From such a novelistic depiction of wholeness, the reader can gain a sense of life and its operations in its entirety, for, as Lukács maintains, "[t]he demand for a 'totality of objects' in epic is essentially a demand for an artistic image of human society which produces and reproduces itself in the same way as the daily process of life" (*Historical Novel* 93).

Guest, of course, writes poetry and plays and not epic novels, yet her own interest in the material items of the office—its devices, furniture, fixtures, and documents—enables her to represent the totality of bureaucracy and its regulatory determination of everyday life. In doing so, Guest assails the profit imperatives and hierarchical organization of midcentury American capitalism as well as its subordination of women in managed workplaces. Guest's inventory of things, her cataloging and depiction of office artifacts, thus offers a "totality of objects" in Lukács's sense, wherein a social totality—including gender politics, the division of labor, and corporate priorities—can be represented and thereby more readily grasped. The representation of a social totality, as Fredric Jameson has commented, particularly comes into focus when the material objects are situated within a set of economic relations, as the "original meaningfulness of objects becomes visible only when their link with human labor and production is unconcealed" (*Marxism and Form* 197). Objects and office materials function in this manner in Guest's writing, as indicators of labor and work—her own as well as others—and offer her a means of repudiating unequal and unfair employment and occupational conditions, with bureaucracy and its principles especially becoming the focal point of her critique.

Guest's attack on bureaucratic systems and their reduction of work into rote, mindless activity finds its most salient expression in her play *The Office*, as she offers a grotesque depiction of bureaucracy and its more alienating and dehumanizing features. Against such grotesquerie, Guest will posit a contrasting imperative, a counter-ideology based on human interconnection and love that repudiates the degrading conditions of work within bureaucracy. Though *The Office* ostensibly centers on the corporate activity of three male executives, the play ultimately aligns, through its female characters, with the committed political program of a "refusal to work," a movement Kathi Weeks has described as a "critique of and rebellion against the present system of work and its values" and a challenge to the "cultural and institutional mechanism by which we are linked to the mode of production" (99).

Beyond the acerbic critique of bureaucracy and administrative systems in *The Office*, Guest's depiction of work elsewhere in her poetry also encompasses her own acts of writing as a material practice. Guest's accountings of "office" work thus notably include her own literary labor as it engages with objects and things—with paperwork, desks, and typewriters. As Guest presents her compositional practices, clerical and administrative tasks not only become figures for the act of writing poetry but also highlight the precarious position of women in the workforce and the literary marketplace. Guest, however, actively intervenes against such sidelining of women: she secures her position within her own writing by consistently and conspicuously foregrounding her own perspective in her writing in a manner that markedly contrasts the air of apprenticeship between H.D. and Pound. Repeatedly and pointedly, Guest announces her role as a writer, embracing her work as a poet, yet her articulation of her poetic career periodically depends upon depicting herself as a clerical worker adept at using objects from the office to record the world around her. Particularly among her first poems, Guest envisions herself as a clerk or scribe as an initial step before more forthrightly claiming a professional identity: her occupation as a poet.

The firmness of Guest's self-regard, her belief in her poetic vocation, clearly and specifically manifests itself in her elevation of a basic typewriter in a poem from 1973, "Olivetti Ode," to which I will return to later in the chapter. The esteem with which Guest endows this simultaneously clerical and artistic machine, though, has an earlier precedent in "Windy Afternoon" (1960), a poem in which she similarly highlights a typewriter and its technology. The reference to a typewriter in "Windy Afternoon" occurs briefly at the outset, coming after the appearance of another piece of machinery—a policeman's truculent and noisy motorcycle:

> Through the wood
> on his motorcycle piercing
> the hawk, the jay
> the blue-coated policeman
> Woods, barren woods,
> as this typewriter without an object
> or the words that from you
> fall soundless (*CP* 8)

In contrast to the noisy, insistent vibrancy of the motorcycle, the typewriter as an instrument at first seems emptied out ("typewriter without an object"), which speaks to Guest's uncertain inspiration or vague poetic purpose. The "you" Guest addresses is similarly indefinite, seemingly designating a desired yet inaccessible lover or the poet's own selfhood. That words "fall soundless" only compounds the sense of hesitancy in the "barren woods" and signals Guest's early tentativeness with both poem-making and world-making. The moment is comparable to the shrinking stance of the speaker in H.D.'s poem "Mid-Day." H.D. invokes a similarly bereft natural scene in "Mid-Day" to convey being at a loss, feeling both fatigued and creatively uninspired: "A slight wind shakes the seed-pods—/ my thoughts are spent" (10). The sense of creative loss in "Mid-Day" is intensified, moreover, by the presence of a prolific, established, male poet in the distance (much like H.D.'s then husband, Richard Aldington), who is figuratively conveyed as a thriving, almighty poplar, "bright on the hill" and "deep-rooted among the trees" (10).

In Guest's "Windy Afternoon," it is the policeman, and not a poplar, who predominates and draws immediate attention. A mixed tone of admiration and rejection characterizes Guest's depiction of the officer. At first, his speeding, bluish blur is likened to a hawk and a blue jay, and his dynamic being is made synonymous with the machine he rides—a virile, triumphant depiction recalling futurist aesthetics. Throughout the rest of the poem, though, Guest tempers the appeal of the policeman, his masculinity, and his speed, an indication of what Sara Lundquist has described as Guest's "subtle reproof of futurist thought and propaganda" in another poem, "The Farewell Stairway" (275). By the end of "Windy Afternoon," Guest rejects the force and velocity of the policeman, finally substituting her own artistic will—as she sits with her typewriter—for the officer's act of racing headlong on his motorcycle.

A symbolic embodiment of authority and the enforcement of rule, the policeman epitomizes what Guest battles when she pits her poetry against the prevailing, male-determined literary order and social totality. There are, Guest implies, social limits to her writing. Guest's choice of a policeman as a symbolic authority figure is apt. David Graeber has argued that the actual role of the police is the application of bureaucratic rules. "Generations of police sociologists have pointed out that only a very small proportion of what police actually do has anything to do with enforcing criminal law—or criminal matters of any kind. Most of it has to do with regulations, or, to put it slightly more technically, with the scientific application of physical force, or the threat of physical force, to aid in the resolution of administrative problems" (Graeber 73). Within the ecosystem Guest depicts in "Windy Afternoon," the policeman and his motorcycle function as figures for a patriarchal literary order, delineating the rules within which Guest must write. In the wake of the "piercing," aggressive movement of the policeman, a certain flatness, docility, and compliance settles upon the landscape and roadway, with "leaves falling over there / a great vacancy / a huge leftover" (*CP* 8). Guest's impetus for poetic volition appears, momentarily, to be voided and "vacant," an impulse washed out and made into an afterthought.

Out of this void and demand for obeisance, however, Guest finds her artistic purpose, as she counterposes her creative will to the force of the policeman, bending the rules toward her own design. Guest concludes the poem with her own imperative, one that authorizes her artistic creation:

> Describe that nude, audacious line
> Most lofty, practiced street
> You are no longer thirsty
> Turn or go straight (*CP* 8)

Owing to the close relationships between poets and painters of the New York School, it is not surprising that Guest might invoke the figure of an artist to convey her poetic impulse. The "audacious line" not only describes the artist's painterly gesture demarcating form and space, but also indicates, self-reflexively, Guest's own labor and work of composition, setting down a line of poetry, the figurative path forward down a "practiced street." Objects here help to produce a Lukácsian sense of totality: the material object or machine of choice, however, is no longer the motorcycle but the once-bereft, "objectless" typewriter from the poem's beginning lines. The objective is, moreover, now clear: the poet directs herself to "turn or go straight," which is to say, to be unregulated and create as she sees fit. If Guest had felt, at first, beholden to rules and a male literary establishment codifying what she may or may not write, the end of "Windy Afternoon" announces her prerogative to write, to venture forth, drawing upon an object, the typewriter and its utility, in the realization of her work.

Like the policeman in "Windy Afternoon," a similarly imposing symbol of bureaucracy and social stricture surfaces in Guest's "On the Way to Dumbarton Oaks" in the form of an artistic institution, the Dumbarton Oaks Museum in Washington, DC. Material objects feature prominently in "On the Way to Dumbarton Oaks," occupying the poet's attention. The Dumbarton Oaks Museum is itself a rather large object containing other objects and stands emblematically as a social totality: the building and its artifacts are meant to imply and represent entire cultures despite their necessarily limited material holdings. Guest's response to the museum in the Nation's capital reflects an engagement with institutional order and bureaucracy, whose very grandness and scale inspire an intensity of emotion and a near-breathless sublime reaction: "The air! The colonial air! The walls, the brick, / this November thunder" (*CP* 12). Though somewhat overwhelmed by the moment, Guest manages to register the sublime monumentalism of the museum and surrounding Washington, DC, by indexing the material objects at hand: the bricks and walls that compose the museum's structure form a material counterpart to the sublime, atmospheric presence of history, both past and current. Guest is able to convey a social totality through her portrait of the museum, whose sheer solidity and size seemingly changes the surrounding atmosphere. That the specialized holdings of the Dumbarton Oaks Museum include art from the Byzantine Empire, renowned itself for intricate bureaucracy, further compounds the poem's prevailing and parallel sense, in 1960, of peaking American empire and administration at midcentury.

Empire, administrative networks, and institutional structures position Guest as a minute figure, and her stance in "On the Way to Dumbarton Oaks" is correspondingly marked by humility, an effect initiated by an overwhelming encounter with the bureaucratic and imperial sublime. Accordingly, Guest imagines herself a modest scribe ("Carrying my scroll, my tree drawing"), as she stands outside the Dumbarton Oaks Museum:

> Chinese tree
> your black branches and your three yellow leaves
> with you I traffick. My three
> yellow notes, my three yellow stanzas,
> my three precisenesses (*CP* 12)

Facing the museum, Guest engages herself with the task of composing the scene, as nature lends her the materials ("three yellow leaves") for work as a copyist. In a sudden turn, the yellow leaves surrealistically become analogs for office documents, with "My three / yellow notes" being akin to either sheets of yellow memoranda or pages from a legal pad. Guest assumes, in the moment, the fused figure of the poet-clerk, like Auden and Ashbery before her (see my chapters 1 and 3). Poetry requires, as Guest implies, the professional attention of a meticulous bureaucrat, attuned to counting and replication as she tabulates her "three notes" and "three stanzas" as "three precisenesses"—a detailed record of observation made in office triplicate (*CP* 12). Guest's vocation, here, is simultaneously poetic and clerical, something she makes clear when she aligns her selfhood with desk work and the very function and dimensions of an office: "This winter day I'm / a compleat travel agency" (*CP* 12).

The humility and self-deprecation that Guest invokes when facing the Dumbarton Oaks Museum, however, ultimately gives way to a keen appreciation of her own value as a poet. Her well-traveled past reduces to a singular moment of sharp, burgeoning aesthetic awareness and appreciation: "I'll betray all my vast / journeying sensibility in a tear dropped before / 'The Treasure of Petersburg'" (*CP* 12). Guest admits to being moved by a painting, yet her response also encapsulates her sensibility as a poet. The epic, institutional scope of "On the Way to Dumbarton Oaks" gets compressed, its focus now on the act of poetic composition, as Guest takes up the question of her ability to recount her experience. At this moment, Guest begins to center her own aesthetic purpose, her poetic will eclipsing the grandness of Washington, DC, and the staggering, byzantine intricacy of its bureaucratic power.

The final stanza of "On the Way to Dumbarton Oaks" accordingly pivots to Guest cataloging the social totality—DC, the museum, and the outside street—anew with the objects that surround her:

> and gorgeous this forever
> I've a raft of you left over
> Like so many gold flowers and so many white
> and the stems! The stems I have left! (*CP* 12)

The sublime moment of Guest's visit to Dumbarton Oaks becomes an intimate act of artistic organization and management, the total experience itself made into an exhibit as if it were an archival floral display: "Like so many gold flowers and so many white." In the excerpt above, Guest's addressee ("you") is indeterminate, whether she speaks to the day, the museum, or even another person loved beyond measure. That this "you" is figured into a metaphorical object, a raft, speaks to a quality in Guest's writing that Barbara Einzig has described as a "liquid balance. Like liquid inside a leveling instrument that determines our horizon line" and to what Timothy Gray terms Guest's "aqueous" environments, water imagery that lends her poems "buoyancy and reflective brilliance" (Einzig 10, Gray 73). The metaphor of the raft, however, also suggests Guest's own compositional act of writing: her weaving together of the pieces and objects of her day is a response to the exceptional and the sublime. There is a clerical order to what Guest retains and accounts for, the archival organization and careful preservation of her memories stirring feelings of jubilation: "and the stems! The stems I have left!" (*CP* 12).

In responding to the magnitude of Washington, DC, and the Dumbarton Oaks Museum as a scribe or a clerk might, Guest manages the moment effectively and efficiently. Nevertheless, Guest concludes the poem with a sublime focus on time itself, as she places temporal matters into the foreground: "gorgeous this forever." With her use of the deictic "this," Guest deftly guides the reader's appreciation of temporality. The invocation of the colonial past, in the form of long-standing capital buildings at the outset of the poem, is eclipsed by the flower stems in the final lines. "Forever" becomes something not to be experienced over centuries but diurnally, recorded and preserved within a poem so that the quotidian sublime might be valued in its own right. Michael Herzfeld has noted that "the effect of daily interactions between bureaucrats and clients is that of making time irrelevant," where navigating lengthy bureaucratic protocol begins to take "on the features of a timeless landscape" (162). Against such bureaucratic, temporal irrelevance, Guest upholds the significance of her immediate, present moment as a way of affirming her specific experience—as well as her artistic purpose—on a particular and extraordinary day.[3]

The tension between bureaucracy on the one hand and the affirmation of existence and creativity on the other assumes greater importance in Guest's *The Office: A One-Act Play in Three Scenes*, a work that more overtly and plainly than "Dumbarton Oaks" critiques patriarchal and capitalist ideology and the bureaucratic measures that sustain them. In the play, everyday office objects serve as incontrovertible markers of bureaucratic norms, their presence conveying a social totality of administrative order and hierarchy, as Guest's stage directions explicitly indicate: "The play takes place in an office. There are three desks. A water cooler. A Dictaphone. A loudspeaker. A blackboard. The desk of X1, who portrays the Executive, is placed in front of the other two desks to form a triangle—or in whatever manner the stage manager may desire, so long as X1 is designated the leading desk" (*Office* 9). Though the stage set is spare, Guest intends for the office dynamics of authority and dominance to be readily apparent to the audience through its objects. The play's list of characters reinforces the features of bureaucratic anonymity and order: the first three roles—all of which are to be played by men—are designated in uniform fashion as X1, X2, and X3. Guest intimates the office's further, unequal stratification with the rest of the cast: Girl 1, Girl 2, and Girl 3 constitute the other characters, along with an "office boy." The final character is an ominous "Figure in Yellow," who enters the play in the third scene and, dressed in the yellow color of memoranda and notepads, lurks menacingly in the background as an embodiment of bureaucracy itself.

The Office was first produced at Café Cino in New York in 1963, three years after the publication of "The Location of Things." The play follows a dark, absurd narrative where capitalism is depicted as menacing as the executives are consecutively "terminated." Two of the male executives are killed offstage when paperwork—memoranda on yellow sheets of paper—is stolen and goes missing. Infused into the play are Guest's allusions to T.S. Eliot's "The Waste Land," wherein the office is figuratively depicted as a hollow, morally bankrupt space in need of purification and spiritual renewal due to unscrupulous business transactions and persistent threats of violence. The office women (Girl 1, Girl 2, and Girl 3) enter intermittently as capricious characters who alternately engage in acts of eroticism, abasement, and subterfuge—as they are the ones who steal memoranda from the executives' desks. At the close of the play, with a single executive left, Guest seeks an alternative to the dehumanizing bureaucratic practices of the office as a social totality. In place of such alienating conditions, Guest advocates for a principled refusal of office work and a disavowal of the job as it had been previously conducted, actions that result, efficaciously, in human connection and love. *The Office* sets human relations as its prerogative, rejecting the ruthless competition inherent to business in favor of human cooperation and interconnectedness instead.

The opening lines of scene 1 establish the administrative habits of the executives and their machinelike existence. Guest emphasizes this regimentation with the close interactions between humans and the objects of the office:

An office. Three men enter, go to desks.

X1 (*placing papers on desk*): Time is. Here is.

X2 (*placing papers on desk*): Time is. Here is.

X3 (*placing papers on desk*): Time is. Here is. (*Office* 10)

Time in *The Office* unfolds in a streamlined, staccato manner. The principles of bureaucratic efficiency reify the executives, their repetitive speech rendering them robotic. Indeed, the three men inhabit a bureaucratic temporality that approximates a punch-card time clock ("Time is. Here is."). Such synchronized movement illustrates what Lukács has described as the systematized essence of bureaucracy, which "bears an extraordinarily close resemblance to operating a machine and ... often surpasses it in sterility and uniformity" (*History* 99).

Along with leading a mechanized existence, the office executives speak a nonsensical language, as Guest parodies the specialized jargon of corporate transactions. Material objects prove central to the drama: using the office Dictaphone, a quintessential instrument of American bureaucratic efficiency, the first executive (X1) speaks words notable for their utter strangeness and stylized lack of coherence:

> X1 (*dictating into machine*):
> The necessaries before the event
> *ual* correspondencies together with
> *ex*plot recant unsized *in*dexes
> *co*operate *uni*laterally *sub*sequent to (*Office* 10; italics in
>   original)

With such phrasing and spacing, Guest imbues X1's speech with a stilted, fragmentary quality, thus reinforcing the alienated, dehumanized attributes of the executives. Guest's purpose is to parody the skewed, tortuous character of corporate speech that reifies the executives even further, making them a mere extension of the office.

Guest's mimicry of business speech illustrates what Charles Bernstein has argued about poetry and its appropriation and deployment of specialized discourse. Poetry "engages the social world directly, by taking on its jargon and its technologies, its blather and displacements, not only as subjects but as methods of organization, as environments, to be sounded and tested ... by and in the poem" (Bernstein 70–71). In rendering X1's speech so mechanistically, Guest constructs a social totality, in Lukács's sense, a comprehensive, bureaucratized social reality, in which objects—the Dictaphone, the rigidly ordered desks, and carefully placed paperwork—constitute the world the characters occupy. That this world appears compromised, a workplace environment of routinization and dehumanization, serves Guest's critique of capitalist ideology, under which unique forms of human imagination and expression get jettisoned for an expedient and routine sameness.

Guest compounds the effects of mechanistic speech and the hierarchically arranged office by depicting the behavior of each of the executives as ideologically regimented and conformist as well. Extending her critique of bureaucracy, Guest illustrates how office principles have infiltrated the very mindset of the executives, creating an authoritarian atmosphere.

After X1's opening speech, X2 offhandedly remarks on the work he must complete at "The branch *office*," and, at the mere mention of the workplace, the "*other two men jump to their feet* [and] *Salute*" (*Office* 10). The executives' reflexive gestures speak to Max Weber's critique of organizational discipline and its compulsory compliance, in which there occurs a "'habituation' characteristic of uncritical and unresisting mass obedience" (*Economy and Society* [2019] 135).[4] Exacerbating the sense of acquiescence, the stage directions subsequently indicate that X2 himself also "*rises to* [his] *feet,* [and] *salutes*" when he observes the actions of the other two men (*Office* 10). Here, with the executives' compulsory saluting, Guest sardonically implies that systematic bureaucracy is a national ideology: capitalist and administrative imperatives have infiltrated the mid-century American mindset, making for an unthinking, automaton-like populace.

Guest further exposes the mechanistic ideology of the office by mocking the executives' attempt at redeeming their regimented work with natural metaphors. As X2 extols his workplace, he likens it to a tree, excitedly proclaiming that the "branch *office*" has "grown from a root we planted / [and] is flowering!" (*Office* 10). Combined with the saluting and standing to attention, X2's declamations come across as jingoistic, an animated proclamation of American bureaucracy and its preeminence. It is not long, though, before this image of a "wholesome" American bureaucratic system becomes corrupted, as X2 proceeds with his speech:

> Sir regard this paper
> (*Holds up yellow sheet.*)
> (*to himself*) it came from a forest
> the logjams of my youth (*Office* 11)

The idealized metaphor ("forest") attempting to naturalize the bureaucratic office is contradicted and gets turned on its head: the artificial yellow color of the memo indexes how far removed from nature the manufactured piece of paper—and, by extension, the office—is. Even the nostalgic aside—X2's invocation of youthful memory—is sullied. The forest of his childhood quickly transforms into a *logjam*, a word oft associated with bureaucratic inefficiency.

The catachresis of the "branch office" metaphor—its failure to uphold a credible image of naturalness—is important in another regard, for it sets up Guest's extended allusion in *The Office* to Eliot's "The Waste Land." Guest draws from Eliot in order to convey the degree to which the capitalist space of the bureaucratic office in her play is ironically barren, despite the premium placed on productivity and efficiency. X2 highlights this lack of production by saying "our flowering Branch needs *water*," recalling the speaker's lamentation in "The Waste Land": "What are the roots that clutch, what branches grow / Out of this stony rubbish?" (*Office* 11; Eliot 51). X2 consequently implores X1 to perform an intervening ritual ("Sign sir Sign   the rain warrant!") that recalls the vegetation ceremonies of "The Waste Land" so that they might be delivered from the office's now-barren conditions (*Office* 13; spacing in original).

In contrast to the men of the play and their barren conditions, Guest introduces her female characters. The three women, all office workers, are vibrant counterparts to the executives and seem at once complicit in and disruptive of the bureaucratic conditions of work. Scene 1 concludes with a flurry of action but little promise of redemption:

(*Enter* GIRLS *dressed as office workers yet very different. The section is in pantomime and simultaneous.*)

(GIRL 1 *approaches* X1, *washes his feet with her hair then slyly steals from desk large yellow sheet of paper.*)

(GIRL 2 *approaches* X2, *attempts to fondle his hair, etc. He repulses her.*)

(GIRL 3 *approaches* X3, *erotic love action on desk.*) (*Office* 13)

A range of behavior, from the obeisant to the erotic, surfaces amidst the previously lackluster, sterile proceedings of the play. Much as the men have done, the women comply with and engage in administrative protocols of hierarchy and subservience. Girl 1's obsequious washing of X1's feet with her hair makes of him a Christ figure. As with the parable of Christ's visit to the Pharisees where his bare feet are washed by a prostitute, gendered norms and sexual suggestiveness suffuse the play's action. Guest, however, instills this scene with ambiguity: the women assertively interact with the men but also seem circumscribed by their stratified roles within the office bureaucracy.

The washing of X1's feet nearly conceals a key detail as Girl 1 "*then slyly steals from desk large yellow sheet of paper.*" The action reveals the contingent nature of bureaucratic work and its objects. Guest here depicts the erratic propensity for paperwork to get lost or misfiled, such that the very forms meant to expedite work end up, paradoxically, hindering it.

This tendency for clerical mishaps and accidents has been characterized by Ben Kafka, who writes about paperwork and its frustrating unpredictability in *The Demon of Writing: Powers and Failures of Paperwork*: "it frustrates those of us who have to write memos or fill out forms as part of our jobs; it frustrates those of us who need a stamp or signature to get on with our lives . . ." (10). Kafka goes on to muse, "What do we want from our paperwork? . . . How do we prepare for its failure? How do we respond when these failures occur?" (15). The remainder of *The Office* will revolve around such questions regarding paperwork, bureaucratic instability, and the significance of such mishaps, as Guest continues to probe the pernicious effects of administrative systems.

One clearly identifiable, if absurd, consequence of the "large yellow sheet of paper" going missing from X1's desk is the lead executive's death, which Guest obliquely depicts offstage. The final lines and closing action of scene 1 stem from a message carried over another quintessential bureaucratic object, the office loudspeaker: "(*Suddenly InterCom: 'Blurt Blurt'*)" (*Office* 13). Despite the incomprehensibility of the order, the executives obediently hasten to the call:

(X1, X2, X3 *jump up from desks and reach for yellow paper which has been lying on their desks. X2 and X3 find theirs. X1 discovers his loss. Consternation. The three men march from the room.*)

(*Gargle of voices over loudspeaker. Shot is heard.*) (*Office* 14).

The fatal penalty for the missing yellow paper is as bizarre and extreme as it is unexpected. With the sequence of events, Guest implies that corporate bureaucracy is cruelly oppressive and authoritarian, and her play offers a hyperbolic caricature of administrative regulation and discipline.[5] The executives' movement through the room, their "march[ing]," redoubles the depiction of bureaucracy as authoritatively repressive. Guest augments the effects of terror and fear by removing the killing from the stage and suggesting death through an auditory gun shot. As a consequence, the menacing power of bureaucracy appears all-encompassing, an effect that is all the more frightening because the theft of the yellow sheet of paper by Girl 1 seems particularly capricious, depicted by Guest as having no discernible motivation.

Guest begins scene 2 with the resumption of office activity, after the death of the first executive, and her implication is that the operation of bureaucratic machinery and power obstinately continues despite the toll on human life. The capitalist, acquisitive imperatives of the office advance inexorably without missing a step, even as the lead executive has been removed and killed. Death subsequently casts a pallor on the environment of *The Office*, suggesting an ominous outcome for the remaining executives. As with "The Waste Land," forewarnings come in the form of cards, as seen in the exchange between the "new" X1 and X2:

(X1 *goes to the water cooler. Brings back a cup of water. Takes bottle of pills, empties several into hand, swallows with water. . . . Now he takes a pack of cards from his pocket. Lays them out. Picks up card just as—*)

X2 (*aloud to himself*): Death by water

(X1 *looks at card. Drops it quickly. Turns off machine.* [The Dictaphone] *gurgles away. He dozes. It clicks off.*) (*Office* 15)

With such everyday objects as a water cooler and Dictaphone, Guest summons a familiar quality of office tedium, yet a prevailing sense of bureaucratic dread is also present. Pills manifest the anxiety and malaise felt by the "new" X1, feelings that he subsequently hastens to quell through self-medication. As Herzfeld has argued, bureaucracy tends to produce an affect of indifference, as "destructive, routinized inaction . . . becom[es] an apparently inevitable dimension of everyday social experience" (33). Such apathy and dreariness arise in *The Office* in a pronounced manner, forming an uncanny counterpart to the more extreme acts of violence in the play.

Guest offers the recurrent and abiding treatment of death in *The Office* as a vehicle to suggest the moral bankruptcy of corporate practices and bureaucratic operations. Whereas Eliot could lament World War I as the cause of social decline in Europe by declaiming "I had not thought death had undone so many," Guest apportions blame to capitalism, implying that the social totality of the midcentury American office, its greed and regimentation, has caused a corresponding moral degeneration and an insufficient ability to comprehend loss. In a seeming parody of Eliot's weightier contemplation of death, Guest presents a shallow debate in *The Office* over payments to the original X1's widow:

> X2: . . . I don't know why the living
> Should charge a dividend. Or why
> The dead should die.
> A serious question. Sir—the expense
> incurred by death?
>
> X1 (waking): Memo.   A skeletal staff
> will remain . . . (*Office* 16)

More actuarial than ethical in nature, the conversation attends to office expenditures rather than any meaningful financial obligation to an employee and his family. The two executives, moreover, talk past each other. Whatever sorrow is to be expected from the loss of a colleague appears null; there is to be no room for mourning in Guest's administrative spaces. X1's memorandum about a "skeletal staff" also continues the play's lugubrious imagery, with the implication being that the two executives are themselves lifeless and already "dead"—a consequence of human impulses being squashed by bureaucratic imperatives.

That Guest views death and bureaucracy as intertwined finds expression in the action immediately following the debate over the widow's compensation. Guest repeats the culminating action of scene 1 in the final moments of scene 2: the office women come in once more to steal an office memo, which again leads to the death of one of the executives. The stage directions indicate that the action of the play will unfold mostly as it had previously, as the undermining of the executives' work goes unchecked with another theft of paperwork: "(GIRL 1 *goes to* X1, *washes feet with hair. Slyly lifts yellow sheet.*)" (*Office* 16). As in scene 1, the punishment for not securing papers—for not following bureaucratic protocol—is severe, and scene 2 ends with another death: "X1 *discovers yellow sheet is gone*. . . . *Gargle of voices on loudspeaker. Gunshot as before*)" (*Office* 16).

The swiftness with which a material object, the yellow sheet of paper, can go missing and subsequently seal an employee's fate undergirds Guest's depiction of bureaucracy as nefarious and harmful. To make the malevolence of administrative protocols more pronounced, Guest will also personify bureaucracy, rendering it in the play as a character in his own right, a "Figure in Yellow," who makes his first appearance at the start of scene 3 (*Office* 17). The iconography of Guest's play is such that yellow stands for the very color of bureaucracy. The memoranda that the executives write are composed on yellow paper, and the Figure in Yellow behaves as a despised supervisory manager might: skulking in the background and monitoring and directing the behavior of the office women.

Guest depicts the Figure in Yellow as odious and greedy, despicably repulsive in his management of others. Now the sole executive remaining, X2 acts according to his own interests and with the approval of the Figure in Yellow:

> (*Switches on* [Dictaphone] *machine.*)
>
> Memo: Pay rise for executives
>   Promote ecstasy in upper income
>   bracket
> (FIGURE IN YELLOW *is nodding ominously*) (*Office* 19)

Here, the writing of the memo, something done by rote, makes of X2 an office automaton, a reified object, hardly more than an extension of the Dictaphone he switches to the "on" position. Guest, moreover, makes the promotion of "ecstasy" appear uncannily abject, a bureaucratic pursuit rendering people categorizable not in terms of their humanity but as tax code, representative of an "upper income / bracket." This is the managerial or bureaucratic sublime at its terrifying apogee, where the last executive of *The Office* functions as a machine and the inert administrative system propagates itself and its own ends, ensuring its profits and executive privilege.

Against these impersonal mechanisms of administration and business transactions, Guest will champion love as a means of rejecting corporate imperatives, leading to refusal of work as it has been formerly conducted. Guest concludes *The Office* and her critique of capitalist bureaucracy with an effort to overturn its logic and replace its teleological drives with something more restoratively human. At the end of her play, Guest encourages her audience to think of interpersonal love as the corrective to bureaucratic principles and what she sees as their dehumanizing tendencies. Appropriate to such a belief in love, Guest presents an interaction between X2 and Girl 1, where he wakes from his memo-induced ecstasy and its allure of higher pay: X2 "(*Shakes himself out of dream. Looks down in alarm at girl washing his feet*)" (*Office* 19). Guest both abides by and departs from the religious motifs that she previously invoked. Girl 1 is abject like the biblical prostitute of Guest's allusion, yet

X2 (now called X1 after the deaths of the other two executives) falls short of wholly being a Christ figure, as he asks:

> Who are you?
>
> (*When she stands up we see she has a grimy, dirt-streaked face.*)
>
> GIRL 1 (*tough*): I'm an office person.
>
> X1: You mustn't do this sort of work.
>
> GIRL 1 (*shrugs*): you're the boss. (*Office* 20)

The stage directions point to Guest's feminist inclinations regarding work and bureaucracy, with Girl 1 resolutely proclaiming her identity and assuming an upright stance. In suggesting that Girl 1 abandon her job—refuse the very work of the office—X1 begins to repudiate the more hierarchical and dehumanizing consequences of bureaucracy. The response of the office woman remains fittingly aligned with Guest's feminist message: though stated in the affirmative, the woman's ironic, shrugging reply ("you're the boss") undercuts both the individual authority behind X1's executive status and the very administrative structure upon which it rests.

Having been mostly relegated to the background previous to this point in the play, Girl 1 gains ascendancy, revealing Guest's interest in a symbolic elevation of women. Girl 1 now becomes a vehicle for challenging the masculine-laden workforce and the patriarchal values that underpin the office. Despite having assertively claimed her identity as an "office person," Girl 1 moments later renounces her job, expressing contempt for what it has hitherto entailed:

> GIRL 1: I won't say I've always liked my work. Or some of the people. I'd just as soon most of them were dead.
>
> (*She slyly, yet unwillingly, reaches out her hand for yellow sheet on desk, then hesitates and looks up at the* FIGURE IN YELLOW. *He returns her look still ominously. She picks up paper and puts it in her blouse.*) (*Office* 21)

The woman's frankness about disliking her job at first appears merely to be a routine office complaint, yet Guest's stage directions denote her more far-reaching concerns with work and the bureaucratic principles that underlie it. Girl 1's nonchalant yet egregious statement that she would not mind if "most of them were dead," overshadows her reluctance to perform her purported role, as she "unwillingly" and "hesita[ntly]" steals yet another memorandum. Guest's emphasis on the woman's hesitation is noteworthy, for it signals an incipient yet foundational refusal of work, a rejection of the avarice, hierarchy, and fatal impulses that have so far characterized the philosophy of her office.

As an alternative to the administrative regimentation of the office, Guest will posit love, whose values of interpersonal connection and relation function as a corrective to bureaucratic and corporate imperatives of capitalist domination and acquisition. The impulse toward love begins simply enough, and even perhaps a bit tritely, as the new X1 asks the office woman, "Could you like me?" (*Office* 21). Girl 1's response to X1's question is comparatively more nuanced, consistent with the scrutiny of motives that Guest wants to infuse into the scene. After looking askance at the only other individual present, the Figure in Yellow, GIRL 1 offers her answer:

(GIRL 1 *looks again at the* FIGURE IN YELLOW. *He returns her look steadily. For a moment she seems perplexed. Then tossing back her head and looking at the* FIGURE IN YELLOW *defiantly.*)

GIRL 1: I might. (*Then almost radiantly:*) Yes, I might. (*Office* 21)

Girl 1's tentative, yet burgeoning, acceptance of X1's overture matches the increasingly defiant stance she adopts toward her job and to the Figure in Yellow, who exists as institutional bureaucracy incarnate. By challenging the Figure in Yellow in such a manner, Girl 1 opens the possibility of replacing the dictates of the office with the counter-ideological program Guest hopes to advance: a belief in the relational, non-hierarchical, and anti-bureaucratic principle of love, indicative of an affirming, revitalizing force, expressed as a possibility ("I might. (*Then almost radiantly:*) Yes, I might").

Girl 1's defiance of the Figure in Yellow consequently enacts a certain refusal of work, whereby the idealization of employment and of work itself is superseded. As Kathi Weeks has argued, the refusal of work allows one to posit a fuller, more enriched existence: "Rather than a simple act of disengagement that one completes, the refusal [of work] is, in this sense, a process, a theoretical and practical movement that aims to effect a separation through which we can pursue alternative practices and relationships"

(100). Guest's advocacy of love in the play is thus a radical substitution of human interconnection over the bureaucratic dehumanization and alienation that has taken up the majority of *The Office*. The implications of Girl 1's repudiation of bureaucracy and embrace of love are immense, providing an inkling of another way of being, one that is emancipatory in nature, as Michael Hardt and Antonio Negri have contended: "the refusal of work and authority, or really the refusal of voluntary servitude, is the beginning of liberatory politics" (*Empire* 204).

Girl 1's budding refusal of work most certainly puts her at odds with the Figure in Yellow, a clash that amounts to the play's ultimate and most important instance of dramatic tension. X1 had signed on to this course of defiant action, voicing his reservations, quoted previously, about her subservient job at the office: "You mustn't do this sort of work" (*Office* 20). What remains, then, is a confrontation with the Figure in Yellow, who seemingly fails to grasp Girl 1's intentions:

> (GIRL 1 *looks now again at the* FIGURE IN YELLOW *who nods his head up and down in affirmation. She takes the yellow sheet from her blouse and slowly tears it into pieces while spot*[light] *fades on her and* X1 *and follows the* FIGURE IN YELLOW *exiting from room.*) (*Office* 21)

The fact that the Figure in Yellow nods in affirmation lends some ambiguity to the scene because this dramatic gesture suggests a sanctioning of what ensues. Girl 1's own performative gesture of ripping up the yellow sheet, however, arguably enacts her final and complete refusal of work and her repudiation of the office and of bureaucracy. That it is the Figure in Yellow who exits—effectively banished from the room—reinforces such a reading, particularly as the destruction of the memorandum does not lead to an executive being shot, as it had done in the previous acts.

In taking up the conflict between Girl 1 and the Figure in Yellow as the pivotal dramatic point of her play, Guest abides by Lukács's belief in collision as the preeminent structuring device of drama. As Lukács argues:

> By concentrating the reflection of life upon a great collision, by grouping all of the manifestations of life round this collision and permitting them to live themselves out only in relation to the collision, drama simplifies and generalizes the possible attitudes of [humans] to the problems of their lives. The portrayal is reduced to . . . what is indispensable to the dynamic

working-out of the collision, to those social, human and *moral* movements . . . out of which the collision arises and which the collision dissolves. (*Historical Novel* 94)

By pitting both Girl 1 and X1 against the Figure in Yellow, Guest dramatizes a collision between the principles of love and those of bureaucracy. The totality of the play had, up until this point, featured the absurd and baleful conditions of the bureaucratic, with the loss of pieces of paperwork epitomizing the pernicious effects of administrative systems: entire lives determined by and succumbing to callous questions of efficiency, organization, and regimentation, with little room for mishaps. Though Guest's depiction of the fatal consequences is without doubt hyperbolic, her aim is to illustrate that bureaucracy entails its share of not just bewildering and frustrating moments but situations that can have real and dire consequences, where clerical error could lead, for example, to a lapse in insurance coverage, a bank account made inaccessible, or a police search warrant executed on the wrong address.

Guest's distrust of bureaucratic systems gains clearer and more direct expression in the marginalization of the Figure in Yellow, yet her advocacy and promotion of love is not without some ambiguity, even in the final line of the play. Guest speaks of love in a somewhat obscure manner as the play ends:

(*With the spot following the exit of the* FIGURE IN YELLOW, *we hear from the half-lit shadows where* X1 *and* GIRL 1 *are standing—*)

X1: A fearful love ascending from the waters. (*Office* 21)

To describe love as "fearful," as Guest does, seems initially not to correspond with her valuation of human interrelationships over bureaucratic alienation and corporate avarice. Guest's diction, however, does ultimately align with her radical vision of altering society and with her sense that the terror of the bureaucratic sublime might be replaced with a truer, ameliorating sublime in the form of transcendent love.[6] Here, the play's earlier allusions to "The Waste Land" return, wherein the deprivations of bureaucracy—its favoring of hierarchy and routinization over human interconnection—get overturned, and love might prosper in astonishing and hitherto unimaginable ways when considered in contrast to the first two scenes of *The Office* and their equation of death and bureaucracy.

Guest's impulse to oppose love to bureaucracy lends her conception of human love an overarching political dynamic that transcends an individual couple, X1 and Girl 1. Instead, Guest posits a belief in love as a social and communal force that is transformative. Hardt and Negri have made similar assertions about the political impact of love, lamenting that love is too often conceived in narrow, uninspired terms: "The modern concept of love is almost exclusively limited to the bourgeois couple and the claustrophobic confines of the nuclear family. Love has become a strictly private affair" (*Multitude* 351). What is needed, Hardt and Negri contend, is an alternate understanding of love: "We need to recover today [a] material and political sense of love, a love as strong as death. This does not mean that you cannot love your spouse, your mother, your child. It only means that your love does not end there, that love serves as the basis for our political projects in common and the construction of a new society"(*Multitude* 352). Though Guest's ending of *The Office* focuses on a singular couple, their action of coupling reasserts a value of love powerful enough, within the context and representative figures of the play, to drive away bureaucracy and its dehumanizing tendencies. Guest, here, does not attempt to construct an intricately detailed social vision or a comprehensive and executable political program. Guest's purpose, rather, is to endorse a world view in which human relations are valued and the dignity of work is restored after a firm refusal of its indignities in the male-determined bureaucratic workspace of mid-century.

A decade after *The Office* was first performed, Guest would focus upon an office device again in her "Olivetti Ode" from 1973. Where *The Office* features a refusal of work and the more baleful conditions of bureaucracy, "Olivetti Ode" takes up work's reevaluation, imagining clerical work anew and wedding it to artistic purpose. Though categorically a poem of elevation and praise, "Olivetti Ode" still bears some of Guest's characteristic ambiguity, for the subject of Guest's celebratory ode might easily apply to the instrument she writes upon, a typewriter, as well as an artistic artifact about which she has presumably been commissioned to write. This task is both clerical and poetic, as she sets out to characterize the artifact, related in italics as the *Building*:

> How difficult it is   to recall you
> Are not Polychrome Limestone
> *Building* received from the administrators (*CP* 133)

Guest's address is intimate, as if she were speaking to a lover, and comes across in a halting manner. In the line above, the caesura and gap in spacing, along with the outright expression of difficulty, signal a confrontation with a sublime object of art, an ancient artifact made of some other substance than Polychrome Limestone. The elevation of love at the end of *The Office* is refashioned here as artistic purpose and so too is the relation to bureaucracy: the "administrators" no longer strike a menacing figure or a hierarchical one. Guest "receive[s]" the work in a manner that suggests her acceptance as an equal and her autonomous position as a poet.

After an initial struggle with the sublime *Building*, Guest assuredly makes herself equal to the artistic object. She proceeds with her simultaneously artistic and clerical task of recording the features of the sculpture, and her Olivetti, too, is raised from a mere bureaucratic machine to a tool for making art: "I must trace your steps / here on the keyboard / I must assign you to space" (*CP* 133). As with the poems of "The Location of Things," she situates objects, secure in her ability to place them. Guest consequently endows herself with significant power and purpose. If she functions as a scribe once more, it is one who can bestow authenticity, her actions having the equivalent veracity and validity of a time stamp:

> Proof of your history
> will be this route
> I am hitting
> this siren note
> I strike
> on a ribbon your archaeology (*CP* 133)

The métier of a clerk mixes here with that of a poet-songstress as well as that of an archaeologist: the clack of her Olivetti resounds, as Guest both creates an alluring song and forges anew the path ("this route") toward artifactual discovery. The raising of a commonplace office material, the typewriter's ribbon, is the final step to making the bureaucrat's job equal to a poet's, for Guest summons an entire cultural history upon a prosaic machine and its constituent parts.

"Olivetti Ode" is Guest's offer of simultaneous acclaim to works of art, bureaucratic skill, and poetry itself and combines reverence for all three, stripping each of their boundaries, into a single poem. In highlighting the typewriter's—and the typist's—functions, Guest recalls her earliest work out of college and the clerical duties she performed for Henry Miller. "Olivetti Ode," however, takes her from a subservient and secondary role and places her squarely and supremely in the position to make art herself. Guest acknowledges her occupation as a composer of poems is a sacred one, but the language of bureaucracy is indispensable to her ability to convey her calling:

> The rituals have been observed
> Vanish   Vanish   *Building*
> Except here on my calendar
> a last iridescent bite (*CP* 133)

As Guest documents the existence of *Building* as an artefact, she elides the differences between sacred ritual and bureaucratic routine and suggests how a relic from the past may be eclipsed by its cataloging, reified into an object for display and paradoxically made to disappear or vanish. "Olivetti Ode," nevertheless, does manage to testify to human industry: Guest's office calendar clearly says so, duly keeping record of acceptance of work and the day she made it her own.

In *The Office* and in her poems, Guest testifies to the social totality of bureaucratic systems by tabulating the various objects and clerical devices that make up her environment. Guest's position in relation to these office objects is largely adversarial. Her opposition arises from a skepticism toward administrative structures and bureaucratic protocol, which themselves are part of a larger patriarchal and capitalist order historically antagonistic to women and their participation in the workforce. With each word and conceit developed in her poems and play, Guest attempts to dismantle the social totality of bureaucracy and its ideology, and though clerical work affords her a reasonable focus for contempt, an office job also provides her with a figure for the responsibilities of a poet. Guest's poems can be unnerving as she unsettles the relation between the world and its objects. As a poet-clerk to the world, Guest finds herself, as in her poem "Knight of the Swan," assuming a sedentary position, "going to [her] desk in the meadow" (*CP* 110). The force of Guest's imagination allows her to put her desk to other uses, until it and its drawers—now dismantled—are made into something else entire, a reality altogether different from a bureaucratic one, shifting nearly perpetually: "in every breath she drew like a swimmer who draws the ocean / or a worm who draws the earth or I who draw / your heaviness as you draw the drawer as / daylight draws to its close all have endings" (110). Drafting and drifting at her desk, Guest draws the world and its bureaucratic ideologies into legibility, only afterwards disturbing and smudging the lines, purposefully and dexterously.

Chapter 5

It Won't Last

Monuments, Counter-Monuments, and James Schuyler's Trials of Affiliation

> Time mocks the rigidity of monuments, the presumptuous claim that in its materiality, a monument can be regarded as eternally true, a fixed star in the constellation of collective memory.
>
> —James E. Young, "The Counter-Monument"

Left alone, bureaucracy will only enlarge itself, exhibiting—it would seem—an endless propensity toward proliferation. Attesting to such a view, D.A. Miller writes that the "definitive dream of bureaucracy" is "to turn the end it serves into the means of its own expansion" (86). Fictional accounts bear out this monumentalist conception of bureaucracy, as do, often enough, actual dealings with large government agencies and corporate entities. The outlook that bureaucracy will inevitably and continuously extend itself could even be expressed as a maxim, or a "a general sociological law," as David Graeber has claimed, such that "any government initiative intended to reduce red tape and promote market forces will have the ultimate effect of increasing the total number of regulations, the total amount of paperwork, and the total number of bureaucrats the government employs" (9).

James Schuyler, not a sociologist but a poet by trade, knows of this bureaucratic tendency toward ceaseless, monumental expansion, calling pointed attention to it in his poem "Hymn to Life," where he describes his odd, alienated experiences in his childhood hometown of Washington, DC:

> Strange city, broad and desolating, monuments
> Rearing up and offices like monuments and crowds lined up
>   to see
> The White House inside (*Selected Poems* [*SP*] 147).

As Schuyler conveys the capital's enormous sprawl, uncanny equations arise in his poetic consciousness: there is little to separate the national monuments of DC from the city's massive federal and corporate office buildings—not to mention the underlying bureaucratic and disciplinary apparatuses—that sustain the city and the nation beyond it.

Schuyler's long poems ironically share some of the breadth and immensity of the national monuments and Washington, DC, office buildings he details in "Hymn to Life." In his introduction to Schuyler's *Selected Poems*, John Ashbery has described Schuyler's longer writings as striking a "Whitmanesqe note" and resulting in "long-lined, long-limbed [and] quasi-epic poems" (*SP* xiii–xiv). The size and scale of Schuyler's long poems, though, commonly exist in tension with their subject matter, which often entails small, quotidian details and the mundane happenings of daily life. A concern with scale, though, occurs even in Schuyler's shorter lyric poems and arises whether he is investigating the minutest diurnal occurrence or pondering his place in cities like New York or Washington, DC. As a consequence, the poems that Schuyler writes routinely exhibit a tension between maximalist and minimalist tendencies, a contrasting structuring principle in his work that reflects how he comes to terms with the world in which he lives.

These rival tendencies to think through scale exhibit what I will call Schuyler's poetics of monumentalism and counter-monumentalism—a practice of poetry that not only attends to the human inclination to build things of great magnitude but also aims to undermine or critique the administrative and professional impulse toward grandiosity. The monumentalist aspect of Schuyler's poetics includes his observations about massive, urban built spaces and the bureaucratic systems that such things as city office buildings evoke by association. As lofty expressions of monumentalism, metropolitan skyscrapers also suggest corresponding human tendencies toward ambition and recognition, about which Schuyler has long had reservations. The counter-monumentalist mode of Schuyler's poetry stems from this ambivalence toward, and skepticism about, what he has often been drawn to: big city buildings, high aspirations, and notoriety. At these moments, Schuyler becomes wary of things becoming too large, grand, or ostentatious. When Schuyler operates within a counter- or anti-monumentalist mode, he becomes doubtful about the purpose and longevity of monuments, their willful function to transcend time, a sentiment he explicitly, and somewhat dejectedly, gives voice to in "Hymn to Life": "And there the Lincoln Memorial crumbles. It looks so solid: it won't / Last. The impermanence of permanence, is that all there is?" (*SP* 149).

Literary reputation is equally a topos within Schuyler's poetics of monumentalism and counter-monumentalism. The towering literary fame of other writers certainly inspires in Schuyler admiration and appreciation, but ambition and recognition, whether his own or that of others, also spur corresponding feelings of either resentment or self-reproach. The nature of—and path toward—literary fame arises periodically as a subject in Schuyler's poetry: renowned poets appear on occasion as figures in his writing, offset by an awareness that Schuyler and his friends must, early in their careers, play a comparative role of humble office apprentice. Later, as an established poet, Schuyler will self-consciously reference the monumentality of his own writing, uneasy with his tendency to hold forth. In long poems like "Dining Out with Doug and Frank" and "The Morning of the Poem," for instance, Schuyler will question why the poems have grown so large, so all-encompassing, and, as he approaches the end of his career, so lugubrious. Schuyler's self-scrutiny reveals at once a poet with aspirations for grand achievement and someone who habitually and skeptically reevaluates his labor as a writer. As a result, the monumentality of writing and literary reputation is a source of consternation for Schuyler, particularly as he struggles to find his place within literature as an institution.

Dubious about monuments and the circumscribing, bureaucratic institutions they represent, Schuyler will repeatedly construct counter-monuments of his poems, writing works that assail the compulsory and narrow institutional affiliation that monuments demand. Turning upon questions of exclusion, Schuyler's poems, for example, attest to the ways in which his military service came under bureaucratic and disciplinary scrutiny as well as legal jeopardy and his romantic relationships necessarily had to remain closeted due to social intolerance and oppression. Schuyler will also question, in a corresponding manner, the sense of affiliation that literary institutions require, acknowledging his longstanding discomfiture with a professional career that began with a clerk-like apprenticeship to W.H. Auden and ends, retrospectively, with a disavowal of any need for his own monumental literary status. Schuyler did not readily capitulate to the institutional and bureaucratic strictures that sought to circumscribe his personal existence and his professional career: his poems persistently sound a note of protest, affirming his desire to interrupt the bureaucratic ethos of midcentury and beyond, challenging the messaging of allegiance that both monuments and literary institutions signify and convey.

Schuyler's affective ambivalence toward monuments typically coincides with his awareness of bureaucratic measures—specifically, the regulatory order and disciplinary set of rules that monuments symbolically convey. That monuments can encapsulate bureaucratic strictures is something that Lewis Mumford argues in *The City in History*, asserting that monuments operate as a means for cultural transmission and regulatory decree. For Mumford, monuments in ancient cities encode and transmit the social and cultural beliefs of city leaders, as their very actions and rulings would become inscribed in stone, expressive of municipal strictures and officialdom: "the rulers of the city lived a multiple life: once in action, again in monuments and inscriptions, and still another time in the effect of the recorded events upon the minds of later people, furnishing them with models for imitation, warnings of danger, incentives to achievement" (97). Similarly observing the ways in which monuments "constitute and found the society [with which it is] concerned" (222), Henri Lefebvre speaks to the administrative and social complicity that monuments enact, through their very elevated dimensions: "The monument thus effected a 'consensus,' and this in the strongest sense of the term, rendering it practical and concrete. The element of repression in it and the element of exaltation could scarcely be disentangled; or perhaps it would be more accurate to say that the repressive element was metamorphosed into exaltation" (220). As Mumford and Lefebvre each maintain, monuments speak to order and rule within civic life, and Schuyler's poems frequently address the tension he feels in abiding by or contravening such regulations.

The type of interpellating, disciplinary role that Mumford and Lefebvre outline for monuments is something Schuyler is highly attuned to, particularly as he himself contemplates cities and urban spaces. In Schuyler's scrutinizing assessment of urban spaces, one recognizes an adept political critique of both monuments and the regulatory, bureaucratic principles that correspond to them. In this regard, "Hymn to Life," published in 1974, owes something of its critique of monumentality to the counter-cultural movements of the 1960s. As David Harvey has contended, monumentality and its relation to bureaucratic strictures were of particular concern for 1960s-era counter-cultural politics: "The critics of . . . downtown monolithic monumentality (like Jane Jacobs) became, as we have seen, a vociferous minority that articulated a whole host of discontents. The counter-cultural critiques and practices of the 1960s therefore paralleled movements of the excluded minorities and the critique of depersonalized bureaucratic rationality" (139).[1] For Schuyler, the exclusion from American civic life he himself felt as a homosexual at mid-century found particular, subtle articulation in his descriptions of, and observations about, municipal spaces and the outsized monuments that populate such spaces. While less vociferous than the activists of the '60s, Schuyler delineates in his poems what David Sibley has described as "geographies of exclusion," or "account[s] of barriers, prohibitions and constraints on activities from the point of view of the excluded" (x).

An alienated point of view, a perspective of the excluded, describes well the social position that Schuyler assumes in many of his poems of the 1970s and '80s and gives expression to a sexual identity that had been condemned and barred in public spaces. The repression that Schuyler faced as a gay man posed limits on his ability to communicate openly his romantic feelings or sexual desires, yet even within the relationships he enjoyed privately, he often felt his existence curtailed, particularly when his partners were closeted, as they themselves felt unable either to act willingly on their sexuality or to commit to him as a partner. In poems written from the point of view of the jilted lover, Schuyler makes a protest of his individual situation, but he also raises a political objection to a society unwilling to grant him freedom to act as a whole human being. Imposing and symbolic, monuments would become the focal points of Schuyler's political and personal agitation, as these structures embodied both the official and unofficial strictures—the bureaucratic and social rules—that regulated his existence and enacted his sense of exclusion.

Though the political dimensions of Schuyler's poems can often seem diffuse and indirect, his objections to monumentality and the ideological and bureaucratic principles aligned with it register nonetheless. For instance, in "Hymn to Life," Schuyler's instinctual, skeptical response to Washington, DC, is to resist its interpellating pull on him:

> Why should a white city dog my thoughts? Vast, arid, a
>   home to many,

So strange in its unamiability. Stony city laid out on an
  heroic plan,
Why are you there? (*SP* 150)

Schuyler's questions about DC ruefully address the city's monumentality, its "vast[ness]" along with its "arid," "stony," and "heroic" architectural features. The same questions also ultimately address his sense of municipal and national belonging. While Schuyler pointedly challenges the authority and ideological function of monumental DC ("Why are you there?"), he also queries his own sense of affiliation or lack thereof ("Why should a white city dog my thoughts?"). Many of Schuyler's poems likewise persist as a contestation of his treatment by others—whether governmental entities or personal friends and lovers—who contribute to his sense of not belonging or being accepted.

The wariness with which Schuyler interacts with Washington, DC, offers an indication of his counter-monumental outlook and poetic approach. James E. Young coined the term "counter-monument" to describe a work of art that functions in opposition to a traditional monument and thereby "en[acts] a critique of 'memory places'" (272). Young's immediate contexts were the counter-monuments of German artists of the late 1980s and early '90s who grappled with ways to confront that nation's Nazi past and the atrocities of the Holocaust of World War II. These artists created works that were "brazen, painfully self-conscious memorial spaces conceived to challenge the very premises of their being," standing self-referentially as anti-monuments in their criticism of Nazi politics of the past (Young 271). As Young further explains, "by defining itself in opposition to the traditional memorial's task, the counter-monument illustrates concisely the possibilities and limitations of all memorials everywhere" (277). Though taking up an altogether different set of historical circumstances and political conditions, Schuyler's poems gain significance when considered in terms of opposition and dissent. Schuyler's "Hymn to Life"—like several of his other poems—functions as if it were a counter-monument, despite being not a physical or material structure but a written text. In its length, "quasi-epic" scale, attention to architectural detail, and address of both national monuments and monumentalist ideology, "Hymn to Life" stands as a counter-memory, expressive of Schuyler's ambivalent relation to his childhood city of Washington, DC, and indicative of his felt lack of national belonging as well as his protest of sexual condemnation and oppression.

To understand the full extent of Schuyler's fluctuating affiliation with and disaffiliation from DC and the United States, it is worth remembering that Schuyler was dishonorably discharged from the US Navy in 1944 for being homosexual. Schuyler had been on trial for going AWOL, for failing to return to his ship after weekend leave, and his sexual orientation was discovered during the trial's proceedings. The Navy's administrative ruling sundered Schuyler from national service, and his military affiliation was dissolved by judicial and bureaucratic fiat. Schuyler's discharge from the Navy notably was not an exception but an integral part of US military bureaucratic policy in the World War II era. As Allan Bérubé has observed, a proposed plan for psychiatric screening of draftees in 1940 initially "included no reference to homosexuality," but was subsequently and explicitly made discriminatory toward gay Americans when reviewed and revised by "a few high ranking [military] officials, many of whom harbored prejudices against both psychiatry and homosexuality" (11). It was, Bérubé argues, the "bureaucratic process itself, by expanding the volume of directives, memoranda, and revisions, [that] helped build the momentum of the military's wartime preoccupation with homosexuality" (11). Such bureaucratic scrutiny continued after 1945. David F. Greenberg writes that an entire bureaucratic system was put in place so that homosexuals would be swiftly removed from the military: "Once [World War II] ended, thousands of soldiers were given dishonorable discharges. In fact, a Senate subcommittee investigating the employment of homosexuals in government noted that the armed services had been much more aggressive than the civilian branches in attempting to exclude homosexuals" (445). The official policies of the US military discriminating against homosexuals unhappily made antipathy toward gay servicemen like Schuyler a matter of efficient procedural and administrative routine.

This deplorable moment in the nation's history regarding sexual orientation and military service certainly warrants a counter-monumentalist reaction. Despite never referencing his dishonorable discharge, "Hymn to Life" exists as Schuyler's skeptical response to, and repudiation of, monumental DC and the personal and political freedoms it is meant symbolically to evoke but has failed to enact for all. Instead of inspiring a patriotic sense of grandeur, the capital underwhelms, exhibiting, for Schuyler, an arbitrary and byzantine urban design bereft of substance: "Quite / A few things are boring, like the broad avenues of Washington, / D.C. that seem to go from nowhere and back again. Civil servants / Wait at the crossing to cross to lunch at the Waffle House" (*SP* 153). Familiar tropes of bureaucratic routine and clerical boredom surface from the laboring—and labored—existence of federal civil servants whom Schuyler observes on their daily trek to the Waffle House. Schuyler's arch stance of dismissiveness, an exhibition of what Susan Sontag identifies as the camp impulse to "dethrone the serious," is aimed precisely at the majesty of the nation's capital, its bureaucratic mechanisms, and its uncritical adherence to established norms (288). Here, also, the image of automaton office clerks serves as an uncanny counterpart to the "crowds lined up to see / The White House," wherein the touristic spectacle of democracy is shadowed by a lethargic bureaucratic apparatus in the form of faceless civil servants out to lunch (*SP* 147).

Appropriate to the critique of memory places driving the purpose of counter-monuments, Schuyler looks, in "Hymn to Life," to banish monumental DC from his thoughts: "As windows are set in walls in whited Washington. City, begone / From my thoughts: childhood was not all that gay. Nor all that gray" (*SP* 157). In revisiting Washington, DC, Schuyler ultimately seeks to control his memory, resolving to counteract bad memories with good ones, as he resignedly notes that "childhood was not all that . . . gray." Schuyler thereby attempts to dismiss his negative feelings about the nation's capital from his consciousness ("City, begone"), overturning his own expulsion from social and military spaces by expunging disciplinary DC from his thoughts.

The intersection between bureaucracy and monumentalism present in "Hymn to Life" obtains as well in another poem, "Wystan Auden," Schuyler's elegy for his friend and former employer, the poet W.H. Auden. As with "Hymn to Life" and its treatment of monuments and the remembered past, "Wystan Auden" revolves around similar sentiments of affiliation and disaffiliation, though these feelings relate not to national or patriotic belonging but to friendship and literary standing. In the elegy, Schuyler recalls his friendship with Auden, chronicling the poet's generosity, his idiosyncratic behavior, and his propensity for grand pronouncements. "Wystan Auden" also raises as subject matter the clerical duties that Schuyler performed for Auden, a working relationship that Ashbery briefly describes in his introduction to Schuyler's *Selected Poems*: "for a time Schuyler worked as Auden's secretary and typed the manuscript of his collection *Nones*" (SP xii). The uneasy tension between being a friend and being an employee forms one axis on which the poem turns, and Schuyler's occasional role as a subordinate clerk colors his view of and writing about Auden. Revealing some of Schuyler's characteristic ambivalence, "Wystan Auden" oscillates between feelings of genuine tenderness and underlying resentment. For instance, Schuyler tellingly must jog his memory at the outset of the poem: "I went to his fortieth birthday / party: was it really twenty-seven / years ago? I don't remember what street he was living on . . ." (*SP* 169). A level of indifference and bitterness on Schuyler's part arises in the elegy, borne out of a close working relationship, literary envy, and the tediousness of his clerical duties. As Ashbery reports, "working on the Auden manuscript caused [Schuyler] to reflect: 'If this is poetry, I'm certainly never going to write any myself'" (*SP* xii).

Auden—at least as he is portrayed in "Wystan Auden"—likewise thought of the working relationship between Schuyler and himself as bureaucratic or administrative in nature. As the poem relates, Auden conceived of his vocation as a poet as being akin to that of a high-ranking diplomat whose all-important paperwork must be safeguarded against misguided actions carried out by office underlings:

> And
> When he learned that in Florence
> I and my friend Bill Aalto had
> fished his drafts of poems
> out of the wastepaper basket,
> he took to burning them, saying,
> "I feel like an ambassador burning
> secret papers." (*SP* 169)

Motifs of State-level dealings and acts of espionage—common features of Auden's poetry—infiltrate Schuyler's elegy, ensuring the poem's bureaucratic context and creating an echo between Auden's writing and Schuyler's. These figures of government agencies and offices also summon, as in "Hymn to Life," feelings of loyalty and betrayal for Schuyler, indicating his one-time sense of affiliation and devotion to his former employer as well as to poetry as an institution. The gesture of securing Auden's manuscripts coincides with not just the task of carrying out one's professional clerical duties but cementing literary reputation: the impulse to secure Auden's papers was one of preservation and memorialization. "Wystan Auden" takes this function of memorialization a complicated, ironic step further, though: the poem itself operates at once as a monument and counter-monument, gently chiding Auden's self-importance while simultaneously acknowledging the poet's stature as worthy of elegy.

Schuyler's own investment in literary reputation and poetry as an elevated art form, however, ought not to be overlooked. Despite giving sardonic treatment to Auden's bombast (" 'My dear, I'm the / first major poet to have flown / the Atlantic' "), Schuyler was not himself immune to the lure or appeal of literary fame (*SP* 170). Auden's bragging, monumentalist claims of stature are offset by Schuyler's own propensity to hold poets in high esteem: "It was in / that apartment [of Auden's] that I just missed / meeting Brecht and T.S. Eliot" (*SP* 169). On one level, the references to Brecht and Eliot in Auden's apartment certainly exemplify the New York School's penchant for casual name-dropping, but Schuyler's mention of the assembled modernist cadre also speaks to his desire for admission into the institution of poetry.[2] David Lehman remarks that Schuyler was prone to agonize about his standing among his New York School peers: "Schuyler was the least prolific of the New York poets, the only one who did not have an Ivy League education [Lehman here excludes Guest], and was susceptible to feelings of resentment and deep insecurity about being overlooked and excluded" (256). The near "miss" of an opportunity to meet Brecht and Eliot indicates both Schuyler's proximity to and sense of remove from a monumental literary class.

Against his own monumentalist aspirations and investment in structures of literary dominance, Schuyler will construct a counter-monumental response. The ironic framing of "Wystan Auden," wherein Auden is shown to be vain and somewhat foolish, enacts Schuyler's anti-monumental depiction of his former employer (*SP* 169). In this manner, approaching his portrait of Auden with wry humor, Schuyler strikes a mildly derisive tone. Auden's generosity with money, for instance, becomes fodder for a counter-monumentalist rebuke:

> He was very kind.
> Once, when I had an operation
> in Rome, he wrote me quite a large
> check: I forget how much.
> When I sent it back and asked
> for (for a more favorable ex-
> change on the black market)
> cash he sent it, along with
> a cross note saying he was
> a busy man (*SP* 170).

In setting down an ambivalent portrait of Auden tinged with both reverence and a degree of spite, Schuyler rehearses feelings of genial affiliation and surly disaffiliation, creating at once a monument to Auden's memory and a counter-monument. Schuyler's gratitude for his employer's benevolence is apparent, yet the transactional nature of their dealings remains sharply in focus, as Schuyler targets for ridicule Auden's impatience and self-importance as a professional, a "busy man"—or businessman—attending to his daily work obligations.

Owing to Schuyler's subordinate position as secretary and office helpmate to Auden, the teetering emotions between animosity and respect revolve not so surprisingly around the issue of work and poetic production. Auden's campy pronouncements about poets and business etiquette lodge in Schuyler's memory: Auden would sit "at Maria's café in the cobbled / square saying, 'Poets should / dress like businessmen,' while / he wore an incredible peach- / colored nylon shirt" (*SP* 169). However campily overwrought or misconstrued Auden's conception of business attire might be, his comment certainly aligns with his sense of requisite expertise for poets, whom Auden has said should be as assiduous as "clerks" and consider themselves as part of a "professional brotherhood" (*Dyer's Hand* 365). Schuyler accordingly attests to Auden's interest in clerical diligence, using the same figurative terminology of the bureaucratic office: "He was industrious, writing away in / a smoky room—fug—in a / ledger or on loose sheets / poems, some of which I typed / for him (they're in *Nones*)" (*SP* 170). In the pendulum swing between monumentalism and counter-monumentalism in "Wystan Auden," the portrait of Auden's industrious work ethic here reinforces the poet's stature even if it is recorded in clerical terms ("ledger"). Schuyler relates his own secretarial production rather meekly by comparison, using a parenthetical, "(they're in *Nones*)," at once to acknowledge his job typing poems and to relegate it to the margins.

Schuyler's conflicted elegy for Auden is borne of contradictory emotions—of loyalty and disloyalty—held by the younger poet toward the more established one. Lehman reports that "Schuyler grew to dislike Auden's poetry and to resent his authority" (257). Another contention Lehman makes is that "it was only when [Schuyler] discarded Auden as an influence that he began to come into his own as a poet" (258). "Wystan Auden" reveals some of the bitterness to which Lehman alludes, and Schuyler makes plain that his feelings of loyalty to his one-time employer have ebbed: "I don't have to burn his / letters as he asked his / friends to do: they were lost / a long time ago" (*SP* 170). The equivocal statement about losing Auden's letters raises the question: Was this an act of personal dereliction—paperwork accidentally going missing—or something different, an outright betrayal—what John O. Brehm and Scott Gates call bureaucratic "shirking and sabotage," that renders Schuyler a disgruntled office worker to Auden's self-conceived "ambassador"?

Schuyler's work displeasure brings to mind the title of Auden's poem "The Treason of Clerks," though Auden's immediate context of poets betraying art by weighing in on politics is altogether absent. Schuyler's campy disregard in "Wystan Auden" for the fate of Auden's letters suggests peevish intentions of reprisal and sabotage, but the counter-monumentalist verve here is also tempered by the elegy's final lines: "So much / to remember, so little to / say: that he liked martinis / and was greedy about the wine? / I always thought he would live / to a great age. He did not. / Wystan, kind man, great poet, / goodbye" (*SP* 170). The end of "Wystan Auden" thus continues in its vacillating monumentalist and counter-monumentalist veins, where direct, plainspoken acknowledgment of Auden's art is also tempered by comments that snipe. Bargaining with his memory in an effort to curtail spite ("So much / to remember, so little to / say), Schuyler finally seeks, as the poem closes, to betray old feelings neither of antipathy nor of fondness, remaining at once loyal and disloyal in his remembrance of Auden.

Questions of fidelity and commitment surface as well in Schuyler's "This Dark Apartment," a poem that possesses a more squarely counter-monumentalist purpose than "Wystan Auden." As the title implies, the narrative of "This Dark Apartment" is an unhappy one and tells of Schuyler's betrayal at the hands of a presumably closeted lover. The premise of monumentalism first appears in the form of the United Nations building, a stately skyscraper whose size is emblematic of the UN's lofty purpose to maintain a just global order through diplomacy and affinity between nations. Schuyler composes "This Dark Apartment" with the UN building situated in the background, a mocking reminder of Schuyler's unsuccessful relationship and its lack of open and sincere communication. Perhaps appropriate to the context of a jilted lover, Schuyler conveys the view of the building from a low, street-level perspective:

Coming from the deli
a block away today I

> saw the UN building
> shine and in all the
> months and years I've
> lived in this apartment
> I took so you and I
> would have a place to
> meet I never noticed
> that it was in my view (*SP* 161)

Schuyler highlights permanence and consistency in his account of the UN building, a structure that functions solidly as a "shin[ing]," immense bureaucratic spectacle, keeping time, consistently ticking off hours—"all the / months and years"—though it oddly has gone unnoticed by him previously.

In its treatment of the disappointments of love, "This Dark Apartment" offers an unexpected, unconscious echo of one of Auden's well-known early poems. Schuyler's first line from "This Dark Apartment" ("Coming from the deli") recalls and reworks—in a prosaic New York vernacular—Auden's first line of "The Letter" ("From the very first coming down") (Auden, *Collected Poems* 29). Auden's prior poem similarly features an unhappy realization about a relationship: like "This Dark Apartment," "The Letter" is about time's advancement, a yearning for constancy, and the discovery of a lover's lack of commitment. Holding out hope for a union with his lover, the speaker in "The Letter" imagines a relationship's would-be machine-like continuity, with "the year's arc a completed round / And love's worn circuit re-begun, / Endless with no dissenting turn" (29). These idealized thoughts of time's persistence and uncompromised love are soon disrupted: Auden's speaker receives a written message that communicates his lover's lack of devotion or even presence: "Your letter comes, speaking as you, / Speaking of much but not to come" (29).

In "This Dark Apartment," Schuyler professes "never [to have] noticed" the UN building's solid and steadfast monumental presence. The comment introduces denial as Schuyler's initial, operative affect, one that prefigures his lack of awareness of his lover's betrayals: "I remember very well / the morning I walked in / and found you in bed / with X" (*SP* 161). Schuyler would subsequently make a wish, at once bitter and naïve, that the relationship was otherwise: "'Can't / you be content with / your wife and me?'" (*SP* 161). His lover—Schuyler comes to understand—is no steadfast monument: "'I'm not built that way,' you said. No surprise"

(*SP* 161). Acknowledging that his own lover is "built" of lesser substance or material, Schuyler here overturns an image from "The Letter," in which Auden likens his uncommunicative and inflexible lover to a solid statue: "The stone smile of this country god / That was never more reticent, / Always afraid to say more than it meant" (*Collected Poems* 29). Broken lines of communication and a lover's reticence, though, are ultimately common to both poems. As Schuyler laments in "This Dark Apartment": "Now without saying / why, you've let me go. / You don't return my / calls, who used to call / me almost every evening" (*SP* 162).

Left with a void and feelings of abandonment, Schuyler must remember his lover in a manner that is opposite the traditional, honorific function of the monument. He must construct, that is, a counter-monument, using the only materials available at his disposal: memories, words, and his own yearning. Absence and the immaterial, indeed, are all that is immediately present for Schuyler: "How I wish you would come / back!" (*SP* 162).[3] The absence of Schuyler's lover prompts the poet to invent a scenario and imagined speech: "I could tell / you how, when I lived / on East 49th, first / with Frank and then with John, / we had a lovely view of / the UN building and the / Beekman Towers" (*SP* 162). Schuyler constructs his counter-monument out of a would-be speech, an invented abstraction that contrasts sharply with the monumental, solid materiality of the UN building and the Beekman Towers. Friendships with Frank and John (references to Frank O'Hara and John Ashbery, presumably) were made of "solid" stuff as well, human counterparts to the two buildings that Schuyler has just named. In the subsequent line, Schuyler rebukes his former lover for being the opposite of reliable and steadfast:

> They were
> not my lovers, though.
> You were. You said so. (*SP* 162)

Assailing his lover's lack of constancy, Schuyler constructs a counter-memorial and counter-monument out of his lover's own words: empty pledges that consequently record loss and absence more acutely. As Young argues, the counter-monument "forces the memorial to disperse—not gather—the memory" and enacts a dissipation, one that "mimics time's own dispersion" (294, 295). Schuyler's clipped, final words of "This Dark Apartment" ("You were. You said so") likewise trail off and disperse, an attenuating echo of an original promise left unfulfilled.

A counter-monument itself, the poem "This Dark Apartment" acerbically memorializes a failed relationship and likewise designates a site ironically diminished by its proximity to the UN building. The United Nations' corresponding diplomatic ideal of promoting "better standards of life in larger freedom" (United Nations Charter) proves unavailable to Schuyler. Many untold factors could have contributed to the split of Schuyler and his married lover, but a certainty is that freedom to love openly was not a legal or historical possibility in New York at midcentury. As Bonny Ibhawoh points out, the Universal Declaration of Human Rights, as adopted by the United Nations in 1948, was not, in fact, universal, for the "story of the human rights movement has been one of progressive inclusion amidst strong exclusionary impulses" (614). The "first resolution recognizing LGBT rights" only came to pass some sixty-three years later in 2011 (Ibhawoh 620). For "This Dark Apartment" and for Schuyler, the UN building would stand as a stark emblem of disaffiliation, indicating that an openly public, loving relationship was not historically viable.

Monuments raise different stakes of affiliation in the poem "Dining Out with Doug and Frank," where Schuyler questions his belonging and that of his friends as gay men and poets withstanding an economic downturn in Manhattan at the tail end of the 1970s. Vanishing historic landmarks furnish the setting and context for the poem and its account of New York's urban spaces, diminished due to financial decline and increased societal violence. Schuyler presents New York City in "Dining Out with Doug and Frank" as antagonistic, where one must persist despite various hostilities, including job instability, income precarity, and criminal violence to survive. Schuyler begins the poem speaking of his reluctance to enter Manhattan's Central Park due to the mugging and subsequent death of his friend, Billy Nichols, "who went / bird-watching there and, for / his binoculars, got his / head beat in. Streaming blood, / he made it to an avenue / where no cab would pick him up" (*SP* 171). Schuyler describes the incident of violence as a mugging ("for / his binoculars"), though it fits a larger pattern of social entropy in the city. Nichols finally arrives "at / Roosevelt Hospital" but is ignored due either to bureaucratic delay or, perhaps, homophobic-fueled neglect: "he waited / several hours before any doctor took him in hand" (*SP* 171). As with "Hymn to Life" and Washington DC, Schuyler in "Dining Out with Doug and Frank" delivers cynical meditations upon a city whose very environs, spaces, and infrastructure, amid a widespread economic downturn, seem inimical to his and his friends' personal security and financial interests.

Against the despairing backdrop of Manhattan, Schuyler tries to muster some contrasting cheer for that evening's plans: the titular dinner with friends and fellow poets, Douglas Crase and Frank Polach. The task is not an easy one. Schuyler relates that Crase cannot come to the dinner as planned. Not unlike Ashbery's technical writer in "The Instruction Manual," Crase must occupy himself with instrumental writing in an office as he attends to his desk job, where he "makes his bread / writing speeches): thirty pages / explaining why Eastman Kodak's / semi-slump (?) is just what / the stockholders ordered" (*SP* 172). Schuyler struggles to remain buoyant during dinner alone with Polach, Crase's partner and lover, at McFeely's bar in the Terminal Hotel. The very name of the Terminal Hotel spurs a series of meditations on endings from Schuyler as he ponders the condition of New York and its monuments, the necessity of clerical jobs to support one's art and poetry, and the will to persevere in a precarious work environment. Even as Schuyler records monumental New York's decimation, however, he reserves within his cartography resilient spaces, where he and his friends try to sustain a vital community that counteracts the degeneration that seems everywhere present.

At first, though, McFeely's bar conjures for Schuyler some of the grandeur of old New York, its monumentality inspiringly intact. An iconic New York architectural space, McFeely's bar has been recently renovated: "someone (McFeely?) has had / the wit to restore it to what / it was: all was there, under / layers of paint and abuse, neglect" (*SP* 173–74). Schuyler couches his next comments about the venue in masculine terms as a means to attest to McFeely's captivating splendor: "The bar is thick and long and / sinuous, virile" (*SP* 174). Schuyler's phallic figuration of the bar as an erection coyly prepares for subsequent references to monumentality within the bar's interior spaces of the past: "I do remember that / above the men's room door the / word Toilet is etched / on a transom. Beautiful lettering, / but nothing to what lurks / within: the three most / splendid urinals I've ever / seen. Like Roman steles" (*SP* 174).[4] The wry simile of a Roman stele makes a monument of men's urinals and confirms Schuyler's preliminary intent to speak to a once-glorious Manhattan with a more robust economic history.

The ghostly past splendor of McFeely's bar that preoccupies Schuyler's memory, though, contrasts starkly with the rest of New York as he begins to ruminate upon the city's downtrodden condition. As mentioned previously, the name of the Terminal Hotel, which houses McFeely's, initiates Schuyler's meditation upon endings and an extended contemplation of loss: "Does the Terminal Hotel / itself still function?" (*SP* 174). Other landmark spaces also prove susceptible to change. The historic Gage and Tollner restaurant in Brooklyn, succumbing to economic need or to consumer demand for renovation, brings in new fixtures: "(Did you know that 'they' sold all the / old mirror glass out of Gage / and Tollner's? Donald Droll has / a fit every time he eats there)" (SP 174). Schuyler codes Droll's distress as camp outburst, a histrionic yet discerning outrage that the beauty of an interior space has been squandered.

The melodramatic reaction to aesthetic loss, however, also anticipates seminal spaces soon to be foreclosed to the gay community. As the poem proceeds, Schuyler's elegy for historic New York encompasses a lament for one of the few municipal spaces that catered to homosexuals: "Pop Tunick's long-gone gay bar," the spot where Schuyler and his lover Bill Aalto had first "picked each other up" (SP 175). Neither Pop Tunick's place nor his relationship to Aalto was able to remain viable, as Schuyler records the end of each. The relationship with Aalto was particularly turbulent and had included threats of violence ("five tumultuous / years found Bill chasing me around / the kitchen table . . . with / a carving knife") (SP 175). Long after their split, Schuyler could not bring himself to visit a cancer-stricken Aalto on his deathbed, solemnly announcing, "I wouldn't go when / he was dying of leukemia" (SP 175). Thoughts of death and diminished prospects for community cast a pallor over Schuyler's experience of the city, and the poem threatens to become bogged down by Schuyler's morbid ruminations.

Schuyler even begins, consequently, to wonder if funereal New York deserves a monumental poem to memorialize it. Other deaths involuntarily surface in Schuyler's consciousness, yet he dismisses the inclination to dwell upon them: "(Shall I tell you about my / friend who effectively threw / himself under a train in / the Times Square station? / No. Too tender to touch. In / fact, at the moment I've blocked / out his name. No I haven't: / Peter Kemeny . . ." (SP 173). A weary Schuyler will subsequently ask, "Why is this poem / so long? And full of death?" (SP 177), as he looks toward the project to chronicle the past with increasing skepticism. The impression of loss becomes ever more expansive: Schuyler next despairs for all of Manhattan, and his lament for New York's obsolete ferry buildings speaks to a pervasive, city-wide atmosphere of deprivation: "And wasn't there [another ferry landing] at 42nd? It couldn't / matter less, they're gone, all / gone . . ." (SP 175).

As evidence of vanishing New York and collapsing of civic spaces mount, Schuyler experiences strong feelings of municipal disaffiliation, which he increasingly expresses in terms of finance and labor. Distressed economic conditions prove unfavorable and inhospitable for poets like Schuyler and friends Crase and Polach who must adjust social outings and creative endeavors around work obligations: Crase had "looked glum, and declined a drink" when acknowledging he had to forgo dinner out (*SP* 172). Questions about commitment and dedication, though, spur an unexpected response for Schuyler, who begins to construct a counter-monument out of his friends' ongoing resilience to employment precarity and their ability to find time to make art outside of work hours. Recognizing a certain fearlessness in his friends' perseverance, Schuyler construes artistic work to be one way of compensating for the disheartening condition of New York and the disarray of its landmarks. Day jobs and office routines may illustrate the degree to which Crase and Polach are beholden to the security and compensation of bureaucratic work, yet Schuyler sees in their ingenuity—in establishing time for their own creative endeavors—a counterpoint to a system that extracts almost all of their attention and energy as office workers.

Dinner conversation with Polach accordingly turns toward an evaluation of poetic labor and its worth, calculated in opposition to bureaucratic timetables and a regimented work week. "Frank," Schuyler explains, "makes his dough as a librarian, / botanical librarian at Rutgers / and as a worker he's a beaver: / up at 5:30, home after 7" (*SP* 172). Such hours leave much to be desired and open up a critique of institutional expectations of, and implicit demands on, workers: "but / over striped bass he said he / had begun to see the unwisdom / of his ways and next week will / revert to the seven-hour day / for which he's paid" (*SP* 172). Polach's refusal to work unpaid hours exhibits what Kathi Weeks has described as an impulse to "contest the necessity of capitalist control" and "to reduce the amount of time spent at work" so that one might "pursue opportunities for pleasure and creativity that are outside the realm of production" (103). Polach's soon-to-be re-worked schedule would allow him "Time / and energy to write. Poetry / takes it out of you, or you / have to have a surge to bring / to it" (*SP* 172). Framing the nature of poetry work in terms of energy, as a loss or gain in vitality, Schuyler illustrates his concern with personal and artistic freedom, both of which are curtailed by the necessity and strictures of office work for his friends Crase and Polach.

Inspired by Polach's interest in reprioritizing creative work, Schuyler reconsiders his depiction of New York. Toward the close of "Dining Out with Doug and Frank," Schuyler vacillates between his attempts to find Manhattan still beautiful and his recognition of just how much of it is in disarray. What wins out is Schuyler's counter-monumental tendencies:

if he had hitherto become preoccupied in the poem with those who have died and the decimation of New York's landmarks, there are other things to recommend living in the city. New York may have succumbed to deterioration, yet Schuyler avers that "Frank and Doug are young and / beautiful and have nothing / to do with that" (SP 177). With this declaration, Schuyler hopes to make of his friends and their work ethic a counter-monument, wherein creativity and poetic labor could stand in opposition to stark economic realities and a corresponding increase in bureaucratization and the demands of work. Of course, creative work and productivity are not remedies for all of the distressed conditions and social ills of Manhattan, yet, for Schuyler, his two friends persist as an enlivening response to what has been dishearteningly chronicled within the poem. Schuyler's pronouncement about Doug's and Frank's vitality effectively ends his record of New York's downfall. Schuyler will consequently curtail his own writing at last, in anti-monumental fashion, concluding that he need not go further: "Why is this poem / so long? 'Enough is as good / as a feast'" (SP 177). The moment and poem will suffice; the brief, counter-memorial to his friends' youthful perseverance offers a momentary reprieve from his troubled account of Manhattan.

Schuyler may champion his friends' literary work, but he is often less generous toward himself when assessing his own merits as a poet. Self-conscious reservations that Schuyler makes about his own writing illustrate that his concerns with monumentality assume other forms, namely, his own literary reputation and enduring achievement. Over the course of his career, Schuyler has preoccupied himself with literary standing, something particularly evident in his late work from 1980, "The Morning of the Poem," a long, spiraling poem that spans forty-eight pages. One perhaps could take the sheer length and mammoth scope of "The Morning of the Poem" to indicate Schuyler's assuredness with monumental poetic works or a confident sense of canonical belonging. "The Morning of the Poem," however, consistently points to a contrasting sense of disaffiliation—Schuyler's abiding belief that he does not quite belong to literature as an institution. Reservations about belonging filter into the poem's form as well: Schuyler's predilection for lists and catalogs here takes the form of a literary balance sheet ("So many lousy poets / So few Good ones"), though he is uncertain as to which side he truly fits (SP 223). In "The Morning of the Poem," a disheveled Schuyler sits "typing in [his] undershorts on this chilly / soggy morning while the rain / Comes and goes," an antithesis to Auden's ideal of a professional poet-clerk. Schuyler has come to suspect that the monumental literary aspirations he once held have been nullified by his waning poetic productivity and ambition (*SP* 199).

Amid free-flowing thoughts about the flora in Western New York, Schuyler's physical health, and, of course, the morning itself, "The Morning of the Poem" offers at least one clear, identifiable narrative strand: Schuyler's long reassessment of both career and life. Reflections about the ambition of his partner and lover, the artist Darragh Park, sixteen years Schuyler's junior, cause Schuyler to review his own early path toward becoming a poet. Schuyler's self-appraisal, though, entails its share of misgivings: his present self lacks the vigor of his youthful being, and current acts of writing leave him feeling tapped out. A notable irony of this very long poem is that Schuyler repeatedly questions his ability to continue to write at all, adding to the troubled sense he has always felt about literary belonging and monumentalism.

In casting a backward glance toward his life and career, Schuyler weighs what has worked out and what has not, and by the end of "The Morning of the Poem," Schuyler will construct an inventory, calculating the circumstances of his existence and taking note of successes and failures. As many have noted, Schuyler raises organizing impulses and cataloging gestures with his poems to a veritable form of art. Ashbery, for instance, has observed Schuyler's propensity "to tabulate," arguing that the impulse to record things constitutes a poetics unto itself: "the list itself, we are given to understand, is a sufficient reason for its own existence" (introduction, *SP* xi). Like Ashbery, William Watkin notes the importance of list-making in Schuyler's poetry, describing its function as a "process of taxonomic autobiography," where "being [is constituted] through the act of naming" (50) and the result is akin to bureaucratic recordkeeping: "an ongoing archive of the thing" (51).

Schuyler's recordkeeping in "The Morning of the Poem" will often resemble actuarial work, a clerical enterprise where he will tabulate and assess his fitness to continue work on poetry toward the end of his career. Personal health, the prospects for longevity, and the ability to endure preoccupy Schuyler's attention. Schuyler, for instance, will undertake an examination of his body as a means of measuring his well-being:

> I know someone who when he wakes up in the
> Morning likes to just lie there and feel himself all over (maybe
>   he's afraid he vanished in the night: I rather
> Wish he would): I like to lie in bed at night and read and feel
>   myself, shoulders, armpits, chest, belly, crotch (*SP* 232)

A nightly review meant to offer reassurance, Schuyler's routine self-examination is an act of both whimsy and discipline, playfully carried out amidst real health concerns, including alcohol abuse and sexual impotence ("mostly it's not / So hard (indeed)"), that he will detail elsewhere in the poem (198). Other sections of "The Morning of the Poem" take a more somber turn, betraying Schuyler's preoccupation with his mortality: "The days go by like leaves / That fall in fall, not yet, soon, so soon, I feel my death in / currents of damp air on the back of my neck, / Filtered through a window screen . . ." (*SP* 217). The accuracy of Schuyler's actuarial analysis is off by several years: death is not "breathing down his neck" but would come much later, in 1991, eleven years after the publication of "The Morning of the Poem." Nevertheless, Schuyler's actuarial calculations about his current existence lead to fatalism and an overriding desire to predict, beforehand, all risks involved with the impending death he has imagined for himself: "Oh goodbye, goodbye. / I want to go away into that blue or dark or / certain or uncertain land: why / Can't we know that it is there . . . ?" (*SP* 191).

One reason that Schuyler becomes preoccupied with death is that age has affected his stamina, particularly as it relates to writing poetry. The prospect of a monumental literary reputation seems out of reach, particularly as Schuyler has lost some of the creative vitality he once had when composing poems: "Writing goes by so fast: / a couple of hours of concentration, then you're / Spent" (*SP* 233). With its connotations of sexual performance, the language here of being "spent" correlates with Schuyler's multiple concerns of longevity, artistic drive, and sexuality. By contrast, Schuyler sees partner Darragh Park's work ethic as unrelenting, possessing an unparalleled, younger intensity. At the start of "The Morning of the Poem," Schuyler associates Park and his artistic drive with Baudelaire's "L'Amour et le Crâne," a poem that has involuntarily intruded upon Schuyler's consciousness. That poem's predominant image of a skull, Schuyler opines, stands "for strength and fierceness, the dedication / of the artist" (*SP* 187). Schuyler resignedly concludes that the divide between himself and Park—with Park in the Chelsea neighborhood of Manhattan for the summer and Schuyler himself in East Aurora, New York—makes patent sense geographically and creatively: "Baudelaire's image" represents "the artist's (your) determination / to be strong / To see things as they are . . . and yet / not too much: in / Western New York, why Baudelaire? In Chelsea, / why not?" (*SP* 187). Elevating Park's resolve to courageous and heroic heights, Schuyler will attribute monumental status to Park yet balk at ascribing similar greatness or prominence to himself.

When it came to writing poetry, Schuyler presumably did not always adopt a self-deprecatory stance, and there are indications, in other sections of "The Morning of the Poem," that he held himself in high esteem especially in his youth. Multiple references in the poem to American writers like Walt Whitman, Marianne Moore, and Wallace Stevens signal Schuyler's feelings of literary kinship and belief in the monumental proportions of his own potential. Schuyler recalls, for instance, the day when, Luther Smeltzer, his high school English teacher

> . . . disclosed William Carlos
> Williams to us, writing a short and seemingly
> Senseless poem on the blackboard—I've searched the collected
> poems and am never sure which it is (Wallace
> Stevens, Marianne Moore, Elizabeth Bishop, I found for
> myself . . . (*SP* 215)

Schuyler's determination to seek out "for [him]self" other modernist poets besides Williams to read and study indicates his desire as a young man to be included among their ranks. The resolve to become a great poet, consequently, sends the teenaged Schuyler on a quasi-epic journey to Upstate New York to find another monumental modernist work, Joyce's *Ulysses*. Schuyler soon ventures "into Buffalo to Otto Ulbrich's book / Shop, where John Myers, to whom the arts stand indebted, then / worked as a clerk: 'You look interesting: / Here's a copy of my new little magazine, *Upstate*'" (*SP* 215–16). The exchange with Myers, who would go from bookshop clerk to partner in the Tibor de Nagy gallery, takes the form of an initiation, with Schuyler newly experiencing a sense of belonging to literary community.

Past aspirations of literary inclusion and youthful certitude, however, are offset by the present time of "The Morning of the Poem." Schuyler's burgeoning sense of his mortality is, in the immediate moment, on his mind. Thoughts of death pervade the poem and are difficult to decouple from his will to write. Having previously associated Baudelaire with Darragh Park's work ethic, Schuyler acknowledges that the comparison is ill-fitting for himself: "Why did Baudelaire wander in? Don't / I love Heine more? Or / Walt Whitman, Walt? No, they come to my death- / bed and one by one take my hand / And say, 'So long, old man'" (*SP* 187). An offhand statement of literary preference thus reveals a predominant genre in which "The Morning of the Poem" operates: self-elegy. As Jahan

Ramazani has written, self-elegy frequently functions as a meditation "on the aging poet in the contexts of his time and place" and can feature a poet "acquiescing to death" with a "gentle self-address" (204). Though ventriloquized through Whitman and Heine, Schuyler's self-address ("So long, old man") is equally gentle and grants him momentary insight into accepting death and the attenuation of his poetic drive. Schuyler's morbid thoughts reveal his concern that he may no longer be confidently at home among monumental literary figures.

The felt lack of belonging also extends in other parts of "The Morning of the Poem" to integral aspects of Schuyler's identity, including, importantly, his sexual orientation and his desire for sex. As Schuyler questions his place within the literary realm, he draws on bureaucratic metaphors to convey his sense of alienation and lack of assuredness. Figures for office work, for instance, infiltrate his dream from the night before, casting "a pall over / This part of the day" and contributing to his sullen, morning mood. The dream begins with "Donald / and Roy exchang[ing] a sharp glance, it meant, / 'Jimmy is going over the hill'" (*SP* 219). Within the dream, Schuyler leaves his friends "in pique," only to encounter a nightmarish bureaucratic spectacle, wherein "businessmen in hats and carrying briefcases were sucking / each other off in cave-like cubicles . . ." (*SP* 219). The overwrought dream imagery is particularly distressing for Schuyler, for it mocks his current medical condition: "did you know a side effect of / Antabuse can be to make / You impotent? Not that I need much help in that / department these days . . ." (*SP* 198). The harrowing dream concludes with an imagined encounter with authorities, which leaves Schuyler with the sense that his entire identity is suspect: "they—the border patrol, the cops, the fuzz—/ Stopped me and asked to see my passport: in my mind I could / see it in a desk drawer in an orange room: / In this land you can't forget your passport" (*SP* 219). Schuyler's dream suggests—and testifies to—the cumulative effects of an entire biopolitics that has, over the course of a lifetime, criminalized his sexuality and intensified feelings of sexual shame.

The events of Schuyler's dream are, of course, fictitious, yet they nevertheless echo a real incident in which his sexuality had been policed and regulated. Earlier in "The Morning of the Poem," Schuyler tells the story of picking up a soldier while on leave in Key West, a sexual liaison that happens to be observed by a policeman:

> I remember walking under the palms on liberty in
>   1943 with a soldier
> I had just picked up and in my sailor suit some-
>   thing stony as the
> Washington Monument I wanted to hide from the
>   officer coming toward me . . . (SP 198)

Even though the encounter happens in Florida, Schuyler's arch reference to the Washington Monument not only alludes to the physical manifestation of his arousal but also underscores the outsized legal, bureaucratic, and regulatory implications of getting caught as a member of the US Navy while engaging in a homosexual sex act. At midcentury, his homosexuality cannot be freely expressed without legal repercussions or administrative penalty. Schuyler subsequently registers a concern that his self-described "monumental" erection would get him disciplined, if the policeman observed it: "I / Guess I was afraid he'd see it, get the picture / of what was about to and in fact / Did happen, and send me back to base" (SP 198). While he may have evaded detection in this particular case, the circumstances echo his eventual court martial and dishonorable discharge from the Navy, when his sexual orientation was discovered during his trial for going AWOL in New York.[5]

The long, retrospective actuarial work of "The Morning of the Poem"—Schuyler's scrupulous task of cataloguing the good and the bad—ultimately points to a final reappraisal of both life and the poem itself. Schuyler's clerical impulse to categorize the circumstances of his life results in a final assessment of his past, a tabulation of gains and losses spread out like a balance sheet:

> Before dawn I woke and made my oatmeal, orange juice and
> Coffee and thought how this poem seems mostly about what I've
>   lost: the one who mattered most, my best friend, Paul
> (Who mattered least), the Island, the California wildflower paper,
>   the this, the that . . . (SP 227)

Defined categories of who "mattered most" and "mattered least" form the basis of Schuyler's clerk-like evaluative efforts, underpinning his aim to record "the this, the that . . ." and make sense of his existence. Tabulating life in this manner offers Schuyler a clearer understanding of his past and grants him an equanimity that has often and previously been elusive.

Schuyler comes to understand, for instance, that the loss of "the one who mattered most" is acceptable. Tolerance for such a loss comes through the composition of "The Morning of the Poem" and the corresponding realizations of the writing process. Schuyler may have dedicated "The Morning of the Poem" to Darragh Park but it is unfinished business with another person, likely the closeted lover from "This Dark Apartment," that must be resolved. Mid-poem, Schuyler admits to feelings of regret, lamenting "that I'll never again / Fall asleep with my head on his chest or shoulder / that kind of bugs me" (*SP* 199). The pangs of romantic longing are irksome and provide a glimpse of Schuyler's propensity to lionize his lovers: "he stood across / The street, in tweed, a snappy dresser, feet / apart, head turned / In an Irish profile, holding an English attaché / case, looking for / A cab to Madison Avenue, late, as usual looking / right out of a bandbox" (*SP* 199). Schuyler's brief portrait of "the one who mattered most" draws upon typical iconography of the mid-century American advertising executive, a statuesque figure on his daily commute to an office within the monumental skyscrapers of Madison Avenue. The dignified, majestic, and, ultimately, inaccessible persona that the man presents offers an index of Schuyler's pain: his lover's propriety is proportionate to his closeted being.

Amid Schuyler's monumental portraiture of "the one who mattered most," though, comes an abrupt, counter-memorializing gesture. Schuyler decides to cut short memories from his account of his lover, all save one: "I won't make a catalogue of all the / times we were together I / Remember: just one more: slim and muscular you / come out of the shower, / Wrap a towel around your waist and lean on the / washbasin with one / Hand . . ." (*SP* 199). Despite being a long poem that foregrounds Schuyler's tendencies to record minutiae, including at one point even a grocery list, "The Morning of the Poem" inheres within itself a final anti-tabulating gesture, wherein he illustrates a paradoxical and atypical restraint. To list all about his one-time lover, Schuyler seemingly concludes, would make of the poem a top-heavy monument. Instead, he opts for balance when ultimately recording the end of the relationship:

> You said, "I'm sorry:
>   everything just got too
> Fucked up. Thank you for the book." That's
>   what I get. Was it worth it?
> On the whole, I think it was. (*SP* 199)

As the relationship is voided, the exchange between the men initially might seem one-sided, with Schuyler's statement of receipt "That's what I get" uttered in a perfunctory tone. Schuyler's morning calculations, however, suggest otherwise and lead to a balance sheet that is offset, considered "worth it," and reasonably accounted for in the end.

The counter-monumental impulse that concludes "The Morning of the Poem" is representative of Schuyler's overall response to those moments in his life when he has felt excluded. Whether his feelings of disaffiliation were initiated in the presence of real monuments, like those of Washington, DC, or quasi-monuments like the UN building, Schuyler has sought to construct his poems to be counter-monuments—memorials of opposition and protest—attesting to discriminatory practices or restrictive cultural norms regarding sexuality. In questioning what literary reputation or standing might mean for himself, Schuyler has also been wary of claiming monumental status for his own work, even if the length of his poems suggests otherwise. Schuyler has even afforded monumental status to individuals, ascribing to lovers inaccessible traits of a statue. Schuyler's poetics of counter-monumentalism fittingly respond to a regimented societal order whose very buildings and monuments encode oppressive strictures. Schuyler's poems thus illustrate well what Henri Lefebvre has said, that monuments unavoidably possess "a phallic aspect, towers exude arrogance, and the bureaucratic and political authoritarianism immanent to a repressive space is everywhere" (49). Schuyler, with his counter-monumental poems, intervenes in such repressive spaces, seeking to nullify them and revise what it means to belong.

Chapter 6

On Being Companionable

Eileen Myles's *Afterglow* and the Administration of Care

> One of the central tasks for people interested in care is to change the overall public value associated with care. When our public values and priorities reflect the role that care actually plays in our lives, our world will be organized quite differently.
>
> —Joan Tronto, "An Ethic of Care"

> The [administrative] grotesque is one of the essential processes of arbitrary sovereignty.
>
> —Michel Foucault, *Abnormal: Lectures at the Collège de France 1974–1975*

Dread of bureaucracy is never more genuine nor fully provoked than when an unexpected letter appears announcing a lawsuit. Such letters of notice not only summon fear of liability and punishment but also outline, in a methodical manner, the procedural steps of seeking justice, including the basis of complaint, establishment of jurisdiction, and legal remedy. *Afterglow (A Dog Memoir)*, by later-generation New York School poet Eileen Myles, begins with such a notice letter, although the more ominous, Kafkan implications of legal and bureaucratic jeopardy are tempered by the fact that the suit appears to be brought by their dog, Rosie. The premise of a lawsuit initiated by one's dog is, on its face, absurd, preposterous beyond measure, but the very fictional and unreal nature of Myles's conceit proves to be their point: Myles would like to dismantle many conventional understandings separating reality from fiction and thereby similarly undermine other concepts like authorship, literary reputation, and the purported sovereignty of humans over other species. In *Afterglow*, Myles will repeatedly draw on various depictions of bureaucracy, its mechanisms, and its agents—in the form of the law, the postal service, politicians, and the government—to undermine authorship as a figure of authority: writing, for Myles, becomes suspect, as careerist an endeavor as any sought by a doggedly ambitious politician or self-interested bureaucrat. It is, however, Myles's portrayal of themself as a pet owner that most fully destabilizes—and refuses—hierarchical power structures associated with bureaucracy and political administration. To advance this critique of administrative power, Myles represents themself as a manager when dealing with Rosie, a key departure from the previous generation of New York School poets who had mainly ascribed to themselves the figurative role of a clerk or office worker in their writing. In so doing, Myles opens a new tack in criticizing bureaucracy and keenly acknowledges their own participation in a hierarchical, administrative apparatus, highlighting the ways in which they had mismanaged Rosie's life and acted as an authoritarian figure and sovereign, precisely as Rosie's lawsuit alleges.

Myles's skeptical self-portrait as an unkind and even oppressive pet owner, as someone who wields administrative authority of their household wantonly, aligns with Michel Foucault's critiques of the abuse of power pervading bureaucratic structures, or what he has called the "administrative grotesque" (*Abnormal* 12). For Foucault, the "administrative grotesque" arises in particular when individuals without merit or distinction undeservedly assume roles of power and leadership: "I am calling 'grotesque' the fact that, by virtue of their status, a discourse or an individual can have effects of power that their intrinsic qualities should disqualify them from having" (*Abnormal* 11). Foucault goes on to explain that "the grotesque is a process inherent to assiduous bureaucracy," due to the intricacy of rules in bureaucratic systems and the unyielding, and often arbitrary, manner in which rules are applied (*Abnormal* 12).[1] In a grotesque, despotic administration or in an arcane and convoluted bureaucracy, the figure in power—whether an autocratic ruler or lowly clerk—wields their influence, Foucault asserts, in a capricious, ludicrous, and cruel manner: "there is in [the administrative grotesque] every degree of what could be called the unworthiness of power, from despicable sovereignty to ridiculous authority" (13). Along the critical lines that Foucault sets out for the administrative grotesque, *Afterglow* records Myles's inquiry into administrative and bureaucratic power, taking up in particular their own hitherto unexamined and unquestioned sovereignty over Rosie.

At the start of *Afterglow*, Myles presents themself as a flawed pet owner, whose callousness, self-interest, and feelings of superiority make them oblivious to Rosie's claims and the legal merit summed up in the letter. Rosie's lawsuit positions Myles as a negligent and unscrupulous owner, which is stipulated in the letter sent by Rosie's lawyer:

> Dear Eileen,
>
> I take the liberty of calling you "Eileen" to begin the unpleasant duty of forcing you to legally take responsibility for the damages you have inflicted over a period of nine years upon the being you have taken to calling "Rosie" . . . Crimes against dogs are ancient and widespread, but dogs having the wherewithal to attain legal representation is new indeed. (2)

Within *Afterglow*'s conceit of a canine lawsuit, what is particularly damning is Myles's portrait of their own behavior, even after receipt of the letter.[2] Myles initially depicts themself as incredulous and dismissive, attitudes that cast doubt on their worthiness to manage the life of their dog or to be in a position of authority when it comes to administering care:

> It seemed unbelievable to me. Rosie was about ten. I looked at her licking an empty wrapper against the fence. She appeared entirely innocent of the letter's content . . . I thought about the letter's content from time to time. I mean for years. I showed it to people. They laughed and smiled. Could Rosie and my entire relationship be framed as blame. I did force her to have sex with Buster that one time. No twice. Could I write about that. (3)

Myles's self-portrait bears out what Foucault details about the administrative grotesque, "in which power [is] derived from someone who was theatrically got up and depicted as a clown or buffoon" (*Abnormal* 13). The blasé remarks made by Myles betray a cruelty made all the more damaging and clownish for its cavalier and haughty indifference. In *Afterglow*, Myles tellingly will not exempt themself from judgments about corrupt or neglectful authority, even if they are not, strictly speaking, a bureaucrat but instead someone in a position to provide or administer care to Rosie. Accordingly, Myles's critique of bureaucracy will take the form of an elaborate caricature of themself and others who—either unwittingly or consciously—abuse power.

Myles's depiction of themself as reckless, as illegitimately wielding authority, subsequently and purposely shifts to their representation of writing and authorship. At the start of *Afterglow*, Rosie the dog makes several claims, coinciding with the lawsuit's accusations of mistreatment and carelessness, that she herself—and not Myles—is responsible for their writing and literary production. In a comical, fantastic, and hallucinogenic scene reminiscent of Burroughs's *Naked Lunch*,[3] Rosie visits a talk show hosted by puppets, where she confesses a host of grievances and ultimately claims responsibility for Myles's writing:

> ROSIE: So yes I taught her to write. I showed her the way. Work changes in 1990 when I came on the scene. Check it out. She admits it but people think she is being poetic, humble, theoretical. (40)

Rosie's disgruntled comments about Myles continue the motif of the administrative grotesque, where she stands accused of clumsily and invalidly appropriating Rosie's work. Rosie's complaint, however self-aggrandizing, paradoxically reveals an unexpected and countervailing premise of *Afterglow*: Myles's sincere and actual belief in collaboration and cooperation with Rosie. As the memoir proceeds and as Rosie's grievances begin to register, Myles starts to acknowledge Rosie's substantial contributions to their literary work. Myles will, in fact, later characterize *Afterglow* itself as ghostwritten, suffused with Rosie's input, presence, and being, after Rosie has passed from a terminal illness. In an echo of Rosie's earlier protest, Myles sorrowfully and elegiacally admits, "I wrote poetry different ever since the advent of you. I got to follow you with my eyes. Take a step behind, next to and in front of you" (55). The narrative structure of *Afterglow* accordingly coheres with Myles's realization: their past behavior of selfishness and disregard—characteristic of the administrative grotesque—is eclipsed by Myles's newfound and keen awareness of companionship with Rosie, as exemplified by their mutual care and the collaborative nature of their writing.

Myles's reappraisal of writing as pluralistic approximates another concept raised by Foucault, that of the "author function" from his landmark "What is an Author?" essay (211). The author function, as Foucault contends, "does not refer purely and simply to a real individual, since it can give rise simultaneously to several selves, to several subjects . . ." (216). Myles guiltily comes, after Rosie's death, to reject the traditional, idealized notions of authorship and literary career that crystallize around a singular individual. Authorship indeed ceases to be a single, unified activity in *Afterglow*, especially as Rosie's and Myles's identities mix in the act of writing "a dog's memoir," much as the lines dividing Gertrude Stein and Alice B. Toklas blur in *The Autobiography of Alice B. Toklas*.[4] That Myles has hitherto been considered the author of their work can be attributed, as Foucault might contend, to the working of the author function: "these aspects of an individual which we designate as making him an author are only a projection, in more or less psychologizing terms, of the operations we force texts to undergo, the connections we make, the traits we establish as pertinent, the continuities we recognize, or the exclusions we practice" (*Abnormal* 213–14).

Authorship in *Afterglow*, though, could also be said to disperse even further, distributed not just among separate, multiple selves but among different discourses as well. If, as Foucault argues, "the author function is . . . characteristic of the mode of existence, circulation, and functioning of certain discourses within society," then one might also apprehend *Afterglow* to be a compendium of competing discourses, ranging from discourses of managerial neglect and disregard—of the administrative grotesque—to those of custodianship and caretaking, or what Joan Tronto has called an "ethic of care" ("Ethic of Care" 211). As Myles succinctly puts it, their relationship with Rosie "is part discomfort and humiliation and part devotion" (4). Rosie's early accusations of mistreatment in the memoir are thus counterbalanced by Myles's belated attentiveness to Rosie, whether in terms of the end-of-life care Myles was able to provide to an incontinent and pain-stricken Rosie or the overdue acknowledgment of Rosie's literary contributions by Myles.

Within *Afterglow*, writing readily dissolves into its constituent and competing discourses, of mistreatment and care, of bereavement and self-reproach, of literary work and its dereliction. Accordingly, *Afterglow* as a work ceases to be a conventional, cohesively unified literary composition. Instead, *Afterglow* represents the *end* of Myles's writing, as both the culmination of a long career of experimental writing, and, in Myles's grief at Rosie's death, a refusal to work as they had done so previously: in an individualistic, singular fashion, without crediting Rosie. Revised as well is Myles's conception of a literary vocation, which Myles admits they had pursued with careerist ambition. By the end of *Afterglow*, Myles entertains a notion of writing that is wholly transformed, as they dispense with the managerial and hierarchical human–dog companionship that had previously typified their relationship with Rosie. Myles will ultimately base their image of writing not on a Romantic belief in an original literary genius but on the model of a bureaucratic cooperative: an idealized collective of mail clerks, including Myles themself, whose diligence and determination as letter carriers—endlessly transmitting words from one place to another—renews the aim of writing and literary work. In this manner, Myles will replace their bad habits that epitomize the administrative grotesque with a more accommodating, benevolent behavior befitting equitable companionship with Rosie.

The last pages of *Afterglow* articulate Myles's visionary conception of writing, in which mail carriers function as mystical figures whose spirited, energetic actions allow for communication among all beings. The image of the otherworldly mail carrier is an elegiac, compensatory one, for Myles would like to believe that they could still be in contact with Rosie after her death, through letters or words, through the very pages of *Afterglow* themselves. The fused figure of the postal clerk/writer is the ideal toward which Myles strives, a monkish being that could bring them closer to Rosie despite her passing: "The postal uniforms could grow softer, longer and looser more like tunics. And the post offices could each be decorated by a tapestry such as this [memoir] by idle postal women and men no longer on a particular route but wandering aimlessly being the . . . letters of our time" (195). Myles proceeds to represent the mail carrier as an apotheosis of attentive care: "The women will be models for all of the other humans. Wild strong mammalian women of the US Postal service carrying nothing but a strong and passionate attitude and a message for everyone . . ." (196). Notably, Myles themself disappears from this image of the postal clerk/writer, emphasizing the collective nature of the work, making it a liberatory vocation generalizable beyond the insular confines of selfhood—beyond the self-centeredness of the administrative grotesque—and focused instead upon communal acts of care.

Myles, however, does not begin the memoir with this idealized, attentive figure of postal workers but, instead, with an image of bureaucratic laxity and disregard as a means of first establishing the administrative grotesque. *Afterglow* indeed starts with an act of carelessness typifying the administrative grotesque, behavior that places Rosie's lawsuit and accusations of disregard against Myles into somewhat sharper relief:

Eileen Myles
308 W. 40th st #2
NY, New York 10078

One day, in 1999, an awkward hand-addressed letter appeared in my hallway. The mailman threw everything on the stairs. (1)

The negligence of the mailman, who undertakes his job responsibilities in heedless fashion, emblematizes Myles's early conception of bureaucracy in *Afterglow* and reinforces their initial depiction of government institutions and their agents as unserious—as clownish or corrupt, or both. The representation of governmental agents as inept or careless provides an index for Myles's own reckless behavior and the remorseful feelings they have regarding the treatment of Rosie. As previously mentioned, Myles will later reclaim the figure of the mailman as an image for themselves and for writers, yet the pattern that develops in the early pages of *Afterglow* is one of administrative and bureaucratic incompetence—shortcomings that the lawsuit adumbrates and that Rosie describes in the interview with the puppets:

ROSIE: . . . and oh yeah and when I was dying, get this, when [Eileen is] wheeling me around town like a man who has money—then she writes on her long legal pad "puppet, puppetry." She gets the idea that I was used. Treated like I was empty. Great. Yeah well how about my whole long life, Eileen. (32)

In Rosie's elaborate telling of their canine-human relationship, Myles is the willful puppet master, an autocratic figure pulling the strings on Rosie's life, selfishly more interested in a novel literary idea than Rosie's pain or the power imbalance that had hitherto characterized their companionship.

Myles's presentation of the administrative grotesque—of themself as a dissembler or as clownishly incompetent—finds a notable parallel in other, recurrent depictions of actual politicians in *Afterglow*. Myles's mordant commentary about Jim McGreevey, former governor of New Jersey, and President George W. Bush, for instance, offers paradigmatic examples of the administrative grotesque and signals Myles's interest in identifying abuses of power, including their own mistreatment of Rosie. Myles likely does not consider themself to be inept or deceitful in the exact manner of McGreevey and Bush, but their portrayal of the two men provides a context for judging Myles's own foibles and shortcomings as a pet "owner": "This morning I was reading in the paper how the governor of New Jersey a secret gay man had hired a poet of all the ludicrous persons on earth to be his director of homeland security. And then the poet realized the governor wanted him. How unabashedly corrupt of a governor to entice a total fool—a poet—practically a clown's occupation to take care of the people of a state" (6). The reference to McGreevey is casual, an offhand remark made as if it were just another, quotidian example of political misconduct, yet the absurd, risible implications of the McGreevey scandal slowly compound. Myles places singular emphasis on the presumed poetic career of Golan Cipel, the man hired by McGreevey, to highlight the illegitimacy of his position within the governor's office.[5]

Myles seems to have taken news accounts of Cipel being a poet at face value, yet their larger point about the work of poetry being "practically a clown's occupation," making one unfit for public service, is a comedic instance of self-deprecation, particularly ironic in light of Myles's own failed presidential bid from 1991 to 1992. Myles, again, does not make themself equivalent to McGreevey in his political missteps, but the scandal serves to underscore Myles's own reevaluation of their treatment of Rosie, especially as they see their caretaking relation to Rosie to be writ through with blame. As Myles proceeds with their assessment of the McGreevey scandal in 2004 as grotesquerie, they frame the matter in terms of increasing imbecility and neglect—a failure of responsibility at the individual and bureaucratic levels. Again, this coheres with Foucault's conception of the administrative grotesque, wherein "an essential feature of big Western bureaucracies has been that the administrative machine, with its unavoidable effects of power, works by using the mediocre, useless, imbecilic, superficial, ridiculous, worn-out, poor, and powerless functionary" (12).

Not only does Myles note the failure of political machinery of McGreevey's cabinet to operate as it should, with properly trained individuals employed in positions suited to their capacities, but they invoke a dog's housebreaking to indicate the scope of misconduct and disgrace: "The fact that the young man was appointed to a position in which he could only reveal his incompetence—who could blame him for that. He was young after all. But the later, more laughable tidbit. Like the room stopped laughing and then the little dog lifts its butt and poops. How could a poet do that. How could a *poet* do that. Twice a fool. And twice the governor's crime" (7). In assessing blame, Myles initially dismisses the young man's responsibility, acknowledging his youth and inexperience. However, it is, as Myles points out, the homosexual extramarital affair, "the later, more laughable tidbit," that is more egregious in society's eyes, which Myles subsequently articulates in an imagined societal and collective homophobic rebuke: "How could a poet do that. How could a *poet* do that. Twice a fool." The repetition reinforces the sense of scolding and heightens the impact of the figurative housebreaking, as the administrative grotesque—its offensiveness—is made scatological: "and then the little dog lifts its butt and poops."

Rather than being tangential, the trope of housebreaking is fundamental to Myles's own sense of personal irresponsibility and administrative shortcomings when it comes to the care of Rosie. Myles's self-conception, as previously mentioned, is that of a flawed pet owner, akin to an incompetent bureaucrat administering to the care of their constituents. The tenor of *Afterglow* suggests that Myles agrees with the claims that Rosie has made in her lawsuit that they had faltered as an owner. Elsewhere, the memoir is, however, devoted to redressing the wrongs Myles has done: hearkening back in particular to the trope of housebreaking, it is in the arena of caregiving that Myles would make amends for what had before made them negligent or inept in their actions toward Rosie. Myles writes: "I took such care of her when she was dying. I relished it. . . . I'd hear the rustling of her limbs and I'd run to her because she couldn't get up and there was generally a puddle already there. In my house, I have beautiful wooden floors. Now I had a pile of facecloths, torn towels, rags. I'd mop up her urine with a clean dry towel and then I'd come back and wash her ass" (12). Myles's image of the "little dog lift[ing] its butt and poop[ing]" in the McGreevey case is here overturned, and the previous figure of a political sex scandal, writ through with shame, deceit, and incompetence, is sublimated into an act of caretaking when transferred to Myles's own deeds.

Myles attends to Rosie with deliberation and proficiency, even beginning, in washing Rosie's "ass," to "relish" what might be considered repulsive or grotesque work. Myles's actions, moreover, comply with Joan Tronto's analysis of care, an ethic of caregiving that Tronto associates with competence: "Although we often do not think of it this way, competence is the moral dimension of caregiving. Incompetent care is not only a technical problem, but a moral one" ("Ethic of Care" 17). In the care that Myles administers at Rosie's end of life, they assiduously deploy skill and consideration that makes their actions transcend the merely technical and begin to take on a moral dimension, which is what they find wanting in McGreevey's clumsy and ineffectual decision to appoint Cipel to his cabinet. Whether it is seeing to the welfare of an entire state or to the functions of a dog with a fatal illness, administering to the needs of others involves an intricate process of evaluation and assessment, which Tronto scrupulously outlines: "the ethic of care, then, both elevates care to a central value in human life and recognizes that care requires a complicated process of judgment. People need to make moral judgments, political judgements, technical judgments, and psychological judgments in their everyday caring activities" ("Ethic of Care" 17). *Afterglow* records Myles's effort to think through their own actions—of both personal and political import—regarding Rosie and to come to terms with whether they have acted competently or incompetently when caring for Rosie.[6]

Afterglow continues to detail another, corresponding set of bureaucratic blunders and political misdeeds by citing the political career of George W. Bush and the incompetence that marked his tenure as governor of Texas and president of the United States. Here, too, the elements of bureaucratic mismanagement and the responsibility for and abuse of others' well-being raise the prospect of care and its political nature. Myles first refers to Hurricane Katrina in 2005 and its aftermath, which occurred almost a year after the McGreevey scandal. The mishandling of the federal response to Katrina by Michael Brown, the FEMA director appointed by Bush, provides Myles with another example of ineptitude and the administrative grotesque: "now that we've seen really good photos of how really bad it was in New Orleans and we've seen also that the man in charge there, Brownie, knew about horses, not safety, there were problems really much bigger than his unknowing, the unknowing is always getting larger . . . and [we] realize that there are always people of greater authority [that are] equally incompetent people like the president . . ." (7). Juxtaposed alongside each other, the McGreevey scandal and the errors made in response to a category 5 hurricane by Brown, FEMA, and the Bush administration illustrate failures to attend to public welfare in an appropriately attentive, competent, or responsive manner. Pursuing self-interest and rewarding political allies with political office in these examples instead are paramount, showing once more how bureaucratic entities and government institutions are mired in corruption and even indifference to public safety and welfare.

As Michael Herzfeld contends, such unconcern is inherent to bureaucracies, where indifference frequently surfaces and "a rejection of those who are different [is] made tolerable to insiders because it is presented in terms that are once familiar and familial" (33). Such lack of concern, Herzfeld further explains, is "arbitrarily selective," and "provides a moral alibi for inaction" (33). Bush's insider nickname of "Brownie" for the FEMA director illustrates the type of "familiar and familial" privileging of which Herzfeld speaks. The response to Katrina was indeed also selective, with a disproportionate amount of harm affecting the African American community: the racial makeup of the hardest-hit communities is oft cited for FEMA's slow response, where four out of seven zip codes that "suffered the costliest damage from Katrina" had populations "that were at least 75% Black" (Frank).

Beyond Bush's selection of Michael Brown for a position for which he was not qualified, Bush's own overblown qualifications and career history are equally scrutinized by Myles for evidence of the lack of merit typical of the administrative grotesque. Myles notes in particular that the gains from Bush's highly touted educational policies as governor of Texas proved misrepresentative of reality: "And supposedly when he was governor, he actually improved schools that was his big claim but now we've learned that in fact the books were cooked, that's all. And the schools even got worse under him . . ." (7). Compounding the problems stemming from Bush's failed educational reform was the rampant and corrupt misreporting of students' standardized test scores and the persistent spread of bureaucratic mismanagement by school districts.

As Myles acerbically points out, the propped-up, fraudulent test scores showing achievement only serve to illustrate his own lack of administrative accomplishment. Myles consequently returns to the scatological to mock Bush's unfounded achievement, his intelligence, and lack of decorum, commenting that, amid his other acts of political mismanagement, he is prone to "fart[ing] in front of interns today" (7). The presidential office is, Myles explains, staffed with highly educated interns, "kids who went to good schools and studied hard" but "[wind up] delivering papers to the oval office and there's the president laughing and farting. And you tried [in school] & he hadn't and now he's your boss and you've got to smell his farts. And you're a dog" (8). Myles's strategy here aligns with what Mikhail Bakhtin describes as the "defecation series" in the novels of Rabelais, where a focus on the body and its excretive functions encourages "laughter [that] not only destroys traditional connections [but] abolishes idealized strata" (170). Myles's aim is not just to portray Bush as uncouth but to reveal his political fraudulence, to show his true disregard for administering to the education of the American populace. Bush's behavior and policies sully the Oval Office, and the "idealized strata" of the presidency and its administration are upended, turning staffers into "dog[s]."

While Myles's takedown of American politicians for their duplicity is incisive in its exposure of the administrative grotesque, the political critique in *Afterglow* pointedly allows them to pivot to self-scrutiny, as they reframe their questioning of competence to an investigation of themselves, their work, and their writing. Bureaucratic metaphors, with an emphasis on mismanagement, incompetence, and disregard, deliver Myles a means to evaluate their actions as a pet owner and ultimately lead to a disavowal of their writing as overly self-important. The nexus between bureaucracy and Myles's guardianship for Rosie begins in a chapter entitled "The Rape of Rosie," where Myles chronicles their dubious efforts to breed Rosie. In the chapter, Myles expresses their sincere desire for Rosie to have puppies, to create offspring that would be an extension of Rosie's life, yet the efforts to "stud her" surprise Myles as especially perfunctory and routine, a procedural feat conducted with stark managerial oversight (60). Myles remarks upon the transactional nature of the act: "it was sex that was impossible to ignore, yet bureaucratic somehow" (64).

Such a description belies misgivings on Myles's part about their administration of care for Rosie and harkens back to *Afterglow*'s beginning, to the claims made in Rosie's letter of "**abuses and crimes against dog kind**" (3). Upon receipt of Rosie's "letter," Myles had acknowledged that they "did force [Rosie] to have sex with Buster that one time. No twice" (3). The businesslike, bureaucratic nature of the breeding and Myles's self-recrimination in doing so situates them within the administrative grotesque, particularly as they frame Rosie's procreation in self-centered terms, revealing a disregard of Rosie's interests and care. The act of securing Rosie for breeding with the other dog, moreover, included regrettable tactics of authority and domination: "We wrapped an extra leash around Rosie's jaw. I felt like she liked being robbed of her choice. . . . I felt like I was hurting Rosie" (63).

Throughout the majority of *Afterglow*, Myles demonstrates irrefutable love for Rosie, yet the act of breeding her is presented in an especially fraught and troubling manner. The power differential between the two dogs involved and their respective owners leads to ambivalent feelings in Myles, writ through with self-reproach: "She was being fucked right in front of me. I felt shame. Regret. Fear. Excitement" (63). The voyeurism surrounding the act and the descriptions of force in restraining Rosie summon images of torture, a facet of the scene reinforced a mere ten pages later, when Myles constructs an absurd, fabulous passage wherein Rosie bears a watchdog's skeptical witness to the horrors of Abu Ghraib: "Rosie had been to Abu Ghraib and ever so gently nudged the soldier who took the pictures—first to take them because he knew in his gut the way they were partying with the prisoners *was* wrong and later (nudge nudge) to send them home . . ." (73).

The juxtaposition of Abu Ghraib and Rosie's breeding so close in the memoir functions as an indirect indictment of Myles, especially as an owner's directed procreation of their dog is seen as commonplace and conventional. The same sense of normalcy, Myles suggests, surrounded the policies and actions of President Bush with regard to enhanced interrogation, black sites, and Abu Ghraib after 9/11, not to mention his general, everyday demeanor: "Even though the President allowed and was around so much that we know to be evil, he did seem to be a very ordinary very essential guy, an American man. Remember the joke about what he was giving his wife for her birthday and he winked lewdly at the press corps" (73). Myles's implicit comparison of themself with Bush aligns each with the administrative grotesque, where the actions of a politician or an everyday individual illuminate how power is wielded differentially and often corruptly, as Foucault has argued: "Political power, at least in some societies, and anyway in our society, can . . . [find] their source, in a place that is manifestly, explicitly, and readily discredited as odious, despicable, or ridiculous" (*Abnormal* 12).

As an ordinary citizen, Myles does not, of course, have the same power as the president of the United States at their disposal, yet Myles would have us acutely recognize the correspondence between themself and the president, as their repeated and cumulative references to bureaucracy and administration suggest. The similarity draws on, again, matters of power as well as bureaucratic oversight and responsibility: having had the casual intention to breed Rosie for a number of years, Myles proceeds in the endeavor much as a disinterested clerk might. Approached by men who asked Myles if they "wanted to stud her," Myles would collect "numbers and put them in my phone book. Tom 549 1694. Sometimes I would write dog next to the name. There's also a few phone numbers in the file where I keep Rosie's health stuff" (60).

While Myles had planned for months to stud Rosie, administering to Rosie's reproductive health was a bureaucratic task that almost did not happen. With files incomplete and phone numbers out of date, Myles's clerical inconsistencies and misfiling nearly derail an opportunity for Rosie's breeding: "Now suddenly she was in heat. I had all the wrong phone numbers and a vacant summer. I kept it free so I could do campaigning, but no one invited me to come anywhere till September, and Rosie's two, so this is the time" (61). Myles's quick, oblique reference to "campaigning" is nonchalant, yet it assures the association between Myles and politicians of a presidential stature, especially as a brief footnote at the bottom of the page reads: "Eileen Myles's presidential campaign, 1991–92, which will be barely mentioned here" (61). The act of breeding Rosie, and their relative lack of competence doing so, consequently begins to take on a political hue, due to their previous critique of Bush and McGreevey. Questioning if the plan to breed Rosie was somehow extralegal, a concerned Myles weighs their competence and conduct, wondering, "if I was doing something illegal. Letting dogs have sex in my building. What was normal in this situation?" (62). Revealing ignorance of the law, Myles self-consciously portrays themself as blundering, if not outright negligent: a would-be clerk or care-worker fumbling the treatment of a being in their charge because their position of power allows them to do so with impunity.

Myles's unaware, self-interested handling of Rosie's breeding not only exemplifies an instance of the administrative grotesque but becomes pivotal to understanding the intersection between bureaucracy and writing that suffuses *Afterglow*. As *Afterglow* proceeds, Rosie's ability to give birth, to reproduce—an act that Rosie calls "copying"—instigates a series of metaphors about writing *as* copying, as re-presentation and duplication, where Myles at once stands accused of and later acknowledges recording Rosie's thoughts as their own literary work.

The initial reference to copying surfaces as Rosie—at the puppet talk show—explains to host Oscar that she has been spayed and no longer has the capacity to produce offspring:

ROSIE: You didn't know that. Spaying?

OSCAR: They take your copy thing away. That's it. Isn't it, Rosie. Still, do you want more dogs. Isn't that the argument. Alleviating dogs' suffering? (33)

Taking away Rosie's "copy thing," her sterilization, speaks to a human discourse of reproductive "care," a stance, from Rosie's view, that smacks of paternalism, eugenics, and the administrative control of canine bodies. Rosie would like to refute this discursive position as self-serving to humans and detrimental to the interests of dogkind and its propagation: "Yes, we want more dogs. . . . We want to outnumber humans. Not in a warlike fashion but gentle, you know" (33). Rosie's thoughts here indicate a politics more conscious of a canine perspective and less focused on humans, a position that Myles themself increasingly gravitates toward as *Afterglow* progresses. As Rosie speaks her mind about canine rights and agency, she offers an alternative to an anthropocentric worldview and ideology under which Myles and other humans have so often operated. Each of Rosie's protests has the cumulative effect of altering Myles's consciousness, raising their awareness of dogs and pushing them to treat Rosie in a less hierarchical fashion.

In the subsequent passages of *Afterglow*, the figure of copying reflects this conceptual shift from the domineering to something more equitable. "Copying" changes its initial reference from dog breeding to indicate the act of writing and literary composition, as Myles comes to insist that a writer like themself merely copies the worldview of dogs. Now more apt to acknowledge Rosie's perspective, Myles asserts that "the writer succumbs[,] the dog gives pictures to the writer which the writer transcribes" (191). Copying, properly reconceived by Myles, becomes an act of literary and existential collaboration, one informed by care: "Everybody's life is just this kind of picture. People get dogs to help them construct it . . . So this is the template of our relationship, exposed, right here" (160). With Rosie's aid, Myles is able to see the world and write it differently. A conventional understanding of pet "ownership" and reliance is, moreover, overturned, where matters of caretaking and responsibility are now revised—comprehended not as unidirectional but as mutual and interdependent.

Figurative descriptions of copying also lead Myles to replace the ego-laden, exhausted conceptions of singular authorial originality that had previously dominated their consciousness. To this end, Rosie considers their aesthetic practice to be interactive and collaborative yet also, necessarily, transcriptive: "It's totally what the little monks did when they were copying the bible" (162). At one point in *Afterglow*, Myles actually attempts an inspired imitation and mimicry of Rosie's perspective by writing in a fluid, stream-of-consciousness style: "Now a baby squeals, dogs barking and across the street on a low wall of brick lions. We look across the street and back. Bark bark bark. Thank god there you go with your sandy back. Oh and now an empty bag of Lay's. I'm trying to *duplicate* what the dog sees like ecstasy but it's not" (106; emphasis added). In this newer sense, copying—duplication—is paramount to establishing the lived experience of a dog, though Myles acknowledges the writing falls just short of fully matching canine experience. Myles here attends to what might be labeled a *transcriptive* poetics, a subset of the bureaucratic sublime, where copying reaches a heady, near-perfect imitation. In the moment, Myles perceives more clearly Rosie's eminence and grace—with Rosie leading them on a neighborhood walk as a perfectly competent, and *not* administratively grotesque, politician might: "[image] of me walking and you. Little mayor with your neck and head covered in light and we turn onto a street that is dirt" (107). The end result is that of collaboration, with Myles more comfortable acquiescing to Rosie's vision of the world.

Ceding the way to Rosie, Myles begins to revise and amend their understanding of both authority and care. The act of yielding is important for it reverses the hierarchy that usually obtains between canines and humans and recognizes an altogether different sense of priority. Myles identifies in Rosie a competence that will guide them: "that's what this book means. We are talking to our 'masters.' Very gently and subtly. Dogs are true leaders and strong teachers as the life of Eileen Myles *after* my own life will show" (33). Myles's deference to Rosie is appealing in its reordering of human and animal power dynamics and its registering of another level of care, wherein Rosie redirects Myles's purpose and existence. The title *Afterglow* itself speaks elegiacally to this restructuring of existence: Rosie's own life and passing has illuminated and animated Myles's existence, inspiring and reviving their life post-Rosie. Within *Afterglow*'s narrative and its acknowledgment of canine mistreatment and power discrepancies, Myles surprisingly proves to be susceptible and open to Rosie's own administration of care, after the fact: "You were always my boat. You brought me space and peace. I put you in the middle of my life and you never steered me wrong" (55). The discourse of the administrative grotesque that had predominated and defined early parts of *Afterglow* no longer obtains; instead, matters of care become paramount, introducing attentiveness and consideration as novel imperatives.

Myles's response to, and acknowledgment of, Rosie's nurturing acts indeed functions as an important dimension of the ethic of care, which, as Tronto argues, is composed of principles of "Attentiveness," "Responsibility," "Competence," and "Responsiveness" ("Ethic of Care" 18). Of particular relevance for Myles's newfound appreciation of Rosie is the matter of "care receiving," which involves "a complex moral element of responsiveness" ("Ethic of Care" 17). As Tronto explains, responsiveness is "complex because it shares the moral burden among the person, thing, or group that has received the care, but it also involves the moral attention of the ones who are doing the caring work . . ." ("Ethic of Care" 17). Myles's recognition of Rosie's caregiving serves as an acknowledgment of Rosie's purpose and competence and underscores the reciprocal nature of their relationship with each other. The practice of care is, for Tronto, a "species activity," a term meant to illustrate the idea that "*how* people care for one another is one of the features that make people human" ("Ethic of Care" 16; emphasis added). Care as a fundamental species activity, though, is not limited to humans but importantly extends to dogs, as Myles would seem inclined to add. The care that ultimately obtains between Myles and Rosie exemplifies canine–human companionship, entailing what Donna Haraway has described as "a story of co-habitation, co-evolution, and embodied cross-species sociality" (4).

Due to Rosie's care, Myles credits Rosie with altering their work patterns and writing habits, as Myles is able to mock both the hackneyed image and actual tendencies of writers to isolate themselves: "The dog has been serving the writer for years, opening up her life and getting her out into the air and onto the beaches and even bringing attractive people into the unattractive life of the writer who often never goes out" (191). Though the humor here primarily turns upon self-deprecation and presumptions of anti-social, misanthropic writerly behavior, Rosie's assistance in getting Myles out into the public ushers in a critique of authorship upon which so much of *Afterglow* turns. Such an interactive process bears out what Haraway describes as fundamental in the human and canine relationship, "Domestication [of a dog] is an emergent process of co-habiting, involving agencies of many sorts. . . . Relationship is multiform, at stake, unfinished, consequential" (30). The companionship between Rosie and Myles produces a new sensibility of writing for Myles, where Rosie's influence, stemming from acts of care, is ongoing, generative, and abundant.

Myles is especially able to concede that Rosie is a driving force behind their writing in part because they jettison their previously held, ego-laden conceptions of their career, a move that enacts a refusal of work—and of writing—to which Myles had formerly subscribed. Myles lambastes their earlier, self-centered idea of a brilliant, accomplished author, related in *Afterglow* in Rosie's voice and customary acerbic manner:

"I listen to her whining and huffing. What's wrong with my life. Why can't anyone see I'm a genius. On and on" (39). The problem, as Rosie sees it, is that Myles has considered writing in terms of their career and literary reputation. From Rosie's canine perspective, a career—literary or otherwise—is an utterly foreign concept, something to which she attests at the puppet talk show, where even the very word "career" causes confusion and bewilderment to the non-human audience:

PUPPETS: What's that?

ROSIE: They put their hands inside of you, don't they? Same idea. Using <u>whatever</u> they've chosen—law, sex, poetry, whatever they choose . . . they try to do that to the world. Animate it. Put their hands inside the thing and shake it at the world and wanting everyone to go whoa. That's pretty much how I understand a human career. (39–40)[7]

Myles's critique of literary careerism as mere vanity allows them to dispense with their identity as an author and to credit Rosie as a writer. The idea of a career proves to be more restrictive than enabling, particularly as Myles has felt beholden to a certain idealized image of writers promulgated by literary disciplines, approximating the restrictiveness that Kathi Weeks argues has long been part of professional and career discourse: "Professional socialization has always served as a disciplinary mechanism, one that can induce the effort and commitment, entitlement and identification, and—perhaps above all—the self-monitoring considered necessary to a profession's reproduction as such" (72). By repudiating careerism, Myles effects a personal work stoppage, as they no longer abide by work as they had previously conceived of it. Their refusal of work is a disavowal of the discourse surrounding authorship and a literary career, and if the concept of a career no longer obtains, then Rosie's own role as a writer becomes ascendant.

Merely replacing Myles's authorship with one solely ascribed to copying or duplicating Rosie as a singular genius would do nothing, ultimately, to unsettle traditional notions of literary composition. In the latter half of *Afterglow*, Myles consequently recasts their relationship with Rosie as one of collaboration, with the production of the memoir now framed as a cooperative act of ghostwriting. Rosie's previous claims of sole authorship of Myles's writing itself seemed to epitomize the blustering, self-celebrating declarations of literary ego. Rosie's assertions, however, were an indispensable step for Myles to recognize the limits of their own authorship—a necessary jolt or correction (as in dog training) that allowed them to see Rosie's literary contributions as actual. Accordingly, Myles turns to ghostwriting as an operative model for composition, framed—not surprisingly—as a creative suggestion by Rosie: "I have one more thought which is dog ghostwriting. Think of it. Funny to ghostwrite for a dog. . . . You liked being my ghostwriter. And you were always that" (158–59). Though the motif of ghostwriting arises here as a humorous suggestion, something easily dismissed, the notion of being Rosie's ghostwriter allows Myles to abandon a conception of authorship that they no longer could abide.

Instead, what is more palatable for Myles is an image of authorship based on partnership and collaboration. Oscar, Rosie's interlocutor at the puppet talk show, puts the question of sole authorship to Rosie, in skeptical fashion:

> OSCAR: Well here's your book. *Afterglow*. It's right on my knee. And what I'm hearing from you is that it's not so clear how much of the work is yours. (OSCAR turns toward the camera waving the book.) *Authorship*! Who's writing who. (34)

The exchange ("it's not so clear how much of the work is yours") is meant to illustrate the initial unraveling of Rosie's claim to authorship, with Rosie subsequently confessing to writing the lawyer's letter at the start of the memoir. The questioning of exactly who wrote what, however, tellingly and indirectly reinforces Myles's own beliefs about ghostwriting for—and collaboration with—Rosie. Myles understands and undertakes the writing of *Afterglow* in the spirit of cooperation, approximating what Michael Hardt and Antonio Negri have described as the interactive and relational character of subjectivity, where subjectivity ought to be defined "not by having, but being or, better, *being-with*, acting-with, creating-with. Subjectivity itself arises from social cooperation" (105). Myles similarly recognizes that the concept of individual authorship no longer obtains due to their relationship with Rosie; their writing is now more properly understood as cooperative and collaborative.

The subject of ghostwriting brings up a corresponding conception of writing for Myles, wherein the collaboration takes the form of a haunting—as discrete beings are united together and exist in mutual interdependence. In ghostwriting, the writer inhabits another being, taking them on as their subject and thinking through another being's perspective. For Myles, that other being is predominantly Rosie, who sympathetically alerts Myles to the idea that they have become ghostlike in trying to channel another being: "No dog writes a book, no dog wants a book written no dog reads a book and the only part [about 'Dog ghostwriting'] that might be interesting is the idea that all writers are ghosts" (159). Amidst the serial negations about what a dog does or does not want, Rosie comes to a singular proposition about writing, "that all writers are ghosts." The assertion is another of Myles's skeptical critiques of work and writing, and—cumulatively—the work of writing. Rosie confronts Myles with a scolding yet caring accusation that the work of authorship has lessened them, rendering them ghostly: "Look at you! The writer spends her life reducing her own existence to that of a ghost. All the vitality floods onto the page while her own existence grows wanner and thinner" (159). In such a state, Myles is living, from Rosie's point of view, anything but the animated fullness of a dog's life. This is what necessitates Myles's turn to collaboration, to intermingling their life with Rosie's and Rosie's story with theirs. *Afterglow* is made substantial with Rosie's input and care; it is the spirit of cooperation that makes ghostwriting a dog's memoir tenable for Myles.

Rosie's recognition that Myles had turned ghostlike ironically reinforces the degree to which *Afterglow* is a work of elegy. Though Rosie is keen to point out that Myles had taken on a haunted, ashen quality before their collaboration, Rosie invokes the idea of ghostwriting once more to acknowledge her own death and, going one step further, to intimate Myles's own mortality:

> Is this ghostwriting.
> Yeah it actually is . . . cause dog is travelling through you. I'm dead but you're *going* to be dead. (169)

Rosie's stern warning from the grave enacts within *Afterglow* a *memento mori*, the dog's memoir now vacillating between elegy and self-elegy. As an elegy, *Afterglow* records the loss of Rosie, with Rosie herself voicing her absence hauntingly: "I've been gone from your life for seven years" (157). Functioning additionally as a self-elegy, *Afterglow* allows Myles to acknowledge the deprivation of her life when she wrote as a "careerist" author, the time period predating their collaborations with Rosie.

Rosie's reminder that Myles, too, will die one day continues the work of self-mourning and initiates an admonishment for them to live more fully.

Afterglow might have concluded with this lugubrious tenor and its focus on death, yet Myles takes up Rosie's memory and the matter of work to reinvigorate their writing. In the final pages of the memoir, Myles seizes upon an image that signifies persistence—that of postal workers—to carry out the job of remembering Rosie properly. Reimagining the purpose of writing, Myles deploys the mail carrier as a figure for writers, as each works with letters, circulating acts of communication and the delivery of words. However, Myles crucially complicates the figure of the letter carrier as writer, highlighting the diligence of postal workers while also referencing—and challenging—stereotypes of postal clerks as apathetic and lethargic bureaucrats. In so doing, Myles distances the persistence of letter carriers from the administrative grotesque, aligning postal work instead with careful attentiveness and deliberateness. The figure of the mail carrier, for Myles, is thus transformed into a being who operates according to their own schedule yet competently facilitates communication between individuals. Imagining writing as work aligned with mail carriers thus also allows Myles to modify previous descriptions of their relationship with Rosie from one of separation, hierarchy, and negligence to one of care—based, that is, on intimacy, parity, and connection.

Myles begins the association between writers and post office clerks first by acknowledging that being a mail carrier has been a familial occupation, a truth that Rosie is keen to point out: "You have mailmen in your family and they were dogs and all mailmen were dogs . . ." (193). As Rosie proposes, this family history forges a connection not only between Myles and their family but between Myles and Rosie herself: "And I am a mailman. Your father was a mailman. Your grandmother's brother Tim O'Riordan from Knocknagoun, Rylane, Cork: mailman. . . . It is a shame, Eileen, that you are not a mailman. The dog smiles. Perhaps you are" (189). In Rosie's association between writing and being a letter carrier, she identifies a key determinant of Myles's being. From Rosie's viewpoint, Myles's fate as a letter carrier/writer is inevitable, a testament to both a familial and personal purpose: "It will always be delivered. The mail will find you. Whose house are you in now, Eileen. No Matter" (193).

That letter writing could stand in for literary composition is something that Myles borrows as well from Frank O'Hara, whose parodic and mocking manifesto "Personism" makes a nevertheless sincere claim of equivalence between a poem and a telephone call. Rosie points out to

Myles that this was "Your favorite moment in literature," when "Frank O'Hara paused . . . and thought *I could just make a phone call*. It was a dog thought" (187). Rosie's canine approval of O'Hara's insight reveals Myles's own desire to liberate literature, to end its confinement in what Laura Riding called "book-death," the inert state of merely existing on a sheet of paper (85). As O'Hara puts it in "Personism," this meant that "the poem is at last between two persons instead of two pages" (499). For Myles, though, the direct address and immediacy of communication that O'Hara values comes in the form not of telephone calls but of a postal letter. Reconceiving the work of a writer in terms of a letter carrier, Myles, like O'Hara, construes writing to be an interactive dynamic, one that is transcendent in its mode of address: "The letter does not stop. You write a letter and it goes somewhere and someone reads it and the letter goes back and forth multitudinously. A letter will never die" (195). In the case of *Afterglow*, the communicative address exists predominantly between Myles and Rosie, where Myles even considers *Afterglow* itself to be a letter, written to Rosie after her death so as to keep the lines of communication open, as Myles relates: "In fact I'm writing this book to *keep* talking to her" (17). As such, *Afterglow*'s very importance is less material than relational and conceptual: "A letter is like a dream of thought. . . . We mourn the loss of the letter but dogs mourn the thought" (195).

In "Personism," O'Hara jokingly relates that the approach to writing he has just outlined has the potential to transform literature radically, even potentially ending in its destruction. Composing poetry with the immediacy of a telephone call, O'Hara contends, could eradicate or nullify writing, a consequence that he glibly considers to be the logical end of Personism: "In all modesty, I confess it may be the death of literature as we know it" (499). Though his bravado is steeped in irony, O'Hara maintains that poetry ought to be stripped of the extraneous, ultimately becoming an immediate and direct form of address. O'Hara thus relates, "Personism has nothing to do with philosophy, it's all art. It does not have to do with personality or intimacy, far from it! But to give you a vague idea, one of its minimal aspects is to address itself to one person" (499). For O'Hara, Personism frees writing from the superfluous to become an unhindered mode of communication, established person to person.

A similar distillation obtains in Myles's conception of writing wherein composition has been emptied out and evacuated, existing foremost as direct address concerned with their well-being. Rosie assures Myles that they no longer need to be hampered by the careerist limitations that they may have subscribed to before: "you are a free soul now and this is why you are doing this great work for us, for me, Eileen. And all dogs. I want to return to the mailman and the letter. What is a letter, Eileen" (192). Rosie prompts Myles to consider that letter writing—literary work—is, ultimately, immaterial, a function of a direct exchange between individuals.[8] Rosie's rhetorical question ("What is a letter, Eileen") understands the letter to be less important than the act of communication, an address to another being. The attenuation and emptying out of letters consequently transform the work of the letter carrier—the postal worker as writer—into a matter of care and duty, attending to acts of communication, as Rosie didactically explains to Myles: "You have such figures all over your family tree. Dogs and letter carriers. Do you know why? I will tell you. To carry the sky. Here we go" (188). To "carry the sky" is to be responsible to another—to bear and to carry out communication between individuals, as Myles describes with visionary diction: "The sky is full of pictures tonight . . . . It is open tonight and tonight . . . all the messages that were ever sent, will ever be sent are written in the sky" (190).

At the end of *Afterglow*, Myles sees a renewed purpose of writing; theirs is a vocation to be undertaken with gravity and deliberateness. Here, Myles will overturn and revise certain features of bureaucratic work, distancing their version and conception of the postal worker from the administrative grotesque. Positing slowness and lassitude as positives, as integral to literary composition and care, Myles will think of their work as a writer as being akin to that of a postal clerk, particularly as the mail carrier's deliberateness refutes careerist demands for speed, ambition, and rote efficiency—characteristics of productivity and professionalism that Rosie abhorred. Against imperatives of speed and career advancement, Rosie will urge Myles to think of *Afterglow* as a book about slowing down, about the restructuring or reorganizing of time: "I'm telling you this because in our time you must make a holy book. A book full of holes about time . . ." (189). Accordingly, Myles postulates for themself a new mode of being and writing, envisioned as a utopian future to come: "time in the hands of the postal worker will become slowly unlabeled. Fed Ex and UPS will continue rushing around but increasingly they will not be carrying anything except speed itself . . . and everyone [else] will be beginning to live slowly in the right time with themselves" (196).

The imperative "to live slowly in the right time with themselves" makes a virtue of clerical traits of persistence and doggedness, especially as these might ensure purposeful communication between individuals.

Espousing the desire to slow down, Myles arrives at a clearer sense of communication with—and understanding of—Rosie. Myles, accordingly, imagines that their grief and pain at Rosie's loss might abate, if the perseverance of the mail carrier can be imitated: "There is no burden anymore. Neither snow nor sleet nor rain shall be considered anything but colors and not problems at all" (196). Myles's release at the end of the memoir stems, finally, from the feeling of being in continuous, posthumous communication with Rosie, an ethereal act Myles associates with the night sky and the messages it contains: "There is only comfort now in working closely with me and all the dogs tracing a path like Johnny Appleseed of blue fruits and sonorities across the sky" (193).

That the postal worker might be selected as a model for such an unearthly job is no mistake. Myles explains that the mail clerk's affinity for the sky derives from the cloth from which their uniforms are cut: "There's a particular blue, a kind of vibrating denim that was adopted by the US postal service in the early twentieth century and it is technically described as 'blue mixed cadet cloth.' The postal uniform is one of my favorite colors . . . illuminated exactly as much and precisely as little as a night sky in winter" (188). In mourning Rosie, Myles finds letter carrying to be an apt figure for the elegiac work of writing, and Myles's recuperation of Rosie—the maintenance of her memory—is made possible only by being in communication with her, conduct made feasible by the vocation of a writer as letter carrier and message purveyor: "The post office needs to walk in the blue uniform of time, the mixed cadet, and be seen knowing your messages are being sent by his footsteps and by your thought[,] the ancient method" (195).

A keen irony of *Afterglow* is that it commences with a fictional and fraudulent letter threatening a lawsuit, a contrivance that Rosie later admits to concocting. Rosie's dog memoir, in short, begins with a lie. By the end of the dog *Afterglow*, though, Myles arrives at a myth, a fiction, that they nevertheless believe in, that mail carriers—figures or stand-ins for writers—are otherworldly figures, capable of transmitting messages to those who need it, unimpeded by time or distance or the elements. Letters, messages, are all important to Myles, for they are the stuff of communication and interconnectedness. Starting *Afterglow* with the conceit of a lawsuit, however, is a necessity, as it allows Rosie to articulate her grievances and Myles to bear witness to the "wrongs" they guiltily felt to have committed. The conceit also allows Myles to admonish themself for their "grotesque" administration of Rosie's life—that lack of competence

Myles labored under when Rosie's needs were not adequately understood or met. *Afterglow* might, consequently, function as Myles's *mea culpa*, yet the memoir is at the same time a rendering of all that they learned from Rosie, including not only how to care for Rosie but also how to collaborate with her. Sardonic and embittered, Rosie articulated her grievances against Myles, but she also instructed Myles about how to be and communicate in the world. The lesson is carefully taken up by Myles, who delivers messages across the night sky, an office bequeathed to Myles by their family and as dictated by Rosie.

Conclusion

Toward a (New) Bureaucratic Sublime

Everyday encounters with bureaucracy commonly dredge up loathing and dismay, if not outright dread. One might comprehend these extreme yet regular responses of alarm and nightmarish repulsion not just as an ordinary reaction to bureaucracy but as affective elements that constitute a distinct cultural and aesthetic category, that of the bureaucratic sublime. In such circumstances, the intractable, Byzantine immensity of administrative networks, workplace organization, and corporate and governmental offices is disconcerting and even terrifying. To grasp the bureaucratic sublime, it is helpful to understand bureaucracy and its apparatus as a technology of records, information, data, and labor—an applied scientific knowledge of human organization and administration—with an aim toward efficiency, expressive of what Rob Wilson calls "the will of technological modernity" (13). For Wilson and his theorization of the sublime, our contemporary age is beset not by overwhelming confrontations with nature—like a majestic mountain range or the expansive, starry night sky—but by monumental postindustrial systems, a postmodern sublime, at once awe-inspiring and terrifying—tied to late capitalism or nuclear power. One could add bureaucratic systems to Wilson's instances of the postmodern, postindustrial sublime, as insurmountable technological forces in their own right and a subset of Capital that alternately evokes feelings of trepidation due to the systems' sheer size and intricacy or amazement as a would-be ideal of efficiency and order.

In making the argument for an evolving conception of the sublime proper to our contemporary era, Wilson situates the sublime within the fast, abstract, and immense operational technology of Capital and its networks. As Wilson writes, "This 'technological sublime' is not so much a *name* as a *site*; the place where the spectacle of Capital produces its idols of production/reproduction, signs of collective colonization of urban and global space. . . . The euphoric/dreadful source of this postmodern sublime is not merely technology per se as icon of material vastness but more unspeakable totalities of commodity infinitude and [information and data] sign-glut . . ." (219). The postindustrial sublime, that is, takes effect not merely in the daily machinations of Capital but in their after-effects and networks. One beholds the sublime spectacle of Capital in all that it sets into motion. Accordingly, bureaucracy—its administration and organization of information, numbers, labor, money, and "commodity infinitude"—might be productively understood as an instrument of Capital and no less disconcerting than Capital itself for its sublime immensity and intractability.

The modernist works of Kafka offer literature's preeminent representations of fear-inducing administrative bureaucracy, yet the writing of the New York School poets enacts versions of the bureaucratic sublime of a type more consistent with Wilson's assessments of the postindustrial sublime. Kenneth Koch's "To My Father's Business," for instance, encapsulates the New York School poets' response to the bureaucratic sublime and exhibits the nexus of dread and euphoria that Wilson identifies in Capital and the postindustrial age. In "To My Father's Business," it is the office furniture company owned by Kenneth Koch's father and uncle in Cincinnati, Ohio—C. Loth, Inc.—that is made the subject of the younger's Koch's ode, whose opening lines invoke sublime affects of amazement and, later, trepidation:

> Leo bends over his desk
> Gazing at a memorandum
> While Stuart stands beside him
> With a smile, saying,
> "Leo, the order for those desks
> Came in today
> From Youngstown Needle and Thread!" (*Collected Poems* 594)

Exclamation points indicate the capitalist-infused euphoria initiated by a transaction of goods at C. Loth, Inc., as does Stuart's gratified smile at the open order for a business deal. It is, however, the "memorandum" that assures the presence of the bureaucratic sublime, for Uncle Leo's gaze is held not by natural wonders—like, for instance, Sharon Woods or Buckeye Falls in nearby Sharonville, Ohio—but by administrative paperwork in a downtown Cincinnati office. The self-propagating mechanisms of bureaucracy are also conveyed in the material objects, office paraphernalia, and paperwork present at the scene: the desk on which the memo sits begets the multiplication and circulation of more desks, suggestive of the exhilarating speed of Capital and the tendency of bureaucracy to replicate itself endlessly—prospects of an economic order that is both exhilarating and terrifying.

Within "To My Father's Office," Koch combines the perspective of a youthful self with the backward glance of an adult poet who understands fully that his life choices would be at cross purposes with his business-owning father and uncle. Koch replaces the joy expressed at the outset of the poem with dread in an apostrophe that compares the family business to an imperialist oppressor, revealing its will-to-dominate:

> C. Loth Inc., there you are
> Like Balboa the conqueror
> Of those who want to buy office furniture (594)

The bureaucratic sublime registers in the young Koch as outright panic and fear, as thoughts of becoming integrated into commerce with his father cause visceral feelings of revulsion: "Kenny, he says, some day you'll work in the store. / But I felt 'never more' or 'never ever'" (594). Koch balks at the prospect of becoming an organizational or company man, and the failure of mimicry—of becoming a mimetic, bureaucratic copy of his father—causes paternal chagrin in the elder Koch: "I am sitting on a desk / Looking at my daddy / Who is proud of but feels unsure about / Some aspects of his little laddie" (594). The shared unease between father and son functions as an indicator of bureaucratic sublime, an expression of corporate dread experienced by both due to the son's lack of conformity to the family business.

The bureaucratic sublime as critical term and concept has slowly entered into scholarly discussions of twentieth- and twenty-first-century poetry. Though Rob Wilson's sweeping and magisterial study, *American Sublime*, does not invoke the bureaucratic sublime by name, his analysis of the technological sublime, as I have tried to illustrate, encapsulates bureaucracy and its apparatuses, its monumental, technological, and systemic totality. In "Grammar Trouble," Brian Reed adopts the specific phrasing of the bureaucratic sublime to identify the zeal with which Gertrude Stein would diagram sentences, a practice fundamental to her understanding of language and approach to poetry. The ecstasy that Stein experiences diagramming sentences, Reed argues, "occurs within a particular frame, the classroom. The U.S. educational system promotes a dizzying affective experience of release into universality and eternity. . . . One could call this dynamic the bureaucratic sublime, a feeling of omnipotence brought on by avid identification with an institution imagined to exist outside the messy contingencies of human history" (147–48). For Reed, it is Stein's pleasurable identification with a gigantic bureaucratic system, the entirety of the US educational system, that inspires feelings of the sublime. Identification is also integral to Paul Stephens's analysis of conceptual poets and their tendency to appropriate data sets in the creation of new poetic forms. These data-rich forms, in the hands of conceptual poets, reveal the degree to which bits of information and corporate statistics stand in for personal identity: Stephens writes "We are data; data is us—whether in bioinformatics or in terms of the bureaucratic sublime's fusion of the personal and the corporate . . ." (779). In their totalizing capacity to represent human existence, massive databases that store our information and are controlled by corporations or government entities determine much of individual lives, including our daily interactions with institutions, whether in banking, shopping, healthcare, or offices of the county or state.

In their antipathy for bureaucratic work and the embrace of the imagination as an antidote to systems administrative regulation, the writings of the New York School poets present their own set of circumstances for comprehending the bureaucratic sublime. These conditions of bureaucracy do not involve the data sets of the conceptual poets nor diagrammed sentences in accord with the US educational system as with Stein but work within an office, clerical matters befitting the "secretarial generation," as Geoff Ward had named the New York School poets (80). Frank O'Hara will, for instance, lament his bureaucratic existence at the Museum of Modern Art in "Radio," an ode that begs for an appropriate, musical end to the office's dreadful and drudging work week: "Why do you play such dreary music / on Saturday afternoon, when tired, mortally tired I long for a little / reminder of immortal energy?" (*Collected Poems* 234). O'Hara's overwrought yearning for auditory pleasure and more energy frames his bureaucratic duties at the museum as stultifying, plodding labor that necessitates a compensatory release:

> All
> week long while I trudge fatiguingly
> from desk to desk in the museum
> you spill your miracles of Grieg
> and Honegger on shut-ins.
> Am I not
> shut in too, and after a week
> of work don't I deserve Prokofieff? (234)

In his campy plea to the radio, O'Hara files a would-be workplace complaint alleging tedium in the insular and claustrophobic spaces of the museum. O'Hara's hyperbolic and overstated comparison of his shuttling between desks at the Museum of Modern Art to the fate of a "shut-in" is uncharitable to his fellow disabled New Yorkers who legitimately cannot leave their apartments, yet O'Hara's protest nevertheless has real implications for the way that an American work ethic is conceived. O'Hara's grudging remarks of employee grievance in "Radio" exhibit what Kathi Weeks describes as "an unwillingness to cultivate, simply on principle, a good 'professional' attitude about work" (77). Instead, O'Hara will protest that he "deserves" more—more Prokofieff, more "miracles" by composers "Grieg / and Honegger"—so that the stultifying and energy-draining aspects of work do not spill over to the weekend.[1] Disguised as campy disquiet, O'Hara's feelings speak to harried workweek schedules and clerical demands that prompt an actual experience of dread and an uneasy and stressed affect characteristic of the bureaucratic sublime. The threat to O'Hara's leisure time signals "an erosion of the temporal boundaries between work and life" and his experience of dread illustrates a collapsing "emotional investment between the times and spaces of work and a life outside it" (Weeks 72).

O'Hara's dismay about the strains of work bleeding into the weekend, the trials of labor exacerbated and made palpable by the lack of pleasure offered by the radio, articulates but one side of the dread and euphoria dichotomy of the bureaucratic sublime. Fantasies of workplace efficiency, immense organizational productivity, and maximal profits fuel the rhapsodic counterpart to bureaucratic dread. Koch's "To My Father's Office" has already given expression to the euphoria of the bureaucratic sublime, a condition suffused with the capitalist imperative always to produce more and to earn more. It is, however, Koch's continued depiction of the family business that rounds out features of the bureaucratic sublime and its ideological underpinnings. In trying to comprehend his father's unreserved embrace of business, Koch figuratively renders the office as a potential romantic partner, whom he addresses with his "heart in an uproar / I loved you but couldn't think of staying with you" (*Collected Poems* 594–95). The infatuated young Koch soon realizes that the love of business is sustained by a doctrinal adherence to bureaucratic stability and dependability:

> I can see the virtues now
> That could come from being in you
> A sense of balance
> Compromise and acceptance (595)

Koch articulates here the allure that a bureaucratic system provides, where organizational and administrative protocol delivers not only certainty and orderliness but pleasant affects of equanimity and accord. The comments by Koch present an uncanny echo of what Max Weber contends are the benefits of bureaucracy: "Experience has demonstrated that [bureaucratic administration] provides precision, consistency, discipline, rigour, reliability, and hence predictability" (*Economy and Society* [2019] 350). Koch perceives in bureaucratic operations a state of rightness and rectitude, whose very appeal is its congenial sense of satisfaction, a sublimely content equanimity where everything seems orderly and organized.

Though the appeal of bureaucracy approaches the sanguine, companionable conditions of an amicable relationship, Koch's sharp reservations about joining the family business not only do not lessen but get stronger. The momentary consideration of becoming an office man like his father and uncle instigates a pendulum swing back to the bureaucratic sublime's feelings of dread and dismay. There arises, in Koch's consciousness, a heightened and skeptical awareness—as with the other New York School poets—of bureaucracy's ideological ends. Accordingly, Koch becomes increasingly attuned to the paradoxical nature of bureaucracy and the capitalist interests it serves: if bureaucracy makes business efficient, disciplined, predictable, and therefore profitable, then why must commercial trade and financial enterprises be continuously propped up by propaganda in the form of advertising campaigns and books about business and leadership? Why does business endlessly promote itself, through widely circulated success stories aiming to recruit new individuals into commerce via pamphlets or various courses promising lucrative career paths? About such business propaganda, prevalent even within his father's office, Koch sardonically observes:

> There were little pamphlets
> Distributed in you
> About success in business
> Each about eight to twelve pages long
> One whole series of them
> All ended with the words
> "P.S. He got the job" (595)

The brochures express a manufactured excitement about both career and financial achievement, an artificial exhilaration constituting its own euphoric instance and illustration of the bureaucratic sublime.

These narratives about finding a job and fulfilling one's purpose through gainful employment are writ through with the ideology of a work ethic that glosses over class differences and capitalist exploitation of labor. As Weeks argues, the ideology of the work ethic perpetuates inequity, promising individual growth and professional success historically available only to a select class of workers: "the work ethic with its various claims about the rewards of work—whether those rewards are coded as social mobility or self-development—shifts from a credible ideal to sheer propaganda depending on the conditions of work and the individual's position within the complex, intersecting hierarchies of the work society. The further the discourse travels, the more its precepts are abstracted from the real conditions of work, and the more often it is reduced to a crudely ideological phenomenon . . ." (60). Koch himself proves to be an astute critic of such discourse and its ideological messaging, as he recognizes that pat instances of initiative and exceptionally ambitious drive are repeatedly woven into narratives: "One a story about a boy who said, 'I swept up the street, Sir, / Before you got up.' Or / 'There were five hundred extra catalogues / So I took them to people in the city who have a dog'—/ P.S. He got the job" (595). The common refrain of the brochures "He got the job"—focused as it is on achievement and success—seals the purpose of such manipulative programming: the reward of employment as the ultimate end is the blissful and sublime outcome of a culture uncritically steeped in the work ethic.

Koch's incipient awareness of, and skepticism toward, the propaganda disbursed in the business pamphlets allows him to interrupt the bureaucratic sublime and thereby combat the ecstatic draw of business ideology and the corresponding dread when one is not in conformity with it. Koch resists such sublime effects with the particular discursive means at his disposal: a counter-rhetoric of poetry and the imagination. Poetry—its forms and discursive tactics—constitutes Koch's defense against bureaucracy and its ideological apparatus. Adopting a lyrical refrain to counteract the rote repetition of the employment pamphlets, Koch riffs cynically on the pamphlet's message of success and ambition:

> P.S. He got the job.
> I didn't get the job
> I didn't think that I could do the job
> I thought I might go crazy in the job. (595)

John Hollander has argued that the efficacy of poetic refrain works via its "rhythm of recurrence" with "each return accru[ing] new meaning" (135). Koch's own illustrative lesson, thus, is that poetic refrain does not operate through sheer and droning repetition as the propagandistic pamphlets might. Rather, poetic refrain, as Hollander further explains, depends upon "rhetorical self-consciousness," resulting, ultimately, in "a lie against repetition" brought on or introduced by slight "lexical and syntactic variation" (Hollander 133, 135).[2] A rupture within the pamphlets' messaging, Koch's lyric consciousness is coincident with his raised awareness of the stifling and delimiting tendencies of work within a corporate setting.

The business pamphlets' rote messaging, an epistrophe premised on getting "the job," is consequently met by Koch's personal testament and lyrical repetition, an anaphora steeped in negation ("I didn't") that repudiates the ideology of the American work ethic and acknowledges that, for Koch, the pamphlets' propaganda would lead not to employment but to the loss of sanity, a dread-filled response of the bureaucratic sublime. Koch's permutations here persist as a form of culture jamming, employing lyrical and syntactic variation to interrupt messaging meant to ensure capitalism's endless bureaucratic reproduction—its replication through paperwork pamphleteering and the operations of businesses themselves.

Koch's rejection of his father's business, as with the responses of the other New York School poets to the culture of bureaucracy, amounts to a refusal of work and an incipient resistance to a highly administered everyday life. Koch's sense that he "might go crazy in the job" signals less a personal failing than a keen awareness of the exploitative nature of work within a capitalist system: in this way, "To My Father's Business" illustrates a savvy understanding of the work ethic under capitalism, where the incessant pursuit of wealth seems fundamentally unreasonable—or, in other words, not sane. In articulating his reluctance to a career in business, Koch once more echoes Weber, who contrasted the Protestant work ethic with what he called a "traditional" or pre-capitalist mindset that conceived of work only as a means to provide one's daily sustenance and no more. As Weber argues, a "traditional" mindset would view working to amass wealth as irrational: "seen from the point of view of happiness," the motivation for affluence and "business with its continuous work" expresses "what is so irrational about this sort of life, where a man exists for the sake of his business, instead of the reverse" (*Protestant Ethic* 24; 32). "To the pre-capitalistic man," Weber continues, that anyone would "make it the sole purpose of his life-work, to sing into the grave weighed down with a great material load of money and goods, seems to him explicable only as the product of a perverse instinct" (33).

Against a capitalistic point of view and the bureaucratic apparatus that supports it, Koch and the other New York School poets would seek out alternative labor practices that intervene against the bureaucratic sublime by pursuing work that is less profit-oriented and affords the opportunity for creative production. Such an aim to find more fulfilling jobs overturns what Weeks identifies as a "the problem with work" and constitutes an appropriate response to the ways in which work is structured under capitalism: "the struggle against work is a matter of securing not only better work, but also the time and money necessary to have a life outside of work" (13). Weeks clarifies that a critique of the work ethic as ideological "is not to claim that work is without value" nor is it to "deny the necessity of productive activity . . ." (12). Instead, the critique of work and current employment practices is "to insist that there are other ways to organize and distribute that activity and to remind us that it is also possible to be creative outside of the boundaries of work. It is to suggest that there might be a variety of ways to experience the pleasure that we may now find in work, as well as other pleasures that we may wish to discover, cultivate, and enjoy" (12).

The New York School poets, the so-described "secretarial generation," would find ways of ameliorating their bureaucratic work as Weeks described, first surreptitiously and subversively by writing poems at work or daydreaming on the job—the type of everyday practice described by de Certeau as *la perruque*, where a worker "diverts time" for creative pursuits and such furtive creative activity is camouflaged or hidden from an employer amid the performance of authorized job duties (25). Later, each of the poets would find other, non-clerical work as art critics and professors, while still writing poetry. The tactics used by the New York School poets to avoid clerical or bureaucratic work, however, present not just individualistic interventions against bureaucracy but a model for widespread and even collective disruptions of capitalism. These disruptive strategies also intercede against the bureaucratic sublime as they neither succumb to euphoric dreams of big business efficiency nor are susceptible to the sense of doom that accompanies intransigent bureaucratic operations indifferent or hostile to individual and societal needs. In other words, the New York School poets and their relationship to employment indicate an alternate praxis for work, organization, and creativity—conditions of labor that could be generative of a new bureaucratic sublime. This novel revision of the bureaucratic sublime would entail a recalibration of work activity to include time set aside for creative activity and maintenance of personal wellbeing. The new concept of the bureaucracy and administration would also embrace human organization of another sort—political action aimed at ensuring just and equitable work conditions.

The critique of work that the New York School have advanced in their poetry in this manner anticipate theories for politics and labor-focused activism that Michael Hardt and Antonio Negri articulate in *Assembly*, a book that elaborates upon the critiques of global networks of capital and power within their *Empire* trilogy. In a chapter entitled "Weber in Reverse" from *Assembly*, Hardt and Negri detail a strategy for combating bureaucratic-capitalist systems by not only maintaining what is effective and necessary in bureaucracy's organizational impulses but reintroducing the affective and human dimension to organized labor that bureaucratic systems seek to abolish. What is necessary, according to Hardt and Negri, is a modification of Weber's views so that the subjectivities of workers have their place within a work environment.

Bureaucratic systems, as Weber writes, follow "the rule of formal impersonality: *sine ira et studio*, or 'without hatred or passion,' . . . .[a principle of] impersonality impelled by concepts of simple obligation. The ideal official fulfills his office 'without regard to person . . .'" (*Economy and Society* [2019] 353). For Hardt and Negri, combating bureaucratic capitalism and its principles of indifference requires a reintroduction of the personal: if bureaucratic measures historically have aimed to neutralize the subjectivity of the worker to promote efficiency and to encourage machinelike productivity, then a personal, affective dimension must be returned to work: "The point is not to be done with Weber but to run Weber in reverse. This is why we have tried to highlight that the same subjectivities that throw modern bureaucracy into crisis also demonstrate the social and organizational capacities, the intelligence, knowledges, and access to information that are required for effective and autonomous social administration" (*Assembly* 134). The implication for Hardt and Negri is that the worker who is fully realized in his or her labor, who utilizes their capacities and knowledge so fully, acts politically, in a manner that also fully realizes human civic potential.

Hardt and Negri imagine a form of social and labor organization so dynamic that it changes the capitalistic, Empire-ordained order that currently presides over our existence. What they propose is a form of "assembly"—a political gathering and mobilization—capable of instituting change that is no less dynamic than the bureaucratic sublime for what it can achieve through concerted organization, though with political ends contrary to the bureaucratic-capitalist systems that presently prevail. Such a restructuring of human organization and political agency is a revision of the bureaucratic sublime toward progressive, utopian ends. As Hart and Negri put it, "the question for today's machinic subjectivities, then, so full of knowledge and intelligence, is how they can invent democratic practices and administrative institutions that organize effectively the life of the multitude" (*Assembly* 134). The manner to achieve such democratic goals and practices is through a reorganization of political models of leadership to make them less hierarchical. Hardt and Negri envision a political movement organized and animated "from below" (*Assembly* 78), deriving its power from a multitude who assembles to take action and use their collective knowledge to enact change, ushering into being a non-hierarchical system of political organization that is an inversion of the bureaucratic sublime.[3]

The type of collective politics that Hardt and Negri imagine may appear on the surface to be about as far from the poetics of the New York School poets as one could conceive. Nevertheless, the critiques of bureaucracy and of work that the New York School poets formulate in their poems do align with the non-hierarchical, anti-bureaucratic theories that Hardt and Negri and other critics of capitalism advance. The habits of work that the New York School poets adopted, writing poems when they could, whether on the job or outside of their hours of employment, reveal a politics of quotidian creation and production, constituting what de Certeau called the "practice of everyday life" (xi). A theorization of everyday practices, for de Certeau, aims "to make explicit the systems of operational combination (*les combinatoires d'operation*) which also compose a 'culture,' and to bring to light the models of action characteristic of users whose status as the dominated element in society (a status that does not mean they are passive or docile) is concealed. . . . Everyday life invents itself by *poaching* in countless ways on the property of others" (xi–xii). As with de Certeau's calculating workers, so may the New York School poets be understood when working as clerks who themselves poached or appropriated time from the office to work on their poetry and, later, intervened into the ideology of capitalism with poems that critiqued the operations of capitalist bureaucracy.

Years before Hardt and Negri, de Certeau envisioned an entire class of workers and clerks engaged in everyday practices of *la perruque* (the diversion of work time and materials for personal, artistic use) that challenge the prevailing socioeconomic order. De Certeau thus imagines, like Hardt and Negri's notion of the "assembly," widespread and daily interventions into capitalist and bureaucratic systems: "With variations, practices analogous to *la perruque* are proliferating in governmental and commercial offices as well as in factories. No doubt they are just as widespread as formerly (though they ought still to be studied), just as widely suspected, repressed or ignored. Not only workshops and offices, but also museums and learned journals penalize such practices or ignore them" (26). The habits, thought, and compositional practices of the New York poets cohere with the diversions from work—the refusal of conventional understandings of work—as outlined by de Certeau and by Hardt and Negri and illustrate a means for contesting the bureaucratic sublime, either in its dreadful or bliss-ridden forms.

The collective dynamics inherent in the interactions of the New York School poets have often been noted by critics as a means of comprehending the group's creative output. The various articulations of collectivity or coterie among the New York School, though, have yet to account for their anti-bureaucratic sensibilities or their refusal of workplace demands and its compulsory ethics of efficient productivity. An anecdote about John Ashbery and Frank O'Hara and their friendship illustrates well the antipathy that the New York School poets had toward the tedium of bureaucracy, for it is one that is centered primarily on work. While working overseas in Paris at the Musée d'Art Moderne, O'Hara enlisted Ashbery to help oversee "the unpacking of the crates for an exhibition of 'The New American Painting'" (Gooch 321). In a manner keeping with the practices of *la perruque*, O'Hara and Ashbery undertake their duties with an eye toward diversion, as Brad Gooch explains:

> Refusing ever to take his work too seriously, or to appear to take it too seriously, O'Hara was pleased to have Ashbery as his accomplice during this working visit. "Whether or not you are interested in doing any work," O'Hara had written ahead, "I do hope you'll make yourself at home in the Musée while I'm there at least, so I won't die of boredom." Ashbery more than fulfilled his mission of diversion. "Thursday afternoon there was a press cocktail at which John and I did not fail to get fairly fried," O'Hara wrote to John LeSueur on January 17. (321)

Gooch is careful here to distinguish between a desire not to *appear* to take work too seriously and sheer idleness, yet the hallmark features of the New York School poets' skepticism toward an American bureaucracy and its underpinning work ethic are on full display. O'Hara treats work and his job not as a singular, all-consuming, and self-defining profession but as something to be shared and enjoyed cooperatively with others. O'Hara's interest is in reorganizing his workload, official responsibilities, and schedule as an antidote to the dread that accompanies the officialdom of bureaucratic duties. O'Hara and Ashbery depart from strictures, literally taking leave of requirements of the job: "Of a later cocktail party following an official public opening at three in the afternoon, O'Hara reported to LeSueur, 'John and I ran out on this to go to Les Dialogues des Carmelites which I loved . . .'" (Gooch 321).

O'Hara's and Ashbery's refusal of work is, then, really a refusal of tedium and repetitive, undemanding tasks and other obligations extraneous to labor itself. Gooch's descriptive words ("accomplice" and "mission") invest the scene with dramatic, adventurous flair, yet they also speak to the sabotaging intentions inherent to de Certeau's "practice of everyday life" and its war on the structures of power everywhere present in a capitalist society. O'Hara's and Ashbery's behavior is remarkably frivolous, a campy scene fit to relate as a lighthearted anecdote in a letter to O'Hara's friend Joe LeSueur, yet it also amounts to a quotidian, cultural practice with a politics of its own. As de Certeau contends, the habits of the *la perruque* can be put toward political ends: "we can divert time owed to the institution; we can make textual objects that signify an art and [collective] solidarities; we can play the game of free exchange, even if it is penalized by bosses and colleagues . . . ; we can create networks of connivances and sleights of hand; we can exchange gifts, and in these ways subvert the law, that in the . . . factory, puts work at the service of the machine . . ." (28).

The impulse to divert, to play, illustrated in the anecdote of O'Hara and Ashbery taking care of their responsibilities but still finding room for enjoyment and allowing themselves to abscond from work, as I have argued, amounts to a politics and a redefinition of the practice of work. This politics resists the alienating and stultifying nature of bureaucratic labor, reorienting workplace obligation from merely a matter of productivity and duty to the realization of human fulfillment that necessarily entails joy and amusement experienced outside of work. Weeks contends that "the struggle to improve the quality of work must be accompanied by efforts to reduce its quantity. . . . [T]he refusal of work—understood as a rejection of work as a necessary center of social existence, moral duty, ontological essence, and time and energy, and understood as a practice of [insubordination] . . .—can speak forcefully to our present situation" (109). In their poetry and fundamental to their poetics, the New York School poets took issue with a bureaucratic culture that hampered their creativity and circumscribed their fulfillment with a work ethic alien to their being. Their poems speak to a radical overturning of work and bureaucratic administration as it was and continues to be culturally prescribed. Though not focused on the politics of work or the hierarchical nature of bureaucracy, Lytle Shaw's conception of "O'Hara's literary coterie" gets at the subversion of such principles in the New York School poets, for he notes the "comparatively horizontal structure of this group," especially in relation to the "clear center of authority" occupied by Ezra Pound amid his fellow modernists (73). Instead of the hierarchical or vertical structure that places Pound in a central and authoritative position, O'Hara's poems demonstrate that "the social field of the [New York School poet's] literary circle is a site of flux, of relatively temporary judgments and invention spurred on by . . . literal collaboration . . ." (73).[4] The tendency for organizational flux and imperative for collaboration that Shaw here outlines approximates the political reorganization and worker cooperation advocated by Hardt and Negri in *Assembly*.

In this way, the impulse toward a horizontal structure that Shaw describes is yet another instance of the anti-bureaucratic, nonhierarchical principles at work in the New York School poets' opposition to administrative culture. Such anti-hierarchical and collaborative values—along with the New York School poets' efforts to modify their work to allow for creativity and achieve a balance while not at work—illustrate their interest in overturning the organizational strictures and material structures of the bureaucratic sublime. In their interventions into the work ethic, the New York School poets initiated a novel organizational sublime—an alternate work praxis astonishing in its intent to maximize individual and collective creativity and contest the prevailing administrative culture of the time. Consonant with the "refusal of work" of the Italian autonomist social movements of the 1960s, the unruly and insubordinate work habits of this "secretarial generation" of poets also pointedly and importantly anticipate contemporary theoretical critiques of capitalist labor, like those of David Graeber, Kathi Weeks, and Michael Hardt and Antonio Negri, among others. In his advocacy for subversive action within the practice of everyday life, de Certeau, for his part, imagines there is an alternate space existing just beyond that of bureaucracy's dominance: "beneath the fabricating and universal writing of [bureaucratic] technology, opaque and stubborn places remain. The revolutions of history, economic mutations, demographic mixtures lie in layers within it, and remain there, hidden in customs, rites, and spatial practices. . . . This place, on its surface, seems to be a collage. In reality, in its depth it is ubiquitous. A piling up of heterogenous places. Each one . . . refers to a different mode of territorial unity, of socioeconomic distribution, of political conflicts . . ." (201). The writings of the New York School poets are such a site of contestation and stubborn, creative resistance, with their poetry at once constituting a literary record and an archival compendium—of work histories, precarious employment, and workplace tedium—collective articulations that imagine and know that alternatives to the cultural dominant of highly administered life and work surely exist.

Notes

Introduction

1. Alongside Whyte's *The Organization Man*, there were several prominent works at midcentury that were critical of bureaucracy and its effects on American culture, including C. Wright Mills's *The Power Elite* (1956) and James Burnham's *The Managerial Revolution: What Is Happening in the World* (1941).

2. For recent work on precarity, see Guy Standing, *The Precariat: The New Dangerous Class*; Lauren Berlant, *Cruel Optimism* (especially chapter 6, "After the Good Life, an Impasse: Time Out, Human Resources, and the Precarious Present"); Emily J. Hogg and Peter Simonsen, *Precarity in Contemporary Literature and Culture*.

3. Gooch remarks that O'Hara's initial duties at MOMA included "the job of typing identical copies of letters (in the days before photocopying), which had made up the bulk of his work on the 'French Masterpieces in American Collections' show" (294). Porter McCray, O'Hara's boss, decided to promote his employee, as Gooch further relates, "believing O'Hara 'too brilliant and too creative for secretarial work'" (294).

4. Weber writes primarily of the Confucian literati in China yet compares these officials to "what the humanist of [the] Renaissance period approximately was: a literator harmonistically trained and tested in the language monuments of the remote past" (*From Max Weber* 92).

5. While the subject of bureaucracy has fascinated poets and fiction writers for centuries, literary critics have of late begun to turn their attention to administrative culture. For recent criticism that speaks to the connections between literature, bureaucracy, and administration, see Evan Kindley, *Poet-Critics and the Administration of Culture* (2017); Benjamin Lewis Robinson, *Bureaucratic Fanatics: Modern Literature and the Passions of Rationalization* (2019); and Yohei Igarashi, *The Connected Condition: Romanticism and the Dream of Communication* (2020).

6. Glen Krutz and Sylvie Waskiewicz provide similar numbers when observing the enormous growth in government agencies at midcentury: "By 1940, approximately 700,000 U.S. workers were employed in the federal bureaucracy. Under President Lyndon B. Johnson in the 1960s, that number reached 2.2 million, and the federal budget increased to $332 billion."

7. While not explicitly anti-bureaucratic, Guest's framing of her poetics in terms of rules and liberation from them upholds the virtues of the imagination against the type of rationality, at its extremes, that one might associate with bureaucracy.

8. Kenneth Koch, in his tribute to Frank O'Hara, "All the Imagination Can Hold," points out the extent to which O'Hara's poetry is likewise steeped in the imagination, arguing that his poetics "are the result of an unfamiliar aesthetic assumption: that what is really right there, in the poet's thoughts, fantasies, and feelings, is what is richest in possibility and worth the most attention" (23). O'Hara himself would also invoke the imagination as a guiding poetic principle in "Ode on Causality," a poem centered on a visit to Jackson Pollock's grave, where O'Hara archly beseeches Pollock's spirit to make him "distant and imaginative / [and to] make my lines thin as ice then swell like pythons" (*Collected Poems* 302).

9. Marjorie Perloff addresses the influence of Dada and Surrealist texts on O'Hara in *Frank O'Hara: Poet Among Painters* (34). David Lehman describes how Ashbery, despite acknowledging the impact of the surrealists, became annoyed "to be considered 'a late-blooming umbilical cord between the French Surrealists and Americans'" (126).

10. See William Watkin's *In the Process of Poetry: The New York School and the Avant Garde* for his perceptive discussion of not only the quotidian as it relates to O'Hara's and Schuyler's work but for his account of the compositional process for the New York School poets as a whole. See also Siobhan Phillips, "Stevens and an Everyday New York School," on the influence of Wallace Stevens on the New York School's quotidian poetics.

11. For recent work on the Italian Autonomists, and the refusal of work, generally, see David Frayne's *The Refusal of Work* and Steve Wright's *Storming Heaven: Class Composition and Struggle in Italian Autonomist Marxism*.

12. That office work can also be alienating is something that Marxist critic Georg Lukács similarly claimed. The bureaucratic system, Lukács argues, becomes all-consuming for the office worker, who is compelled by a sense of personal obligation to the office, resulting in "a specific type of bureaucratic 'conscientiousness'" (*History and Class Consciousness* 99). In such circumstances, office workers experience reification, where their "own activity, [their] own labor becomes something objective and independent of [them], something that controls [them] . . ." (87). An individual worker beset by reification, whether in the factory or the office, does not "appear as the authentic master of the process; on the contrary, he is a mechanical part incorporated into a mechanical system" (89).

For clerks and office workers, Lukács maintains, the experience of reification is especially acute and "becomes all the more clear, the more elevated, advanced, and 'intellectual'" the work is (99).

13. Anthropologist Michael Herzfeld identifies this apathetic phenomenon as "the social production of indifference," a consequence of bureaucratic society that "provides members of the public a means of conceptualizing their own disappointments and humiliations [at the hands of clerks and bureaucratic measures] and . . . under some circumstances [if performing clerical work themselves] may lead them to acquiesce in the humiliation of others" (13). Dealing with a bureaucracy and its agents often begets the perception of an actively hostile bureaucratic entity or system conspiring against one's individual interests, indifferent to one's humanity.

14. Weber goes on to describe an "ideal official" of a bureaucratic system: "the ideal official fulfills his office 'without regard to person': 'everyone' is treated with formal equality, that is, everyone who finds themselves in the same actual situation with regard to interest" (*Economy and Society* [2019] 353). This description, however, also succumbs to an ironic reading where bureaucratic torpor and impersonality prevail even as the goal of equal treatment is obtained.

15. As Graeber argues, "The bureaucratization of daily life means the imposition of rules and regulations; impersonal regulations and rules, in turn can only operate, if they are backed up by the threat of force" (32). Graeber goes on to explain that the threat of violence is not conceptual but real, mobilized in particular to protect property rights: "All of these [HMOs, banks, etc.] are institutions involved in the allocation of property rights regulated and guaranteed by governments that ultimately rests on the threat of force. 'Force' in turn is just a euphemistic way to refer to violence: that is, the ability to call up people dressed in uniforms, willing to threaten to hit others over the head with wooden sticks" (58).

Chapter 1

1. Richard R. Bozorth offers this explanation of Auden's perception of his own sexuality: "At the core of Auden's effort are two contradictory views: that homosexuality signifies diseased self-consciousness, arrested development, and cultural degeneracy; and that the self-acknowledged homosexual can embody liberation from repressive bourgeois norms" (12).

2. For an account of British diplomatic relations with Hitler and his cabinet, see Gilbert and Gott, *The Appeasers*. As Gilbert and Gott write, British diplomacy worked in secret to make repeated unscrupulous concessions to Hitler that contravened British promises made to the Polish: "Once again 'British' policy was created by a handful of men and carried out by those men in utmost secrecy. The public had no idea that behind the strength of public utterances lay so strong a determination to make the Poles surrender" (276)

Chapter 2

1. The influence of Dadaism and Surrealism on O'Hara's poetry has been frequently observed. Marjorie Perloff, for example, has commented on the connection between the Dadaists and O'Hara, noting that "Dada and Surrealist texts begin to assume importance" in his reading toward the end of his years at Harvard (34). See also pages 96–99 in *Poet Among Painters*, where Perloff discusses O'Hara's interest in "poem-painting." The entry "Dada and Surrealism" in *Encyclopedia of the New York Poets* also details the influence of both movements on the New York School poets in general and O'Hara specifically.

2. Cold War motifs are also present in "For the Chinese New Year & For Bill Berkson," where O'Hara alludes to the B-movie *Village of the Damned*. See my "Parading the Undead: Camp, Horror and Reincarnation in the Poetry of Frank O'Hara and John Yau."

3. For a concise history of the events, see chapter 19, "The Revolt," in Tsepon W.D. Shakabpa's *Tibet: A Political History*.

4. Diggory, Shaw, and Epstein have each persuasively argued for the importance of community, coterie, and social groups to O'Hara's work.

Chapter 3

1. William Watkin speaks of Ashbery's view of art as a site that is full of risk yet also provides security for the artist: "We get a double dream of art, both as a place of invigorating risk-taking very akin to Ashbery's own descriptions of the New York scene of the 1950s, but also as a place of security; a space where we can linger even if we cannot live there" (181).

2. Harold Bloom also remarks upon Ashbery's "Wet Casements," arguing that the poem owes some of its tone to Kafka's short story, "Wedding Preparations in the Country": "That dark reflection [present in 'Wedding Preparations in the Country'] is the ethos, the universe of limitation, of the poem *Wet Casements*, whose opening irony swerves from Kafka's yet only to more self-alienation" (*Agon* 280).

3. Many sentiments Kafka had about writing verge upon the melodramatic, betraying a deep sense of failure if he is unable to engage in creative work: "When not writing, I feel myself to be pushed out of life by unyielding hands" (*Letters to Felice* 116). See also the comments of Stanley Corngold, who remarks that Kafka's struggles with writing routinely plagued him, noting that "the period preceding the writing of *The Trial* was increasingly full of Kafka's expressions of his shortcomings vis-à-vis his writing" (241). That episode of difficult writing had coincided with Kafka's broken engagement with Felice Bauer in July 1914 and the start that same month of a war that would consume Europe.

4. Ashbery is perhaps most ambivalent about—and critical of—the writing process when attempting a new and different style, as when he explains his

aspiration to develop a more formally experimental approach in *The Tennis Court Oath*, after the publication of *Some Trees*: "I was kind of scrounging around to find some new way of writing that would appeal to me because I was already satisfied with *Some Trees* but didn't want to go on writing in that way. . . . It was mainly a question for groping for different things, knowing what I didn't want to do and not really knowing what I did want to do" (Koethe 181).

5. For Epstein, Ashbery's poetry, particularly with regards to its depiction of subjectivity, reveals an "insistence that human selves, however atomized, independent, and isolated are inextricably bound to one another, wound within one another" (128).

6. The creature's various remarks about reinforcing his burrow bear out allegorical implications that compare building to literary writing, as he likens aspects of his constructed burrow to a "*tour de force*" that, despite some flaws, is "perhaps theoretically brilliant" (Kafka, *Complete Stories* 331). For the mole, the burrow is an aesthetic endeavor engaging in and of itself: "All this involves very laborious calculation, and the sheer pleasure of the mind in its own keenness is often the sole reason why one keeps it up" (325).

7. According to Karin Roffman, John perceived that his brother Richard, an athletic young boy who, when photographed playing football, "was exactly the image of what John believed Chet most desired in a son" (55).

8. Jonathan Morse writes of another letter in Ashbery's "The Tomb of Stuart Mill," arguing that such communications in Ashbery's poetry always and ritualistically allude to an original absence: "Whatever its origins off the page, therefore, the letter as read has become a part of the ritual that lies at the heart of Ashbery's poiesis: a perpetual tribute of nostalgia offered to 'you,' the lover absent in time" (19).

9. If one were to read the sequence of Ashbery's career in an Oedipal manner, "Fragment" suggests an overarching schema in which the poet first contends with a paternal figure and subsequently later turns to his creative rival in Parmigianino in "Self-Portrait." Ashbery's most pressing compositional challenge or subject, however, has always been contending with himself. In "Fragment," Ashbery sets out to discover an individual self, which he comes to realize is inextricable from his history with his father.

10. Ashbery's militaristic phrase "mounted on a charger" echoes another term, a *chargé d'affaires*, the title for a bureaucrat who has assumed duties in the absence of the ambassador and one that seems to pertain more closely to his present responsibilities of coordinating the paperwork surrounding his father's death.

Chapter 4

1. Guest relates H.D.'s romantic relationship and eventual engagement with Pound in the first pages of *Herself Defined: H.D and her World*, where Guest

notes, "Only a freshman when Pound became her mentor, she knew nothing of literature or art, except fairy tales, myths, music, Moravian legends" (4). Hugh Kenner describes the meeting between H.D. and Pound as being filled with clerk-like revisions and occurring "by one account in the British Museum tearoom, where Pound with a slashing red pencil made excisions from her 'Hermes of the Ways' and scrawled 'H.D. Imagiste' at the bottom of the page before sending it off (October 1912) to Harriet Monroe at *Poetry* . . ." (174).

2. Nelson extrapolates from the questions in "The Location of Things" a mode of inquiry that guides Guest's self-conception and concerns about her fitness as a poet: "Why am I here, and not somewhere else? Do objects change, or only our perception of them? . . . Are all material events somehow interrelated? If so, how attuned am I as an instrument to perceive their correspondence; how attuned can (my) poetry be?" (Nelson 35).

3. Here Guest is at work countering bureaucratic time, as Herzfeld describes it: "First, the sheer tedium [when dealing with an obstinate clerk] of constantly having to 'come back next week' deadens one's sense of the passage of time, especially in its repetitiveness. Second, the ability to demand this level of obedience expresses the bureaucrat's control over the client's time, making the latter unimportant by comparison: 'Can't you see I'm very busy?'" (162).

4. Weber makes these comments in his analysis of political organizations, as he diagnoses the types of rule and authority inherent to such systems. As Weber writes, "Rulership is the *Chance* that a command of a particular kind will be obeyed by given persons. Discipline is the *Chance* that, because of a practised disposition, a command will find prompt, automatic, and schematic obedience among a definite number of persons" (*Economy and Society* [2019] 134).

5. Though Guest's depiction of a corporate functioning of the office seems extreme or exaggerated, the scene coheres with what Graeber argues is fundamental to market capitalism: "History reveals that political policies that favor 'the market' have always meant even more people in offices to administer things, but it also reveals that they also mean an increase of the range and density of social relations that are ultimately regulated by the threat of violence. . . . The bureaucratization of daily life means the imposition of impersonal rules and regulations; impersonal rules and regulations, in turn, can only operate if they are backed up by threats of force" (32). Graeber's paradigmatic example is the university library and the repercussions of not complying with its rules, for if students "insisted on their right to enter the stacks without showing a properly stamped and validated ID, armed men would have been summoned to physically remove them, using whatever force might be required" (58).

6. Maggie Nelson provides a contrasting reading of this strain of transcendent love to the one I offer here, where she argues that Guest is inclined at times "to mock—however faintly—the kind of access to the transcendent or intangible traditionally offered to women (i.e., mediated through a male figure)"

(41). Nelson quotes Jacqueline Rose to reveal the ways in which Guest's work might be situated within "a discourse, which is fully and historically specific, in which transcendence is not a way of being that women seize for themselves but something handed to them with all the weight of male sexual fantasy and demand" (Rose 149–50). Nelson does acknowledge that Guest "privileges a state of suspension" in a more positive fashion elsewhere in her poetry, and my reading of this scene from *The Office* rests upon the apparent agency in her character's reaction to her male addressee, albeit made in a provisional manner: ("I might. (*Then almost radiantly:*) Yes, I might") (*Office* 21).

Chapter 5

1. Harvey outlines the counter-cultural sentiment of the 1960s as acting against bureaucratic efforts to "monumentalize corporate and state power" (38). As Harvey explains, the anti-bureaucratic sensibility of the counter-culture is fundamentally anti-authoritarian and anti-establishment: "Antagonistic to the oppressive qualities of scientifically grounded technical-bureaucratic rationality as purveyed through monolithic, corporate, state, and other forms of institutionalized power (including that of bureaucratized political parties and trade unions), the counter-cultures explored the realms of individualized self-realization through a distinct 'new left' politics, through the embrace of anti-authoritarian gestures, iconoclastic habits (in music, dress, language, and lifestyle), and the critique of everyday life" (38).

2. Though Andrew Epstein excludes T.S. Eliot from a list of influences, he argues that the coterie that developed between the New York School poets was shaped in part by common interest in "their different choice of artistic models," an "other" tradition that includes "Whitman, Williams, Pound, Stein, the more experimental side of Stevens and Auden . . ." (64).

3. James E. Young describes the tendency of counter-monuments to memorialize through absence and the use of negative space when he references a memorial to the Aschrott Fountain in Kassel City, which was demolished by the Nazis for bearing the name of a Jewish benefactor. As Young writes, Horst Hoheisel, the artist who designed the counter-monument, would make an inverted structure to represent the fountain that was once present but is now gone: "How does one remember an absence? In this case, by reproducing it. Quite literally, the negative space of the absent monument will now constitute its phantom shape in the ground. The very absence of the monument will now be preserved in its precisely duplicated negative space" (290).

4. A typically pedestrian, practical space, the bathroom with its urinals is here transformed by elegance, epitomizing a space where, as José Esteban Muñoz has shown, "nonfunctionality and total functionality merge" (7). Schuyler's

aesthetic appreciation of the historic bathroom, along with his phallic imagery, hints at a lost, erotically charged, and queer underground world that Schuyler will subsequently address in "Dining Out." The bathroom of McFeely's bar may not have explicitly been a site of homosexual public sex, yet Schuyler's sexualized rendering of the bathroom and its seduction of "what lurks / within" exhibits what Muñoz has called the "ghosts of public sex" or a "hauntology" the examination of which "situ[ates] semipublic phenomena such as public sex within queer history and politics" (42).

5. As Graeber notes, "Police are bureaucrats with weapons. . . . We think of [the police] as fighting crime, and when we think of 'crime,' the kind of crime we have in our minds is violent crime. Even though, in fact, what police mostly do is exactly the opposite: they bring the threat of force to bear on situations that would otherwise have nothing to do with it" (73).

Chapter 6

1. In raising the concept of the administrative grotesque, Foucault identifies clear literary references to bureaucracy and precursors but also emphasizes real-world counterparts in actual bureaucratic organizations: "The administrative grotesque has not been merely that kind of visionary perception of administration that we find in Balzac, Dostoyevsky, Courteline, or Kafka. The administrative grotesque is a real possibility for bureaucracy" (*Abnormal* 12).

2. Rosie admits to writing the letter and making the entire lawsuit up in a subsequent passage "Okay so I totally wrote the letter" (34). Rosie continues to explain that the conceit is collaborative, an idea shared between herself and Myles, as I discuss below: "There's no lawyer. There's no money. I . . . I never said it because it kind of confuses things. I put it in her head. It's what we always did. She feels she wrote it" (35).

3. Myles identifies *Naked Lunch* as one of the novels that they most want to read again for the first time, calling the novel a "gorgeous abomination" in an interview ("Reading with . . . Eileen Myles") posted on the website *Shelf Awareness*.

4. Myles references Gertrude Stein, describing Stein as "a great weaver" (192). Myles associates their own writing with weaving as well, likening parts of *Afterglow* to a tapestry: "The tapestry is like an advanced memory" (169).

5. There is little evidence that Cipel was a poet, beyond a self-published book in youth. The press covering the scandal and McGreevey's subsequent resignation often labeled Cipel a poet, likely to reinforce his lack of qualification to work in matters of homeland security.

6. On the politics of care, see Joan Tronto's *Moral Boundaries: A Political Argument for Care* and *Caring Democracy: Markets, Equality, and Justice*.

7. The puppets' incomprehension of a "career" is especially acute because the deadening, life-sapping qualities of a careerist ambition seem antithetical to

what gives their existence meaning: animation. As Kenneth Gross argues, "The puppet reminds us of our powers of animation. It may remind us by contrast of our human tendency to turn ourselves, our thoughts, our memories, and our words into fixed, frozen, inanimate, or mechanical things . . ." (33).

8. At one point, Myles acknowledges an impulse to get rid of letters altogether: "It's little wonder that mailmen would-wide do not simply destroy the mail" (190). This may intimate a dream on Myles's part of pure, immaterial communication, but it also attests to the lack of societal appreciation afforded to postal clerks and the mail system: "the mailman wants nothing better than . . . to destroy the mail. Why? All these men and woman who are carrying these bags and carriages through the streets of the world, all of them are dogs" (190).

Conclusion

1. O'Hara's admission of end-of-workweek exhaustion cuts against an ingrained American work ethic, as Kathi Weeks notes: "Work is not just defended on grounds of economic necessity and social duty: it is widely understood as an individual moral practice and collective ethical obligation. Traditional work values . . . continue to be effective in encouraging and rationalizing the long hours US workers are supposed to dedicate to waged work and the identities they are expected to invest there" (11).

2. Hollander argues that poetic refrain always points to itself in a self-referential manner, calling conspicuous attention to itself as a device: "And the ultimate point is that for poetry, rather than mere verse, to employ a refrain, it must thereby, therein, therewith propound its own parable of the device itself, its etiology, or its effect, or its emblematic reading" (147).

3. Hardt and Negri here have in mind a new model of political organization that is less dependent on singular, charismatic political leadership in whom power is centralized. Instead, they imagine political movements to be horizontal in nature, led by the multitude: "There are, of course, and will continue to be, issues that because of their urgency or technical nature require centralized decision making of various sorts, but such 'leadership' must be constantly subordinated to the multitude, deployed and dismissed as occasion dictates. If leaders are still necessary and possible in this context, it is only because they serve the productive multitude. This is not an elimination of leadership, but an inversion of the political relationship that constitutes it, a reversal of the polarity that links horizontal movements and vertical leadership" (*Assembly* xv).

4. Shaw references the work of Georgio Agamben to articulate the fluid, non-hierarchical nature of coterie embraced by O'Hara: "Agamben's writing helps to focus the idea of communities as temporary, tactical social compositions based on contingent rather than organic bonds, dissipating and reforming themselves frequently" (8).

Works Cited

Albérès, René Marill, and Pierre de Boisdeffre. *Kafka: the Torment of Man*. Philosophical Library, 1968.
Allen, Donald. Editor's Note. *The Collected Poems of Frank O'Hara*, U of California P, 1995.
Ashbery, John. "Frank O'Hara's Question." *Book Week* 25 Sept. 1966: 6.
———. *Houseboat Days*. Viking, 1977.
———. Introduction. *The Collected Poems of Frank O'Hara*, by Frank O'Hara, edited by Donald Allen, U of California P, 1995.
———. Introduction. *Selected Poems*, by James Schuyler, Farrar, Straus and Giroux, 2007.
———. *The Mooring of Starting Out*. The Ecco Press, 1997.
———. *Rivers and Mountains*. Harper Collins, 1977.
———. *Self-Portrait in a Convex Mirror*. Penguin, 1976.
———. *Shadow Train*. Penguin, 1981.
———. *Some Trees*. The Ecco Press, 1956.
———. *The Tennis Court Oath*. Wesleyan UP, 1957.
Auden, W.H. *A Certain World: A Commonplace Book*. Viking, 1970.
———. *Collected Poems*. Ed. Edward Mendelson. Vintage, 1976.
———. *The Complete Works of W. H. Auden: Poems, Volume I: 1927–1939*. Princeton UP, 2022.
———. *The Dyer's Hand and Other Essays*. Vintage International, 1989.
———. *Selected Poems*. Expanded edition, edited by Edward Mendelson, Vintage Books, 2007.
Bakhtin, Mikhail. *The Dialogical Imagination*. U of Texas P, 1981.
Beckett, Samuel. *Three Novels by Samuel Becket: Molloy, Malone Dies, The Unnamable*. Grove Press, 1955.
Benjamin, Walter. *The Arcades Project*. Belknap Press of Harvard UP, 1999.
Bergius, Hanne. *"Dada Triumphs!": Dada Berlin, 1917–1923: Artistry of Polarities*. G.K. Hall, 2003.

Berlant, Lauren. *Cruel Optimism*. Duke UP, 2011.
Bernstein, Charles. *My Way: Speeches and Poems*. U of Chicago P, 1999.
Bérubé, Allan. *Coming Out Under Fire: The History of Gay Men and Women in World War II*. U of North Carolina P, 2010.
Blasing, Mutlu Konuk. *Politics and Form in Postmodern Poetry: O'Hara, Bishop, Ashbery, and Merrill*. Cambridge University Press, 2009.
Bloch, Ernst. *The Principle of Hope*. Vol. 1., translated by Neville Plaice, Stephen Plaice, and Paul Knight, MIT Press, 1986.
———. *The Utopian Function of Art and Literature*. Translated by Jack Zipes and Frank Mecklenburg, MIT Press, 1988.
Bloom, Harold. *Agon: Toward a Theory of Revisionism*. Oxford UP, 1982.
———. *The Poems of Our Climate*. Cornell UP, 1976.
Bozorth, Richard R. *Auden's Games of Knowledge*. Columbia UP, 2001.
Breton, André. *Manifestoes of Surrealism*. Translated by Richard Seaver and Helen R. Lane, U of Michigan P, 1972.
Britan, Gerald M. and Ronald Cohen. *Hierarchy and Society: Anthropological Perspectives on Bureaucracy*. Institute for the Study of Human Issues, 1980.
Buell, Frederick. *W.H. Auden as a Social Poet*. Cornell UP, 1973.
Burke, Edmund. *A Philosophical Inquiry Into the Sublime and Beautiful*. Routledge, 2008.
Burke, Kenneth. *A Grammar of Motives*. U of California P, 1969.
Burnham, James. *The Managerial Revolution: What Is Happening in the World*. The John Day Company, 1941.
Butler, Judith. Introduction. *Soul and Form*, by Georg Lukács, edited by John T. Sanders and Katie Terezakis, Columbia UP, 2010.
Callan, Edward. *Auden: A Carnival of Intellect*. Oxford UP, 1983.
Corngold, Stanley. *Franz Kafka: The Necessity of Form*. Cornell UP, 1988.
Costello, Bonnie. "John Ashbery and the Idea of the Reader." *Contemporary Literature*, vol. 23, no. 4, 1982, pp. 493–514.
———. "John Ashbery's Landscapes." *The Tribe of John: Ashbery and Contemporary Poetry*, edited by Susan M. Schultz, U of Alabama P, 1995.
Coutts-Smith, Kenneth. *Dada*. Studio Vista/Dutton Pictureback, 1970.
Crase, Douglas. *The Revisionist and The Astropastorals: Collected Poems*. Carcanet, 2019.
"Dada and Surrealism." *Encyclopedia of the New York Poets*, edited by Terrence Diggory, Facts on File, 2009.
Davidson, Michael. *Guys Like Us: Citing Masculinity in Cold War Poetics*. U of Chicago P, 2003.
de Certeau, Michel. *The Practice of Everyday Life*. U of California P, 1984.
Dickinson, Emily. *The Collected Poems of Emily Dickinson*. Little, Brown, 1960.
Diggory, Terence, and Stephen Paul Miller. *The Scene of My Selves: New Work on New York School Poets*. National Poetry Foundation, 2001.

Einzig, Barbara. "The Surface as Object: Barbara Guest's Selected Poems." *American Poetry Review*, vol. 25, no. 1, 1996, pp. 7–10.
Eliot, T.S. *Selected Poems*. Harvest Books, Harcourt, Brace & Co., 1936.
Epstein, Andrew. *Beautiful Enemies: Friendship and Postwar American Poetry*. Oxford UP, 2006.
Ferris, Sarah. "Workerism's Inimical Incursions: On Mario Tronti's Weberianism." *Historical Materialism*, vol. 19, no. 3, 2011, pp. 29–62.
Finkelstein, Norman. *The Utopian Moment in Contemporary American Poetry*. Revised ed., Bucknell UP, 1988.
Forgács, Éva. "Revolt and Authority: From Kassák to Erdely." *Cannibalizing the Canon: Dada Techniques in East-Central Europe*, edited by Oliver A.I. Botar et al., Brill, 2024.
Foster, Stephen C. *Crisis and the Arts: The History of Dada, Vol. 5*. G.K. Hall, 1996.
Foucault, Michel. *Abnormal: Lectures at the Collège de France, 1974–1975*. Picador, 2003.
———. *Aesthetics, Method, and Epistemology*. Edited by James D. Faubion, The New Press, 1999.
———. *Discipline and Punish: The Birth of the Prison*. Vintage, 1979.
———. *"Society Must Be Defended": Lectures at the Collège De France, 1975–76*. Edited by Maurio Bertani and Allesandro Fontana, Picador, 1997.
Frank, Thomas. "Flooding Disproportionately Harms Black Neighborhoods. *Scientific American*, 2 June 2020, www.scientificamerican.com/article/flooding-disproportionately-harms-black-neighborhoods.
Frayne, David. *The Refusal of Work*. Zed Books, 2015.
Galambos, Louis. *The New American State: Bureaucracies and Policies Since World War II*. Johns Hopkins UP, 1987.
Gangel, Sue. "John Ashbery." *American Poetry Observed: Poets on Their Work*, edited by Joe David Bellamy, U of Illinois P, 1988, pp. 9–20.
Gershoy, Leo. *The French Revolution and Napoleon*. F.S. Crofts & Company, 1947.
Gilbert, Martin, and Richard Gott. *The Appeasers*. Houghton Mifflin, 1963.
Gooch, Brad. *City Poet: The Life and Times of Frank O'Hara*. Alfred A. Knopf, 1993.
Graeber, David. *The Utopia of Rules: On Technology, Stupidity, and the Secret Joys of Bureaucracy*. Melville House, 2015.
Gray, Timothy. *Urban Pastoral: Natural Currents in the New York School*. U of Iowa P, 2010.
Greenberg, David F. *The Construction of Homosexuality*. U of Chicago P, 1990.
Gross, Kenneth. *Puppet: An Essay on Uncanny Life*. U of Chicago P, 2011.
Guest, Barbara. *The Collected Poems of Barbara Guest*, edited by Hadley Haden Guest, Wesleyan UP, 2008.
———. *Forces of Imagination*. Kelsey St. Press, 2003.
———. *Herself Defined: H.D. and Her World*. Schaffner Press, 2003.
———. *The Office*. *Chicago Review*, vol. 53, no. 4, 2008, pp. 9–21.

Guest, Barbara, and Mark Hillringhouse. "An Interview By Mark Hillringhouse." *American Poetry Review*, vol. 21, no. 4, 1992, pp. 23–30.

H.D. *Collected Poems*. New Directions, 1983.

Haraway, Donna. *The Companion Species Manifesto: Dogs, People, and Significant Otherness*. Prickly Paradigm Press, 2003.

Hardt, Michael, and Antonio Negri. *Assembly*. Oxford UP, 2017.

———. *Empire*. Harvard UP, 2000.

———. *Multitude*. Penguin, 2004.

Hardt, Michael, and Paul Virno, eds. *Radical Thought in Italy: A Potential Politics*. U of Minnesota P, 1996.

Harvey, David. *The Condition of Postmodernity: An Enquiry into the Origins of Cultural Change*. Blackwell, 1990.

Heinemann, Richard. "Kafka's Oath of Service: 'Der Bau' and the Dialectic of Bureaucratic Mind." *PMLA*, vol. 111, no. 2, 1996, pp. 256–70.

Herzfeld, Michael. *The Social Production of Indifference: Exploring the Symbolic Roots of Western Bureaucracy*. Berg, 1992.

Hogg, Emily J., and Peter Simonsen. *Precarity in Contemporary Literature and Culture*. Bloomsbury, 2021.

Hollander, John. *Melodious Guile*. Yale UP, 1988.

Huizinga, Johan. *Homo Ludens: A Study of the Play Element in Culture*. Taylor & Francis, 1998.

Ibhawoh, Bonny. "Human Rights for Some: Universal Human Rights, Sexual Minorities, and the Exclusionary Impulse." *International Journal*, vol. 69, no. 4, 2014, pp. 612–22.

Igarashi, Yohei. *The Connected Condition: Romanticism and the Dream of Communication*. Stanford UP, 2020.

Jackson, Laura (Riding). *Collected Poems*. Random House, 1938.

Jameson, Fredric. *Marxism and Form: Twentieth-Century Dialectical Theories of Literature*. Princeton UP, 1971.

———. *The Political Unconscious*. Cornell UP, 1981.

———. *Seeds of Time*. Columbia UP, 1994.

Kafka, Ben. *The Demon of Writing: Powers and Failures of Paperwork*. Zone Books, 2012.

Kafka, Franz. *The Complete Stories*. Schocken Books, 1971,

———. *Letters to Felice*. Knopf Doubleday, 2016.

Kafka, Franz, and Hannah Arendt. *The Diaries of Franz Kafka: 1914–1923*. Edited by Max Brod, translated by Martin Greenberg and Joseph Kresh, Schocken Books, 1949.

Kenner, Hugh. *The Pound Era*. U of California P, 1971.

Kiesling, Lydia. "The Office Politics of Workplace Fiction by Women." *New Yorker*, 27 July 2016.

Kindley, Evan. *Poet-Critics and the Administration of Culture*. Harvard UP, 2017.

Koch, Kenneth. "All the Imagination Can Hold." *New Republic*, vol. 166, January 1 & 8, 1972, pp. 23–25.

———. *Collected Poems*. Alfred A. Knopf, 2005.

Koethe, John, and John Ashbery. "An Interview with John Ashbery." *SubStance*, vol. 11/12, 1982, pp. 178–86.

Krutz, Glen, and Sylvie Waskiewicz. *American Government 3e*. OpenStax, 2021.

Lagapa, Jason. "Homely Persons, Rude Speeches: Camp Personalities, Cold War Sensibilities and Dystopian Impulses in Frank O'Hara's Loves Labor, an Eclogue." *Beat Drama: Playwrights and Performances of the 'Howl' Generation*, edited by Deborah Geis, Bloomsbury, 2016.

———. "Parading the Undead: Camp, Horror and Reincarnation in the Poetry of Frank O'Hara and John Yau." *Journal of Modern Literature*, vol. 33, no. 2, 2010, pp. 92–113.

Lefebvre, Henri. *The Production of Space*. Blackwell, 1991.

Lehman, David. *The Last Avant-Garde: The Making of the New York School of Poets*. Doubleday, 1998.

Lukács, Georg. *The Historical Novel*. U of Nebraska P, 1983.

———. *History and Class Consciousness: Studies in Marxist Dialectics*, translated by Rodney Livingstone, MIT Press, 1971.

———. *Soul and Form*. Edited by John T. Sanders and Katie Terezakis, Columbia UP, 2010.

Lundquist, Sara. "Reverence and Resistance: Barbara Guest, Ekphrasis, and the Female Gaze." *Contemporary Literature*, vol. 38, no. 2, 1997, pp. 260–86.

McDiarmid, Lucy. *Saving Civilization: Yeats, Eliot, and Auden Between the Wars*. Cambridge UP, 1984.

Mendelson, Edward. *Later Auden*. Farrar, Straus and Giroux, 1999.

Miller, D.A. "Discipline in Different Voices: Bureaucracy, Police, Family, and Bleak House." *Representations*, no. 1, 1983, pp. 59–89.

Mills, C. Wright. *The Power Elite*. Oxford UP, 1956.

Mommsen, Wolfgang J. *The Age of Bureaucracy: Perspectives on the Political Sociology of Max Weber*. Harper Torchbooks, 1974.

Moore, Marianne. *New Collected Poems*. Farrar, Straus and Giroux, 2017.

Morse, Jonathan. "Typical Ashbery." *The Tribe of John: Ashbery and Contemporary Poetry*. Edited by Susan M. Schultz, U of Alabama P, 1995.

Mumford, Lewis. *The City in History: Its Origins, Its Transformations, and Its Prospects*. Houghton Mifflin Harcourt, 1961.

Muñoz, José Esteban. *Cruising Utopia: The Then and There of Queer Futurity*. New York UP, 2009.

Myles, Eileen. *Afterglow (A Dog Memoir)*. Grove Press, 2017.

———. "Reading with . . . Eileen Myles." *Shelf Awareness*, 23 Nov. 2022, www.shelf-awareness.com/issue.html?issue=4366#m58324.

Nelson, Maggie. *Women, the New York School, and Other True Abstractions*. U of Iowa P, 2007.

Notley, Alice. *Disobedience*. Penguin, 2001.
O'Hara, Frank. *The Collected Poems of Frank O'Hara*. Edited by Donald Allen, with an introduction by John Ashbery, U of California P, 1995.
———. *Lunch Poems*. City Lights Books, 1964.
Perloff, Marjorie. *Frank O'Hara: Poet Among Painters*. U of Chicago P, 1998.
Phillips, Siobhan. "Stevens and an Everyday New York School." *Wallace Stevens Journal*, vol. 36, no. 1, Special Issue: Stevens and the Everyday, 2012, 94–104.
Ramazani, Jahan. *Poetry of Mourning: The Modern Elegy from Hardy to Heaney*. U of Chicago P, 1994.
Reed, Brian. "Grammar Trouble." *boundary*, vol. 2, no. 36, 2009, pp. 133–58.
Remnick, David. "John Ashbery in Conversation with David Remnick." *Bennington Review*, no. 4, 1980, www.benningtonreview.org/john-ashbery.
Reverdy, Pierre. *Pierre Reverdy*. Edited by Mary Ann Caws, The New York Review of Books, 2013.
Robbin, Nancy. "A Friendship." *Chicago Review*, vol. 53/54, 2008, pp. 137–40.
Robinson, Benjamin Lewis. *Bureaucratic Fanatics: Modern Literature and the Passions of Rationalization*. De Gruyter, 2019.
Roffman, Karin. *The Songs We Know Best: John Ashbery's Early Life*. Farrar, Straus and Giroux, 2017.
Rose, Jacqueline. *The Haunting of Sylvia Plath*. Harvard UP, 1992.
Schultz, Susan M., editor. *The Tribe of John: Ashbery and Contemporary Poetry*. U of Alabama P, 1995.
Schuyler, James. "Interview with James Schuyler." *Agni*, no. 37, 1993, pp. 152–82.
———. *Selected Poems*. Farrar, Straus and Giroux, 2007.
Shakabpa, Tsepon W.D. *Tibet: A Political History*. Yale UP, 1967.
Shapiro, David. *John Ashbery: An Introduction to the Poetry*. Columbia UP, 1979.
Shaw, Lytle. *Frank O'Hara: The Poetics of Coterie*. Iowa City: U of Iowa P, 2006.
Shoptaw, John. *On the Outside Looking Out*. Harvard UP, 1994.
Sibley, David. *Geographies of Seclusion: Society and Difference in the West*. Routledge, 1995.
Sontag, Susan. *Against Interpretation: And Other Essays*. Farrar, Straus and Giroux, 2013.
Standing, Guy. *The Precariat: The New Dangerous Class*. Bloomsbury Academic, 2011.
Stein, Gertrude. *The Autobiography of Alice B. Toklas*. Knopf Doubleday, 1990.
Stephens, Paul. "Vanguard Total Index: Conceptual Writing, Information Asymmetry, and the Risk Society." *Contemporary Literature*, vol. 54, no. 4, 2013, pp. 752–84.
Stevens, Wallace. *The Palm at the End of the Mind*. Vintage Books, 1971.
Susik, Abigail. *Surrealist Sabotage and the War on Work*. Manchester UP, 2021
Tronti, Mario. *Workers and Capital*. Verso, 2019.
Tronto, Joan C. "An Ethic of Care." *Generations: Journal of the American Society on Aging*, vol. 22, no. 3, 1998, pp. 15–20.

———. *Moral Boundaries: A Political Argument for Care* and *Caring Democracy: Markets, Equality, and Justice.* Routledge, 1994.
"United Nations Charter." United Nations. www.un.org/en/about-us/un-charter/full-text. Accessed 6 Dec. 2024.
Vendler, Helen. "Understanding Ashbery." *John Ashbery: Modern Critical Views*, edited by Harold Bloom, Chelsea House, 1985.
Ward, Geoff. *Statutes of Liberty: The New York School of Poets.* Palgrave Macmillan, 2001.
Watkin, William. *In the Process of Poetry: The New York School and the Avant-Garde.* Bucknell UP, 2001
Watten, Barret. "The Conduit of Communication in Everyday Life." *Aerial 8*, edited by Rod Smith, Edge, 1995.
Weber, Max. *Economy and Society: A New Translation.* Edited and translated by Keith Tribe, Harvard UP, 2019.
———. *Economy and Society: An Outline of Interpretive Sociology.* Edited by Guenter Roth and Claus Wittich, U of California P, 1978.
———. *From Max Weber: Essays in Sociology.* Oxford UP, 1946.
———. *The Protestant Ethic and the Spirit of Capitalism.* Translated by Talcott Parsons, Routledge Classics, 2001.
Weeks, Kathi. *The Problem with Work: Feminism, Antiwork Politics, and Postwork Imaginaries.* Duke UP, 2011.
Whyte, William H. *The Organization Man.* U of Pennsylvania P, 2002.
Wilson, Rob. *The American Sublime: The Genealogy of a Poetic Genre.* U of Wisconsin P, 1991.
Wright, Steve, et al. *Storming Heaven: Class Composition and Struggle in Italian Autonomist Marxism.* 2nd ed., Pluto Press, 2017.
Young, James E. "The Counter-Monument: Memory against Itself in Germany Today." *Critical Inquiry*, vol. 18, no. 2, 1992, pp. 267–96.

Index

Aalto, Bill, 133
administrative grotesque, 19, 29–30, 144–45, 150, 154–55, 163, 192n1
Agamben, Georgio, 193n4
Albérès, R.M., 74
Aldington, Richard, 97
Allen, Donald, 47
American midcentury, 5, 22
Ashbery, Chet, 84
Ashbery, John, 2, 6, 10, 20–21, 28, 47, 62, 66, 67–90, 99, 118, 124, 130, 136, 180–81, 188nn1–2, n4, 189nn8–10; and *Beamtengeist* (bureaucratic mindset). See *Beamtengeist*; and Franz Kafka, 6, 67, 69–70, 72, 80, 82, 84, 86, 90, 106, 170, 188nn2–3; and office work, 67–72 *passim*, 76–77, 79, 82, 88
Ashbery's Works
  "A Boy," 69
  "Business Personals," 4
  "Flow Chart," 4
  "Fragment," 4, 69, 82–90
  "The Instruction Manual," 6, 10–11, 13, 15, 25–26, 62–63, 67–68, 71, 73, 76–77, 81, 90
  "The Leasing of September," 4
  "Litany," 69
  "The Painter, 69, 72–74

  "Self Portrait in a Convex Mirror," 69, 74–82, 90
  "The Skaters," 67, 69
  "Untilted," 70–72, 73–74, 90
  "Wet Casements," 69, 86
  "A White Paper," 4
Auden, W.H., 5, 19–20, 25–46, 99, 120, 124–28; and clerklike professionalism, 18, 34, 127, 135; and homosexuality, 42, 187n1; depiction of managers, 19, 22, 35–36, 43–44; and Mortmere, 31–33, 36; and play, 27–29; 37–38, 46; influence on New York School poets, 17, 28
Auden's Works
  "The Age of Anxiety," 41
  "At the Grave of Henry James," 34
  A Certain World (commonplace book), 25
  Dyer's Hand, 18, 25, 27, 46
  "The Fall of Rome," 17, 28, 30
  "In Memory of W.B. Yeats," 30, 35–40
  "Forty Years On," 17–18, 29–30
  "The Letter," 129–30
  "September 1, 1939," 30, 40–46
  "The Treason of Clerks," 128
  "The Unknown Citizen," 17, 30–33, 36

203

Bakhtin, Mikhail, 154
Baudelaire, Charles, 137–38
Bauer, Felice, 188n3
Beamtengeist (bureaucratic mindset), 21, 70–71, 73, 75–76, 79, 81–82, 90
Beat Generation, 7
Beckett, Samuel, 65
Benjamin, Walter, 90
Berechnungskunst (art of calculation), 82, 87
Berlant, Lauren, 32, 185n2
Bernstein, Charles, 103
Bérubé, Allan, 123
Blasing, Mutlu Konuk, 58, 60
Bloch, Ernst, 60, 64
Bloom, Harold, 50, 188n2
Boisdeffre, Pierre de, 74
Bozorth, Richard R., 187n1
Breton, André, 9
Brehm, John O., 128
Britan, Gerald M., 29
Brown, Michael (former FEMA director), 152–53
Buell, Fredrick, 27, 31, 36–37
Bureaucracy: culture of bureaucracy, 2, 4, 9, 21, 26, 176, 182; midcentury growth of, 7–9
Bureaucratic sublime, 78, 80, 158, 169–83
Burke, Edmund, 78
Burke, Kenneth, 56
Burnham, James, 185n1
Burroughs, William S., 7, 146
Bush, George W., 150, 152–56
Butler, Judith, 94

Callan, Edward, 34, 40
Carpenter, J.E.R., 55
Certeau, Michel de, 1, 12, 37, 39–40, 67, 177–83 *passim*; *See also* "la perruque"

Cipel, Golan, 150, 152, 192n5
Cohen, Ronald, 29
Cold War, 7–8, 20, 48–50, 52, 54, 57–60, 66
Corngold, Stanley, 72, 188n3
Costello, Bonnie, 69, 73
Crase, Douglas, 22, 132, 134–35

Dadaism, 9–10, 51–52, 55, 186n9, 188n1
Davidson, Michael, 58
Dickinson, Emily, 43
Diggory, Terrence, 58, 61, 188n4
Droll, Donald, 133
Dumbarton Oaks Museum, 98–100

Einzig, Barbara, 100
Eliot, T.S., 6, 102, 104–105, 107, 191n2; "The Waste Land," 102, 104–105, 107, 113
Epstein, Andrew, 61, 71, 188n4, 189n5, 191n2

Ferris, Sarah, 14
Finkelstein, Norman, 65
Foucault, Michel, 19, 22, 29, 30; 32, 37, 40, 143–45, 147, 150, 155, 192n1; "What is an Author," 147; *Discipline and Punish*, 30; *See also* administrative grotesque
Frayne, David, 186n11

Galambos, Louis, 7
Gates, Scott, 128
Gershoy, Leo, 63
Gilbert, Martin, 187n2
Ginsberg, Allen, 7
Gooch, Brad, 48–49, 180–81, 185n3
Gott, Richard, 187n2
Graeber, David, 16, 52–53, 60, 72, 97, 117, 183, 187n15, 190n5, 192n5
Gray, Timothy, 100
Greenberg, David F., 123

Gross, Kenneth, 193n7
Guest, Barbara, 2, 5, 21, 91–116, 186n7, 189n1, 190nn2–3, 190nn5–6, and clerical work, 92, 95–96, 99, 101–16 *passim*
Guest's Works
"Forces of Imagination" (essay), 8
Herself Defined, 92–93
"Knight of the Swan," 116
"The Location of Things," 93–94, 102
The Office (play), 21, 91, 95, 101–16
"Olivetti Ode," 21, 91, 96, 114–16
"On the Way to Dumbarton Oaks," 98
"Windy Afternoon," 96–98

Haraway, Donna, 159
Hardt, Michael, 14, 18, 45–46, 112, 114, 161, 178–83 *passim*, 193n3
Harvey, David, 121, 191n1
H.D., 92–93, 96–97, 189n1
Hegel, G.W., 94
Heine, Heinrich, 139
Heinemann, Richard, 21, 70, 72, 77, 82
Heller, Joseph, 6
Herzfeld, Michael, 101, 107, 153, 187n13, 190n3
Hoheisel, Horst, 191n3
Hollander, John, 44, 176, 193n2
Hogg, Emily J., 185n2
Huizinga, Johan, 20, 27, 37–38, 44, 46

Ibhawoh, Bonny, 131
Igarashi, Yohei, 185n5
Isherwood, Christopher, 31
Italian Autonomists, 13–14, 183, 186n11

Jameson, Fredric, 4, 36, 95
Johnson, Lyndon B., 186n6

Kafka, Ben, 84, 106
Kafka, Franz, 6, 67, 69–70, 72, 80, 82, 84, 86, 90, 106, 170, 188n2, 188n3; "The Burrow," 72, 80; "The Metamorphosis," 67
Kenner, Hugh, 190n1
Kerouac, Jack, 7
Kiesling, Lydia, 7
Kindley, Evan, 185n5
Koch, Kenneth, 6, 170, 170–77, 186n8; and antipathy for office work, 171, 175–76; "To My Father's Business," 6, 170–77
Krutz, Glen, 186n6

Lagapa, Jason, 58, 188n2
Lama, Dalai, 59
Lefebvre, Henri, 120, 142
Lehman, David, 28, 49, 186n9
LeSueur, John, 181
Lukács, Georg, 94–95, 98, 102–103, 112, 186n12
Lundquist, Sara, 97

Man, Henri de, 77
McCray, Porter, 185n3
McDiarmid, Lucy, 34
McGreevey, Jim, 150–52, 156
Melville, Herman, 7
Mendelson, Edward, 40
Miller, D.A., 117
Miller, Henry, 5, 92, 115
Mills, C. Wright, 7, 185n1
MoMa, 3, 5, 12–13, 48–49, 61, 172–73
Mommsen, Wolfgang, 51
Moore, Marianne, 8, 138
Morse, Jonathan, 189n8
Mumford, Lewis, 120
Muñoz, José Esteban, 191n4
Musée d'Art Moderne, 180
Myers, John, 138

Myles, Eileen, 22, 143–67, 192n2, 192n3, 192n4, 193n8, and bureaucratic work, 144; and caregiving work, 151–52, 159
Myles' Works
Afterglow: A Dog Memoir, 22, 143–67

Negri, Antonio, 45–46, 112, 114, 161, 178–83 *passim*, 193n3
Nelson, Maggie, 94, 190n2, 190n6
New York School poets, and clerical work, 2, 4–6, 8, 10–11, 14–20, 26, 49, 152; critique of bureaucracy, 4–5; 17, 19, 22–23; and the Beat Poets, 7; and Dadaism, 9–10, 51–52, 55; as "secretarial generation," 5, 172, 177, 183; and Surrealism, 9, 14–15
Notley, Alice, 22

O'Hara, Frank, 1, 12–13, 15–16, 20, 28, 57–67, 130, 163–64, 172–73, 180–81, 185n3, 186nn8–10, 188nn1–2, 193n1; and bureaucratic work, 48, 50, 59–62; and camp sensibility, 48, 60
O'Hara's works
"Adieu to Norman, Bon Jour to Joan and Jean-Paul," 54, 60–66
Amorous Nightmares of Delay (Play), 58
"A City Winter," 15, 47
"The Day Lady Died," 53–54
"Getting Up Ahead of Someone (Sun)," 50
Lunch Poems, 3–4, 12, 15, 20, 48
"Music," 58
"Personal Poem," 56, 62
"Personism: A Manifesto," 51–52, 163–64

"Poem (Khrushchev Is Coming on the Right Day!)," 58
"Radio," 172–73
"Rhapsody," 54–60
"A Step Away from Them," 53–54

Park, Darragh, 136–38, 141
Parmigianino, 74–81 *passim*
Perloff, Marjorie, 186n9, 188n1
"la perruque," 12, 67, 177, 180–82. See *also* Michel de Certeau
Phillips, Siobhan, 186n10
Polach, Frank, 132, 134–35
Pollock, Jackson, 186n8
Pound, Ezra, 92–93, 96

Ramazani, Jahan, 138–39
Reed, Paul, 171
refusal of work: 13–14, 18–19, 21, 54, 60, 92, 95, 102, 109, 111–12, 114, 134, 148, 159–60, 176, 180–83, 186n11
Remnick, David, 70
Reverdy, Pierre, 65
Riding, Laura, 164
Robbin, Nancy, 92
Robinson, Benjamin Lewis, 185n5
Roffman, Karin, 84, 189n7
Rose, Jacqueline, 191n6

Schuyler, James, 2, 5, 13, 21–22, 117–42, 186n10, 191n4, and clerical work, 124–25, 127–28, 135–36, 139
Schuyler's Works
"Dining Out with Doug and Frank," 119, 131–35
"Hymn to Life," 21, 117–24 *passim*, 131
"Interview with James Schuyler," 13
"The Morning of the Poem," 119, 135–42

"This Dark Apartment," 128–31, 141
"Wystan Auden," 124–28
Shakabpa, Tsepon W.D., 188n3
Shapiro, David, 69, 73
Shaw, Lytle, 61, 182, 188n4, 193n4
Shoptaw, John, 4, 11, 28, 69, 77, 88
Sibley, David, 121
Simonsen, Peter, 185n2
Sontag, Susan, 60, 124
Standing, Guy, 185n2
Stein, Gertrude, 147, 172, 192n4
Stephens, Paul, 172
Stevens, Wallace, 6–7, 50, 85, 138; 186n10; "Description without Place," 85; "The Idea of Order at Key West," 50
Surrealism, 9, 14–15, 186n9, 188n1
Susik, Abigail, 9, 14–15, 18

Toklas, Alice B. 147
Tronti, Mario, 13–14

Tronto, Joan, 143, 147, 152, 158–59, 192n6

United Nations, 131
Upward, Edward, 31

Vasari, Giorgio, 78
Vendler, Helen, 75

Young, James E., 117, 122, 191n3

Ward, Geoff, 5, 172
Waskiewicz, Sylvie, 186n6
Watkin, William, 136, 186n10, 188n1
Weber, Max, 6, 8, 14, 16–18, 22–23, 34, 51, 57, 62, 78, 104, 174, 177–78, 185n4, 187n14, 190n4
Weeks, Kathi, 1, 4, 13, 18–19, 95, 111, 134, 160, 173–83 *passim*
Whitman, Walt, 55, 138–39
Wilson, Rob, 169–71
Whyte, William, 2–3, 185n1
Wright, Steve, 186n11

www.ingramcontent.com/pod-product-compliance
Lightning Source LLC
Chambersburg PA
CBHW022019220426
43663CB00007B/1140